How? Come Planet Earth

How Come? Planet Earth

By Kathy Wollard
Illustrated by Debra Solomon

Workman Publishing, New York

Library of Congress Cataloguing-in-Publication Data
Wollard, Kathy.
How come? : Planet Earth / by Kathy Wollard ; illustrated by Debra Solomon.
p.   cm.   Includes index.
Summary: Answers to approximately 125 of kids' science questions about people,
animals, and the natural world, such as why cats purr and why our fingers wrinkle in water.
ISBN-13: 978-0-7611-1239-6; ISBN-10: 0-7611-1239-1
1. Science—Miscellanea Juvenile literature.   [1. Science—Miscellanea.   2. Questions and answers.]
I. Solomon, Debra, ill.   II. Title.   III. Title: How Come?: Planet Earth.
Q173.W788   1999
500-dc21   99-14294   CIP

Workman books are available at special discount when purchased in bulk for special premiums
and sales promotions as well as for fund-raising or educational use. Special editions or book excerpts
also can be created to specification. For details, contact the Special Sales Director at the address below.

Workman Publishing Company, Inc.
225 Varick Street
New York, NY 10014-4381
www.workman.com

Manufactured in the United States of America

First Printing October 1999
20 19 18 17 16

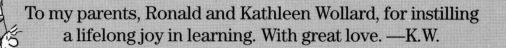

To my parents, Ronald and Kathleen Wollard, for instilling a lifelong joy in learning. With great love. —K.W.

For my wonderful mom, darling Alex, and my fave science wiz and good friend Kathy. —D.S.

Acknowledgments

MANY THANKS GO TO: Margot Herrera, tireless and meticulous editor; Peter Workman, designer Erica Heitman, Suzanne Rafer, Kylie Foxx, and everyone else at Workman who contributed toward making a second beautiful book; Tony Marro and Bob Keane of *Newsday*, for continuing faith; Reg Gale and Marcie Kemen, editors of the Health and Discovery section at *Newsday*, for incisive comments and unfailing encouragement; Mary Burke of *Newsday*, who has tracked down missing addresses, people, and checks, and sent out books week after week, making *How Come?* possible; Janis Donnaud, wise (and fierce) literary agent; Evan Morris, my husband (a.k.a. The Word Detective), for loving support; and Debby Solomon, whose unique sensibility and humor have made *How Come?* a never-ending adventure.

—K.W.

Contents

Safari

Bodyworks 153

What Are You Wondering About?

All the questions in this book were asked by real kids.

They mailed and e-mailed them to the syndicated "How Come?" newspaper column from all over the world: from Brooklyn, New York, to Madras, India, to Melbourne, Australia, and from points in between—Brazil, Thailand, Jamaica, Oman. Letters from younger kids were often decorated with crayon drawings in all the colors of the rainbow. Some letters were carefully hand-printed. Older students often typed their letters on a computer. All of them helped create the book you are holding in your hand.

The "How Come?" column started in 1987 at *Newsday*, the wonderful and eclectic newspaper based in Long Island, New York. Since then, expanding its reach through the Los Angeles Times Syndicate, the column has gone planet-wide. In 1993, the first book of questions and answers, *How Come?*, was published. This is its companion volume.

How Come? runs the gamut of science questions, from "Why is the sky blue?" to "Why are bubbles round?" and "Why do stars twinkle?" *How Come? Planet Earth* zeroes in on our small blue world—its exploding volcanoes, drifting icebergs, arching rainbows. It explores Earth's astonishing variety of animal life, from cows chewing their cud in meadows to electric eels sparking under the Amazon. It examines our peculiar human bodies, from our bath-wrinkled fingers and 100-mph sneezes to our onion tears and growling stomachs. And finally, it explains our unnatural but uniquely human creations—from bubble gum to chocolate bars to compact discs.

Enjoy the trip. And feel free to send in your own questions, by postal mail or e-mail. We may use them in a future column or book. Here's how to reach us:

How Come?
P.O. Box 4564
Grand Central Station
New York, NY 10163

howcome@word-detective.com

I'm looking forward to seeing what *you* are wondering about!

Kathy Wollard

TURBULENT EARTH

Out of darkness came our turbulent planet. Earth started its babyhood as a rock, growing bigger and rounder from a steady hail of debris raining in from the early solar system more than 4 billion years ago.

Today, it is a blue-white world, blue from the waters below, white from the water vapor afloat in the skies above. As Earth spins like a daredevil carousel at 1,000 mph, volcanoes belch rivers of hot hot rock from its insides. Icebergs the size of houses break off its ice sheets and drift into its oceans.

Bowls carved out of glaciers fill with rain. Islands thrust themselves up from the bottom of the sea. And above it all, shape-changing clouds send bolts of lightning thundering to the ground.

Why are storm clouds dark and menacing-looking? Why does dew form on the morning grass? Why are mountain peaks blue, and the sunset sky red and purple? Take a journey around our home planet, and find out.

How does Earth maintain its speed of rotation? Why doesn't it slow down?

Ever hear of the Broadway play called *Stop the World, I Want to Get Off!*? Much as we might like to take a break from the whirl of life, Earth keeps right on spinning, turning day into night and back into day again.

Just how fast is our planetary amusement ride going? A large wooden merry-go-round turns at about 13 mph; Earth, meanwhile, merrily spins along at 1,000 mph at the equator. Dramamine, anyone?

No one needed to give Earth a shove to start it whirling like a top. Earth and its planetary siblings were born from a cloud of spinning gas and dust in space, so the planets began their lives tumbling. (The young planets' speed and direction of rotation also depended on what collisions they suffered in the early years of the solar system, when the area around the Sun resembled a demolition derby.)

Even though Earth was born spinning, its speed was never constant. Our planet, after all, didn't come equipped with cruise control. Earth was an incredibly speedy little planet in the very beginning, whirling around at about 4,000 mph—making days 6 hours long. But over the centuries, Earth's rotation slowed.

How come? One of the main causes of the deceleration is the swelling and falling of Earth's immense oceans. Sloshing ocean tides affect a planet like the brakes on a speeding car. Since the tides are created mainly by the gravitational pull of the Moon, it's fair to say that Earth's rotation is slowing in large part because our planet has a big moon. (For more on tides, see page 74.)

Scientists say that Earth is slowing each century by 1 to 3 milliseconds a day (a millisecond is one-thousandth of a second). So every hundred years or so, a day has lengthened by anywhere from about 30 seconds to nearly 2 minutes. In another 4,000 years, the slowing will have probably added a full hour to each day.

But events other than moon-whipped tides also affect the rotation of a planet. For example, scientists say that by damming up

A large wooden merry-go-round turns at about 13 mph; Earth, meanwhile, merrily spins along at 1,000 mph at the equator.

much of the fresh water of Earth into giant reservoirs, human beings have slowed Earth by several milliseconds.

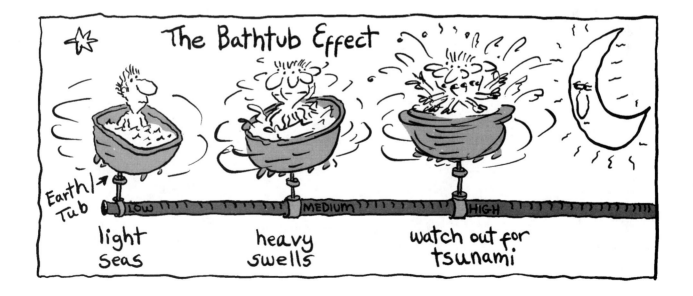

The Bathtub Effect

Earth/Tub

LOW — MEDIUM — HIGH

light seas   heavy swells   watch out for tsunami

Ocean currents and weather systems also affect rotation speed. A typical hurricane temporarily slows Earth a tiny amount, increasing day length by about 2 microseconds (two-millionths of a second). El Niño, the warm Pacific Ocean current that wreaks havoc with Earth's weather, also slows Earth. According to NASA scientists, El Niño at its peak causes the day to get longer by about 0.6 milliseconds. (For more on El Niño, see page 43.)

Sounding like something in a science fiction novel, the International Earth Rotation Service (IERS) keeps track of the fluctuating speed of our planet for the rest of us. And it's the IERS that decides whether or not to add an extra second to the world's Coordinated Universal Time, to keep clocks in sync with fickle Earth.

How was Earth formed, and what was it like in the beginning?

A STAR is Born...
and then some planets

Somewhere in the Milky Way...

Clouds of dust and gas attract and compress...

Seen from space, Earth looks familiar, like home: bright blue oceans; gray, snow-capped mountains; sandy deserts; patches of green. But once upon a time, there was a very young Earth. And the baby planet was as different from the grown-up planet as Earth today is from Mars.

About 4.6 billion years ago—when the universe was already about 10 billion years old—our Sun and planets were born. The Sun is one of about 100 billion stars in the Milky Way galaxy, born out of a cloud of gas and dust between other stars. Newborn stars are surrounded by orbiting debris— gas and dust—circling in a flattened disk. Particles collide and make bigger particles, like snowflakes clumping in a storm. It took

and the next thing you know...

It's a sun!

about 100,000 years for tiny grains to grow into rocky bodies the size of asteroids in the inner part of our solar system.

Earth itself started as a rock, slowly growing as a rain of debris, from sand- to mountain-size, fell onto its surface. (In the beginning, more than 60 million tons of material fell onto Earth each day. Now, the daily dose is about 150 tons of stuff—most of it too small to notice.) Earth grew to its present size in about 70 million years.

The unceasing impacts heated the rocky surface to a liquid. Earth was covered in a sea of molten lava, topped with a thin layer of dark, cooler rock, like the scum on a pond. Cracks revealed the fiery glow

beneath; dust hurled into the sky made days as black as nights.

Over millions of years, the impacts grew fewer. Why? There were fewer objects tumbling through the solar system that hadn't been swept up into planets. So Earth's surface began to cool, and a true crust formed.

Volcanoes belched carbon dioxide and steam into the air, which until then had been mostly hydrogen gas. The cooled, cratered surface was soon covered with water, as steam condensed and rained down in drops. Icy comets from the outer solar system added more water as they crashed in. By about 4.4 billion years ago,

Baby Earth was as different from the grown-up planet as Earth today is from Mars.

Earth was entirely covered by a warm-water ocean, pelted continuously by rain. By about 4.2 billion years ago, there was some land visible, mainly the rims of craters, jutting above the water's surface here and there.

The newly formed Moon was nearer than it is today, so tides surged wildly. Asteroids striking the ocean created monstrous tidal waves, which crumbled land into the sea.

Much of the air's carbon dioxide gradually dissolved into the ocean. As the air thinned, days brightened. The global ocean began to evaporate, exposing more and more rocky, fractured land.

By 3.4 billion years ago, broad landmasses broke up the expanse of ocean. The first plants appeared by 3 billion years ago, adding oxygen to the air's mix. (See page 10 for how plants do it.) But it took another billion years for oxygen to build up to its current 21 percent. By altering the atmosphere and making it breathable, plants created the conditions for the spread of animal life that took place about 700 million years ago. Thanks to plants, you are reading this today. And the rest, as they say, is history.

10 million years later, after much clumping, colliding, compression, and attraction...

grandchildren!

Does air weigh anything?

ARE YOU UNDER A LOT OF PRESSURE?

ON Venus

ON Mars

ON Earth

You don't notice the air unless there's a breeze. But billions of gas molecules are constantly banging against your head and stomach and arms and legs. A typical nitrogen molecule, for example, zooms around at about 1,030 mph at room temperature. These energetic gas molecules are clutched to Earth by our planet's gravity; otherwise, they would simply escape to space. (Some escape anyway, especially the lightest ones, flying off the top edge of the atmosphere toward parts unknown.)

Earth's air is more than 77 percent nitrogen molecules. Another 21 percent is oxygen molecules, and the rest other gases.

Other planets have their own special recipes of gases enveloping them like shrouds.

Scientists weigh air by measuring how much it presses against objects on Earth. At any average spot on Earth's surface, the air is pressing against each tiny square inch of you with about 14.7 pounds of force. (Pick up a 15-pound dumbbell, and you'll see that the air packs a significant force.)

The higher you go, however, the thinner the air gets. At 18,000 feet, way up a mountain, the air is pressing with only about 7.4 pounds of force. (However, don't rejoice at the weight off your shoulders— this also means that you are breathing in only half the air molecules you normally do. That's what causes the dizziness, shortness of breath, and nausea of altitude sickness.)

Life on Earth evolved to live comfortably on or near the surface, with the air weighing down just the amount it does. Some ocean animals and plants evolved to withstand much higher pressures, deep under the combined weight of the atmosphere and the ocean.

Other planets, of course, have different-weight atmospheres—or virtually no atmospheres at all. Mercury, for example, has a wispy, barely-there atmosphere made mainly of sodium gas.

But just next door, on Venus, it's a vastly different story. Venus is enveloped by a suffocatingly thick layer of carbon dioxide gas. Attempting to stroll across a plain in Venus would be like trying to walk across a swimming pool underwater. Drop a penny

At any average spot on Earth's surface, the air is pressing against each tiny square inch of you with about 14.7 pounds of force.

through Venus's air, and it would flutter slowly to the ground as if it were falling through liquid. The weight of the air would be literally crushing—more than 1,300 pounds on each square inch of you. Jupiter, a gaseous world in the outer solar system, has an atmosphere that would weigh down on you with an elephant-like force of nearly 1,500 pounds per square inch.

By contrast, Martian air, which is also mainly carbon dioxide molecules, is very thin. If you were standing on the rusty surface of Mars, the atmosphere would press down on each square inch of you with only about 1 pound of force.

Why do trees and other plants take in carbon dioxide, while we take in oxygen?

All over the world, as you read this, oxygen is escaping from plants—from the trees on your street, the algae in the park pond, the tiny cactus in your window. On land, the process is invisible: We can't see oxygen gas leaving plants, any more than we can see it in the air we breathe. But underwater, we can actually see bubbles of oxygen seep out of plant leaves and float off into the water. Thanks to plants, Earth's air is more than one-fifth oxygen—perfect for us to breathe.

Scientists began to figure out in the 1600s that plants were responsible for oxygen. They wondered about where all the oxygen was coming from. The air around us, they reasoned, should be losing oxygen. After all, fires burn day and night all over the planet, consuming oxygen as they burn. Billions of animals, including human beings, breathe in oxygen, use it up, and then breathe out carbon dioxide. Why doesn't carbon dioxide gas build up in the air? And why doesn't oxygen simply disappear?

Some scientists noticed that when a candle went out after using all the oxygen in a small closed space, it could be relit after a living green plant sat in the space for a while. It became obvious that green plants give off oxygen gas. But how—and why?

Here's how it works. Green plants use energy from the Sun to manufacture their own food—sugar. To make sugar, they also pull water from the soil and carbon dioxide from the air. Oxygen is released as plants make their own dinner. In a way, oxygen coming from food-making plants is like the lovely scent emanating from a factory making bread.

The color green is an important part of the food-making process for a plant. The green color in a plant's leaves comes from the pigment chlorophyll. Remember the water the plant pulls from the soil? Each water molecule has two atoms of hydrogen and one of oxygen. The chlorophyll in a plant's leaves uses energy from sunlight to split water molecules apart, separating hydrogen and oxygen.

Some of the atoms glom right back together, reforming into water. This gives off more energy than the plant can use; the plant

Earth's atmosphere is rich in oxygen because plants have a sweet tooth.

uses this energy to form a compound called ATP (adenosine triphosphate). ATP takes carbon from carbon dioxide and hydrogen atoms it got from the split-up water and

makes sugar—plant food! (Each year, all over the planet, busy plants make 150 billion metric tons of sugar.)

Meanwhile, the oxygen left over from splitting the water molecules escapes into the air. And that's why Earth's atmosphere remains rich in oxygen—all because plants have a sweet tooth. The whole process is called "photosynthesis," which comes from Greek words meaning "putting together with light."

The photosynthesis of plants, which adds oxygen, and the breathing of animals, which adds carbon dioxide, tend to balance each other out. But since the 1800s, carbon dioxide levels have been slowly increasing. Since carbon dioxide absorbs heat from the sun, too much may mean a "greenhouse effect," trapping warmth and raising Earth's average temperatures. Even a little rise can cause droughts, make deserts expand, and decrease our food supply.

Figuring out ways to run cars and factories without burning as much gasoline and coal, which make carbon dioxide, should help. But equally important is putting an end to tearing down the rain forests. They are Earth's largest supply of green plants, cleansing the air of excess carbon dioxide and giving us fresh oxygen to breathe.

FAST FACT

At night, when there is no light, plants actually behave more like we do: absorbing some oxygen from the air and giving off carbon dioxide as a waste product. In daylight, plants still "breathe in" a little oxygen, but mostly they photosynthesize, giving off far more oxygen than they take in.

What makes a volcano erupt?

Have you ever gotten really mad, started yelling, and then calmed down? Like opening a vent on a boiling teakettle, that was your way of letting off steam. A volcano is a planet's (or moon's) way of letting off steam.

Think of a fired-up furnace. When hot gases build up inside, they push out, trying to escape. To relieve the pressure, people build vents to release the gases. These vents are the familiar chimneys we see on nearly every building.

Volcanoes are natural vents in the ground—Earth's chimneys and smokestacks. Hot gases pour out, just as they do from a chimney or a laundry vent. But hot, melted rock may also push up out of Earth's chimneys. And Earth may toss solid pieces of rock out through the holes, too.

Here's how it starts. Deep underground, rock is pressed down by the enormous weight of the land and oceans overhead. Also, the deeper you go, the hotter it is.

(In Earth's core, the temperature may reach 4,000° F.) Under such great pressure and temperature, rock melts.

The liquid rock underground is called magma. Melted rock tends to well up through cracks in solid rock because it is

Hot Ash, Cold Climate

After a big volcano erupts, all of Earth may be treated to deep red sunsets each evening for months—an important clue that volcanoes affect the atmosphere. As ash rises into the atmosphere and spreads around the globe, it hangs in the air, scattering sunlight and tinting sunsets more vivid colors.

But the effects of volcanoes on a planet's atmosphere can go far beyond gorgeous sunsets. Take what happened several hundred million years ago in Siberia. If you travel there today, you can visit the "Siberian traps," an expanse of solid volcanic rock stretching across 870 miles. Scientists who have tested the rock say it is about 250 million years old. Before the rock cooled, it was all hot, flowing lava. And judging from the sheer amount of the rock, which would stretch from New York City to Atlanta, Georgia, the volcanoes that spilled it must have been monstrously large.

Scientists believe the Siberian volcanoes erupted again and again, pouring hot, melted rock out of Earth's insides for about 600,000 years. And each time they erupted, they blasted tons of ash into the skies of Earth.

less dense. When magma erupts through the surface, it is called lava, and its temperature may be 1,700° F.

How does a volcano form? Think of the surface of Earth as the top of a soda can, and a weak area of the crust as the place where the pull tab is. Carbon dioxide gas in a shaken soda expands, and may push through the thin outline of the pull tab—punching a hole in the can. Likewise, hot gases and magma can punch a hole through a weak area in Earth's crust and come bursting out.

They also spewed out deadly, choking gases. Melting minerals released sulfates, which, as they heated up, changed into sulfur dioxide gas.

The ash and gas belched out by the Siberian volcanoes rose high into the atmosphere. The ash blocked some sunlight from reaching Earth. Meanwhile, the sulfur dioxide gas combined with water in the air to make burning sulfuric acid. The acid droplets reflected some of the Sun's rays back into space, further cooling the air.

Gradually, temperatures dropped everywhere. The polar ice caps grew enormous, as ocean water froze. Eventually, much of Earth lay frozen under a coating of ice. Hot volcanoes had begun a new ice age. Meanwhile, acid rain pelted the ground, and acid snow drifted down from the clouds.

Around the same time as this planetary catastrophe, more than 90 percent of all the plant and animal species in the seas of Earth gradually died off, leaving only their fossils. Many scientists blame this mass extinction, which took thousands of years, on those erupting volcanoes and the chain-reaction events that followed them. (See page 151 for another view on what might have caused this catastrophe.)

When we think of volcanoes, we often think of a conical mountain spewing lava and steam out of its funnel-shaped top. Volcanoes that spew lava for many thousands of years may indeed build up into huge, steep cones—as did snow-capped Mt. Fuji in Japan. But there are also shield volcanoes, wide domes that resemble skillet lids, such as those in Hawaii.

The gas that comes out of a volcano is mostly water, along with carbon dioxide (soda pop gas). There are also traces of nitrogen, chlorine, argon, and sulfur.

Volcanoes are natural vents in the ground — Earth's chimneys and smokestacks.

Surprisingly, most volcanoes on Earth are underwater. When hot magma wells out of cracks in the ocean floor, it finds itself flowing into cool seawater. So when a little magma seeps out of a vent, it may quickly cool into thin sheets around the vent that are as shiny as glass. A bigger magma flow that pushes out and away from the vent will harden into lava "pillows" of solid rock.

FAST FACT

The largest lava flow in history was in Iceland in 1783. The vent that the lava pushed through was nearly 20 miles across. The lava streamed 40 miles from one end of the vent and 30 miles from the other end. Scooped up, the lava would have filled a box 2 miles wide by 2 miles high.

Vents tend to form along the edges of the continental plates, the huge puzzle pieces of Earth's crust. Vents can also open up above hot spots in the crust. Hawaii's shield volcanoes are located above such a hot spot.

There are some 500 active volcanoes on Earth, and many more dead ones. But Earth is not the only place in the solar system with volcanoes. The other rocky planets and moons have handy vents in their surfaces, too. Mars has the largest volcano, Olympus Mons, the height of three Mt. Everests. But Io, one of the big moons of Jupiter, has some of the most active. Scientists have glimpsed a number of big plumes rising from that far-off moon's surface.

Why don't we have ice ages anymore?

Although on a sweltering summer day it may seem hard to believe, Earth has *not* stopped having ice ages. Luckily, we happen to be living through a time between ice ages right now. When is the next one due? Not for another 20,000 years or so. (Whew!)

For now, much of Earth is still enjoying a temperate climate, with temperatures moderately cool to warm. In temperate zones, where the weather is warm at least part of the year, we can grow vegetables and grains in the spring and summer, and some flowers will bloom from early spring into the fall.

But it wasn't always so. In the early 1800s, scientists began to notice signs that glaciers—huge, moving shelves of ice—had once visited places far away from the ice and cold. It soon became clear that the average temperature falls and glaciers creep out from the Arctic and Antarctica on a regular basis. Looking at a speeded-up movie of Earth's past, you'd see ice spreading toward the equator and then retreating back toward the polar ice caps in cycles of tens or hundreds of thousands of years.

At the peak of the last ice age, 30 percent of Earth's land area was covered by ice (as opposed to only 10 percent today).

Take the last major ice age. As the climate cooled, huge ice sheets formed near the Arctic and Antarctica and began creeping outward. In North America, an ice sheet slowly enveloped all of what is now Canada and the northern United States, extending as far south as St.

Louis, Missouri. All of Great Britain was also locked in ice. The ice sheets crept southward and retreated several times over tens of thousands of years.

Meanwhile, as temperatures dropped, already-existing glaciers in mountain ranges all over the world, such as the Himalayas, Andes, Rockies, and Alps, grew larger. At the peak of the last ice age, 30 percent of Earth's land area was covered by ice (as opposed to 10 percent today). It's been about 10,000 years since the ice sheets melted away, or pulled back to places like Alaska.

The weight of the ice (in some places, 13,000 feet thick!) was so great that Earth's crust sagged underneath it. Now that the ice is gone, some parts of the crust, such as in Canada, are still slowly rising to their former levels—like dough springing back after being squashed.

All that ice had to come from somewhere, and most of the water was supplied by the oceans. As ice stole ocean water, sea levels fell as much as 650 feet (the height of a 60-story building). Land formerly underwater was uncovered everywhere. For example, you could walk from England to France across a dry English Channel, and from Asia into North

America across the Bering Strait into what is now Alaska.

What makes ice ages come and go? Scientists think it's a combination of two factors. The first is Earth's changing relation to the Sun. Earth's orbit varies over time from circular to more oval, and its tilt shifts slightly, too. This can mean more or less energy from the Sun reaching Earth over thousands of years. The second is continental drift. In regular cycles, Earth's continents slam together and then break apart. This alters the direction of ocean currents and temporarily elevates land, changing climate and temperatures.

Past ice ages have prodded human beings and animals from their usual haunts. For example, take southern France, with its Côte d'Azur (Blue Coast), otherwise known as the French Riviera. The Côte d'Azur is famous all over the world for its sunny, balmy beaches. Well, during one ice age, a new group showed up on the Côte d'Azur—reindeer—giving new meaning to "wintering on the Riviera."

FAST FACT

If all the ice covering the Antarctic and Greenland suddenly melted, oceans all over the world would rise about 215 feet, enough to cover a 21-story building.

If you dug all the way through Earth, would you end up in space?

Looking at a miniature globe of Earth, tilted on its axis and spinnable with a finger shove, it's easy to picture: Tunnel through Earth like a gopher, and you simply pop out the other side and float off into space.

Unfortunately, tunneling through the real Earth is as yet impossible. So far, human beings have tunneled down only about 5 miles. How come? The deeper you go, the higher the pressure, or weight on you, gets. So even a steel gopher would get squashed as it burrowed down and down.

But if it *were* possible, here's what you would encounter on an imaginary dig—and what you'd find when you popped out the other side.

First, some distances. The distance all the way through Earth, also called the diameter, is more than 7,900 miles. Those miles run through a varied terrain—from soil to rock to metal.

You could start your big dig in your backyard. Shoveling down through the dirt, you'll eventually hit rock. That's because the dirt in your yard lies atop Earth's crust. Most of the crust under the continents is made of a rock called granite (visible at places like the Grand Canyon). The crust extends down about 15 to 30 miles under the continents, such as North America, Europe, and Asia. But under the oceans, the crust is made mostly of basalt rock, and extends only about 3 miles below the ocean floor.

At the center of Earth may be a ball of solid iron.

Below the crust is a much wider layer—some 1,800 miles thick—called the mantle. The mantle is made of both solid and melted rock under enormous pressure.

Finally, if you could blast through the mantle, you'd reach Earth's heart, the core, which extends down another 2,000 miles. The core is searingly hot, perhaps 4,000° to 7,000° F. The core is so hot that part of it is made of liquid, melted metals, mainly iron.

Topped (and surrounded) by most of the planet, the core is under the most crushing pressure of all. Since the core's matter is very dense (squeezed tightly together), scientists think there is a ball of solid iron under the liquid metal. Even though the temperature is blast-furnace hot, the extraordinary pressure keeps the iron molecules jammed so tightly together that the iron can't melt.

If you could bore all the way through Earth's solid iron center, you'd travel

through the same layers (liquid core, mantle, crust, and soil or sand) on your way through the opposite side of the planet. As you dug up through those last

The distance all the way through Earth is more than 7,900 miles.

few feet of soil on top of the crust, you might find yourself standing in someone's garden (or basement) on the other side of the world.

You won't be upside down, either. Anywhere you go on the surface of Earth, there you are: The ground is down and the sky is up. You'd simply be standing there, dazed and dirty.

If your luck were particularly bad, you might find yourself on a freeway at rush hour—or at the bottom of an ocean, looking up toward daylight through miles of seawater. In fact, since oceans cover more than 70 percent of the planet, the odds are that's exactly where you'd be.

Where you wouldn't be is in outer space. Unfortunately, the only way to get yourself into space is to blast off from the surface of Earth with enough speed (at least 25,000 mph, called "escape velocity") to free you from our planet's gravity.

What causes quicksand?

Fans of the old *Lassie* TV show from the 1950s and '60s—or just about any kids' adventure show from that period—have fond, scary memories of quicksand. A character is strolling along, minding their own business—little Timmy, or Flicka the horse, or Rin Tin Tin the dog—and suddenly they feel the solid ground give out from under them. Whichever character hasn't fallen in goes for help. And using tree branches or brute force, Gramps or Lassie or a horse named Fury slowly pulls the sinking someone out of the quicksand and safely onto hard ground.

What is quicksand? Quicksand is ordinary sand that has become what scientists call "quick." Clay can also become quick, and there are quick bogs and swamps too. "Quickness" is the way water flowing through sand, clay, or other material can lift and separate its small grains.

In ordinary sand, whether wet or dry, sand particles are pushed up against each other. But when sand becomes quick, an invisible cushion of water holds sand grains a bit apart. So what looks like a solid surface is really— oops!—liquid, a thick soup of water and sand.

In most quicksand patches, ordinary sand is sitting on top of a body of water, such as a bubbling spring. The water is trying to push upward; the sand is weighing the water down. The sand becomes "quick" when the water pressure underneath balances out or exceeds the weight of the sand above. As each grain is surrounded by a thin film of water, the sand particles lose contact and friction. Toss a rock onto what looks like solid sand, and you'll see it disappear below the surface, just as if you'd thrown it into a lake.

Any kind of sand—rough or smooth, mixed with pebbles or not—can become quick. But heavier grains need a more powerfully surging spring to lift them, while the finest-grain, roundest sand can become quick even from weakly flowing water.

Quicksand is found everywhere water and sand live side by side—creek beds and ocean coasts, prairies and mountains. One good place to find it is in hilly country, with lots of limestone caves dotted with underground springs; such springs breed quicksand above. When you're hiking, watch out—quicksand may be hidden under leaves, or by a dried-out crust of mud.

Even if you stumble into a quicksand patch, you'll probably live to tell the tale. No matter what you see in movies or old TV shows, quicksand doesn't suck you in, any more than a lake does. In fact, quicksand is actually more buoyant than water. So unless you're wearing a ton of camping equipment, you'll float quite nicely. To extricate yourself from quicksand, squirm out of anything heavy, such as a backpack, and calmly swim or dog-paddle to solid ground.

Big, heavy objects do sometimes fall into quicksand, with disastrous results. In the 1800s, a freight train derailed off a Colorado bridge and plunged into a "dry" creek bed, made quick by a recent flood. Railroad workers found most of the cars, but the 400,000-pound engine had sunk without a trace.

FAST FACT

A patch of quicksand isn't really a bottomless pit. The average "pit" is only a few inches to a few feet deep.

Why do some mountain ranges look blue if they are covered with green forests?

In the distance you see them: peaks of hazy blue. But as you get nearer, the blueness frustratingly fades from the mountaintops. Up close, you realize the mountains aren't blue at all—simply covered with ordinary green trees. The Blue Mountains of Australia, the Western Ghats in India, and the Blue Ridge and Great Smoky Mountains in the United States all share this quality of blueness-at-a-distance.

How come? Think of a big city, such as Los Angeles. From far off on a hot day, Los Angeles may appear gray or gray-brown. The peaks of its buildings seem shrouded in gray, just as the mountain peaks were enveloped in blue. Get closer, however, and the gray seems to fade. Green glass or white stone buildings are revealed; what caused them to appear gray from afar?

In the case of Los Angeles, you probably know the answer: smog. Big cities are polluted, and smog hangs around them on warm days, enveloping their man-made peaks in gray. Some people think that the blue appearance of mountain ranges is caused by fog on the peaks or smoke (hence the name "Great Smokies"). Actually, the blue haze worn by some mountain ranges has more in common with the smoggy haze of big cities than it does with fog (or smoke).

Unlike smog, fog is a kind of low-hanging cloud, made of water. Water is always present in the air around us, even when the sky looks clear. The water is in the form of invisible, wispy vapor. When a cloud forms, it's as if the water had jumped out of hiding.

How? When the air is saturated with water vapor, the water can collect into droplets around particles in the air, such as clay dust, salt, and soot. Tumbling and falling in a big group, the water droplets, each with a bit of something at its heart, make a visible cloud.

Haze, such as smog, is different. Haze is common in the summer, when the air is either too warm or contains too little water vapor to make droplets and clouds. If there is no wind, the airborne particles that

Blue mountain haze is a kind of natural pollution, created by plants like pine trees on warm, windless days.

would be taken up by water instead collect in the air, forming a dusty haze. In the polluted, particle-laden air over big cities, a thick smog can be the result.

Smoggy haze is a form of human-made pollution, caused by cars, trucks, and factories. Blue mountain haze is a kind of natural pollution, created by plants like pine trees on warm, windless days.

Imagine a high mountainside covered with pine trees, on a hot day, when the air is still. Sticky resin oozes from the pines; get it on your hands, and it's hard to wash off. In the resin are terpenes, fragrant hydrocarbons. (Many plants, from purple sage to wild squashes, produce terpenes. Paint-thinning turpentine is a terpene; so is aromatic, soothing camphor.)

As the temperature rises, pine-tree terpenes evaporate into the air as tiny, oily droplets. Floating in the air, the droplets can collide with ozone, which has sifted down from the upper atmosphere. (Ozone is a kind of oxygen made of three oxygen molecules [O_3] instead of the ordinary two [O_2].)

FAST FACT

Terpenes are what give pine and fir trees their Christmas-tree fragrance; orange peels get their scent from terpenes, too.

The terpenes and ozone chemically react in the air, forming a haze. The tiny particles of the haze scatter blue light from sunlight, tinting the haze blue. With no wind, the haze hangs around the mountaintop.

When mountains like the Great Smokies are seen from a distance, their blue haze looks thick, just like the smog over L.A. But up close the particles are so spread out that the haze can barely be seen, and the blueness disappears.

How come there are deserts?

It's easy to think of the desert as an exotic place. Movie images of the desert show shifting sand dunes, men in flowing scarves, plodding camels, and teasing mirages.

However, you might be surprised to know that deserts are actually commonplace, covering a little over one-third of the landmass on Earth. The main reason most of us look out our windows and see green grass and trees, or a shimmering lake, or even the ocean, is because most people (96 percent of Earth's population) don't even try to live in the desert.

Scientists divide deserts into two kinds: the familiar "deserts of dryness," like the Sahara, and the "deserts of cold," including all of Antarctica and areas on the fringes of both the North and South Poles.

The dry deserts, which cover about 18 percent of Earth's land, are the hottest places on the planet. One of the highest temperatures ever measured on Earth, for example, was recorded on a sweltering day in 1922 in the Libyan Desert of North Africa, when the thermometer read 136° F.

Dry deserts get little rain, usually less than 10 inches a year. Rain clouds may gather; raindrops may even fall. But the drops usually evaporate before they ever

Clarence of Arabia talks about deserts...

When they're hot, they're HOT!

situated between 20 and 30 degrees of latitude on either side of the equator.

Hot deserts are found mainly in that strip because of the way Earth's air flows around the planet. In the desert areas on the coastlines, winds tend to stay offshore, bringing no clouds or rain. In desert areas

Cold deserts have lots of water, but it's locked under the surface, frozen in crystals.

reach the ground. Months or years can pass between real rainstorms. And then there may be a storm of unusual violence. Dry stream channels quickly overflow with rushing water, often destroying desert villages and their gardens.

Strangely enough, in the hottest of deserts, the nights can be bitterly cold. With little or no cloud cover, heat stored in the sand and soil radiates directly into space, and the temperature can quickly drop from 125° F to 25° F.

If you look at a map of the world, you'll find that most hot, dry deserts begin on the west coasts of their continents and then reach inland. These sandy expanses are usually

further inland, winds have traveled so far from any big source of water, like an ocean or lake, that they carry little water vapor to condense into clouds and rain.

Cold deserts are another story. These deserts, which cover about 16 percent of the land on Earth, have lots of water, but it's locked under the surface, frozen into crystals. The cold temperatures at or near the North and South Poles are the culprit, making for expanses of land with stunted plant growth and vast sheets of ice. (Greenland is home to one of the world's largest regions of cold desert.)

Many other planets and moons in our solar system are complete desert worlds. Mars is one vast, cold desert of shifting red sands, deep-cut valleys, and soaring, rocky mountains. Water on Mars is trapped in a layer of permafrost, under the topsoil. Venus, on the other hand, is a boulder-strewn desert inferno, where daytime temperatures can hit 900° F.

Considering the alternatives, we should count ourselves lucky, here on Earth, that there are vast patches of green and basins of blue surrounding our own planetary deserts.

A Sampling of the World's Largest Deserts

Desert	Location	Size (square miles)
Sahara	North Africa	3,500,000
Gobi	Mongolia and northeast China	500,000
Libyan	Africa	450,000
Patagonian	Argentina	260,000
Rub al-Khali	Africa	250,000
Great Victoria	Southwest Australia	150,000
Great Basin	Southwest U.S.	190,000
Chihuahuan	Mexico	175,000
Great Sandy	Northwest Australia	150,000
Kyzyl Kum	Kazakhstan/Uzbekistan	115,000

Sources: The New York Public Library Desk Reference *and* The Cambridge Factfinder

How do lakes form?

Make-A-Lake Cycle
Create valuable waterfront property and retire!

Hire a meteor to excavate your backyard...

After the dust settles...

Fill with water, and build a...

...lakefront subdivision, fill the lake with lawn clippings, sewage, and junk cars...

...then move and hire a glacier, and start over...

Just as there are many recipes for cakes, there are many recipes for lakes. If hollowed-out ground is in the right place, it can be filled by melting ice and snow, rushing rivers and springs, and pouring rain. And there you have it: a lake.

One recipe for lakes has glaciers as the main ingredient. As these moving sheets of ice pulled back north after their cold reign, they carved out basins. They also dammed up rivers, caging them into lakes.

Another moving mass—Earth's unstable crust—has also dug out plenty of basins. Huge sheets of crust thrust up, while other pieces of earth subside, leaving big bowls in the land. Volcanoes explode, and when the dust settles, there are craters to fill (like Crater Lake in Oregon). Earthquakes trigger rockslides that dam up depressions, turning them into waiting tubs.

The flow of water itself can also create lakes. Ocean currents can push sediments to block off rivers. Underground water can wear down soft rocks, carving out nice bowls.

More exotic recipes for lakes involve wind, animals, and outer space. Strong winds push sand to dam up rivers. Animals—from beavers to humans—create artificial lakes. And meteorites, slamming into Earth, can leave craters that later fill up. One such it-came-from-space lake is Ungava Lake in Quebec.

Just as there are many recipes for cakes, there are many recipes for lakes.

We may think we know a lake when we see one, but the scientific definition is a little vague. A lake, scientists say, is any largish body of water that fills a big hole carved into the land—and whose water moves slowly or stands still. Even scientists debate whether some bodies of water are lakes or seas. And just when does a pond graduate to lake status, anyway?

One lake that is surely no pond—in fact, it's the deepest on any continent—is Lake Baikal, in Siberia, a basin surrounded by mountains. If you dropped a rock in at the lake's deepest point, it would come gently to rest 5,314 feet (1,620 meters) down. Lake Baikal stretches 395 miles across Siberia. An astonishing one-fifth of all our planet's fresh surface water is sitting in the bowl of Lake Baikal. The water is kept supplied by 336 rivers and streams pouring continuously into the lake.

Big or small, lakes come and lakes go. A beautiful lake dotted with sailboats may someday be history. Lakes can become extinct, just like animals. In fact, scientists who study lakes say that of all the geologic features on Earth, lakes have among the briefest lives.

A lake can die because its water has been evaporated by droughts, or when its feeding rivers dry up or become dammed up. A lake can also vanish when it fills up with sediment. And a lake can become overgrown with plant life, gradually turning into a marsh. Some little lakes created by beavers last only a few days, as the woody dams pull apart. Vast lakes, on the other hand, can shimmer in the moonlight for millions of years.

Then there are the lakes that still exist but are so polluted that for all intents and purposes, they are dead. In the grand history of lakes, we humans need to switch sides, from polluting to caretaking.

If the rivers drain into the oceans, why don't the oceans fill up and overflow?

Human beings have always been confounded by the puzzle of rivers. "All rivers run into the sea; yet the sea is not full," notes one of the writers of the Bible.

From space, rivers look like faucets, continuously turned on, ceaselessly flowing into the oceans. The 4,000-mile-long Amazon River pours continuously into the Atlantic Ocean, as does the 3,000-mile Congo River. The 1,200-mile Columbia River empties day and night into the Pacific Ocean; the 1,700-mile Zambezi River gushes nonstop into the Indian Ocean. And yet the oceans, unlike a bathtub, never seem to get any fuller. It's a genuine mystery: What happens to all that water?

First, some fast river facts. A river is a stream of water bigger than a meandering creek or babbling brook. Rivers are etched by rain and melted snow that run off the land like tears run off your face. (That's why scientists call the water "runoff.") Water flows down the gentle hills and towering mountains of Earth in streams; streams collect together into rivers. Rivers widen as water joins them from more streams along the way. Some rivers, like the Mississippi, become mighty, fed by smaller rivers. And all the water flows down, down, down toward the sea.

Big rivers dump stadiums full of water into the oceans. The greatest runoff occurs in areas of the world with the most precipitation, such as the rainy tropics, with their torrential monsoons. Some rivers in the tropics can pour out 700,000 cubic feet of water each second. The immense Amazon River drains an astonishing one-fifth of the world's runoff into the Atlantic in northern Brazil.

To understand why the oceans don't simply overflow, it helps to think of an ocean as a fountain in a public square. In a fountain, water sprays into a basin. But the basin doesn't overflow, because water is

pulled up from the basin to spurt out of the top of the fountain once again. The water continuously recycles.

Some rivers in the tropics pour out 700,000 cubic feet of water into the ocean each second.

It's the same with oceans and Earth. Water rains down on the land and flows into the oceans. But on the surface of the oceans, water continuouly escapes into the

sky—a process known as "evaporation." Molecule by molecule, water breaks free from the oceans, saturating the air and forming clouds. Clouds rain and snow, causing runoff on the land. And water from the land makes its way back to the oceans in pouring rivers.

All this is not to say that the amount of water in the ocean basins never changes. Earth's periodic "ice ages" have a big effect on sea level. When glaciers locked up much of the land, the level of water (sea level) in the oceans was much lower than it is today. Why? Water continued to evaporate from the oceans, forming clouds. But rain and snow falling on the continents quickly froze onto the massive sheets of ice, rather than flowing back into the sea.

However, as centuries passed and the ice slowly melted, sea level rose once again. In fact, sea level has risen at least 325 feet since glaciers last began to melt, about 18,000 years ago.

FAST FACT

The Amazon River pours out more than 456 million cubic feet of water each minute.

How do islands form?

When we think "island," we may picture palm trees, sandy beaches, and warm trade winds. But islands form everywhere, even in the coldest north. Chilly Greenland, for example, is Earth's biggest island, with 840,000 square miles of land.

Scientists define an island as a chunk of land smaller than a continent (such as Africa or North America) and surrounded by water. An island can be an inviting place to swim out to in the middle of a lake, or a whole country surrounded by the sea, like Jamaica or the Japan islands.

Some islands that look like separate pieces of land are actually part of nearby continents. So scientists call them "continental islands." New Guinea, a Pacific island just north of Australia, is one of them.

Here's how it works. The Earth's crust is really a patchwork of plates that float on a layer of extremely hot, liquid rock. Like rafts on the sea, the plates slip and slide along the surface of the molten rock. Continents ride on the plates, and plates underlie the oceans.

The island of New Guinea, which looks so separate on maps, is actually anchored to the same plate as its continental neighbor, Australia, with water covering the connection. The rising sea often creates such continental islands by flooding valleys around hills on the coastline of a continent. Voilà: Part of the continent is suddenly "offshore." Great Britain is a continental island. In the United States, islands off the coast of Maine were hills on the shoreline before the ocean flooded inland.

In addition to the continental islands, there are the "oceanic islands" that were never connected to any landmass. Most of the world's islands are oceanic, truly islands unto themselves.

Volcanoes are the artists that sculpt oceanic islands. Underwater volcanoes erupt, spewing lava, which cools and hardens. Over many years, the lava piles up and up, until it finally juts above the ocean's surface. The island of Hawaii, for instance, is really a pile of lava 32,000 feet high.

When volcanic islands are eroded by wind and rain, or sink back toward the sea, tiny sea animals known as coral sometimes build a ring around the island in shallow water. This "coral island" is called an atoll.

Where do volcanic islands get their lush plants and trees? Plants sprout when seeds blow in on ocean breezes, float in on seawater, or are dropped in by birds. In fact, birds and insects are often the only creatures living on such islands until human beings show up, bringing unwanted guests like rats and mice.

New oceanic islands are always being created. Scientists have even found an infant island hidden among the Hawaiian Islands. If you could peer down into the murky depths of the ocean, 17 miles from Hawaii, you'd see the island, dubbed "Loihi." Now a half mile underwater, Loihi is building slowly upward to the surface, one lava flow at a time. When it emerges, palm trees, hibiscus flowers, and beachfront hotels will undoubtedly take root and grow, given enough time.

Volcanoes are the artists that sculpt oceanic islands.

Besides the two major kinds of islands, there are also barrier islands, made of sediment (fine soil and sand) that has slid off the shoreline and into the water. Floating islands, mounds of matted plants and dirt, can often be found in lakes or rivers. In the coldest waters, such as those of the Arctic, you'll find floating ice islands.

How do icebergs form?

When a baby cow is born, the farmer says the mother cow has "calved"— given birth to a calf. Well, when an iceberg forms, scientists say it has been "calved," because it has broken off from a big ice shelf (or a bigger iceberg) to make its own way in the world.

Where do icebergs come from? They break off glaciers that cover Antarctica at the bottom of Earth and part of Greenland and Ellesmere Island at the top of Earth. So icebergs are born near the North and South Poles and then move out toward the middle of the planet, into warmer waters.

The parent glaciers formed from snow and freezing rain, spreading over the land and pushing into the sea at the coastline. There, the ice sheet edges are held up by the water. Glaciers are one of the more permanent features of our planet. They spread and retreat, depending on the climate, but they never completely disappear.

The glacier covering Antarctica, called an "ice sheet," stretches across nearly 5 million square miles and averages nearly a mile thick. The smaller "ice cap" of Greenland is still enormous, covering four-fifths of the island's 840,000 square miles.

Icebergs are born near the North and South Poles, then drift toward the middle of the planet, into warmer waters.

Over time, as ocean waves lap against the ice, the wind blows, and currents push, chunks of ice break off from the glaciers. (This usually happens in summer, when seawater is at its warmest.) This is called calving, and it's where icebergs come from.

How big are icebergs? Scientists say the average icebergs range in size from a kitchen stove to a 10-story office building. Scientists have even come up with cute names for different-sized icebergs. The littlest are called "growlers"; those the size of a small house—not very big as icebergs go—are dubbed "bergy bits."

The biggest chunks that break off in the Arctic region are rarely more than 400 to 500 feet long. But Antarctic icebergs can be monstrously large; one berg sighted was 208 miles long and 60 miles wide. Big icebergs can extend down 1,000 feet or more underwater and tower 200 feet high.

The life of an iceberg is short compared to ours, but long compared to Frosty the Snowman's. Imagine an iceberg calving from the mother ice sheet on the west coast of Greenland. As it separates, it slowly moves out to the open sea, carried along by ocean currents and pushed gently by the wind. For the first 3 months to 2 years of the iceberg's life, it floats south through Baffin Bay, a stretch of water between Greenland and Canada. During its vacation in the bay, much of the berg's ice melts off in the sun, while, now and then, small chunks of it splash into the ocean. If it reaches the coast of Newfoundland in Canada, more than 800 miles away, 90 percent of its original ice may have disappeared, leaving the iceberg a shell of its former self.

As the iceberg floats on into the Grand Banks, off the southern coast of Newfoundland, it encounters the warm water of the Gulf Stream. The remaining ice quickly melts as the bathtub-warm water mixes with the colder water from the north. In less than two days, a 400-foot-long iceberg can melt to a snowball and then disappear. If it's also raining and the wind is blowing, the iceberg melts all the faster, like a sad-sack snowman in a December downpour.

But some hardy icebergs make it nearly all the way to sunny Bermuda—truly an incredible journey.

Once in a while, somewhere on the Atlantic, a green iceberg floats by. Called "emerald icebergs," the bergs look green because of thousands of tiny ocean plants studded in their ice. How did it happen? In a typical case, as an iceberg melts unevenly, it may roll over in the ocean. Suddenly its undersea side, coated with frozen seawater and plankton, is now its topside. Presto: an iceberg ready for St. Patrick's Day.

FAST FACT

Since 1704, ships and icebergs have collided at least 200 times.

What are the jet streams, and what causes them?

You can't see them, but they're up there: miles above your head, blowing like a hurricane. They're the jet streams, and they're whizzing around the planet at this very moment.

People have hidden from tornadoes and battened down the hatches against hurricanes for as long as there've been humans. But we didn't know the jet streams existed until World War 2, in the 1940s.

The jet streams were actually discovered by fliers on their bombing runs. Because of ferocious winds, the fliers ran into problems hitting their targets when they tried to drop bombs from great heights. Some planes even found themselves at a standstill as they tried to fly into the wall of wind. Scientists later christened the winds "jet streams." (A jet is a forceful flow of fluid, either liquid or gas.)

Like a strong ocean current running through the water near a beach, jet streams are narrow, rushing currents in the air high above Earth. The winds in jet streams usually blow at speeds ranging from 60 to 150 miles (96 to 242 km) an hour. But at their peak, these high-flown winds can reach 310 miles (500 km) an hour.

Although TV weather forecasters often talk about *the* jet stream, there is more than one jet stream in the upper atmosphere. Jet streams are

Cruisin' in the...
Jet Stream
With it...

We're 10 minutes early!

usually found 30,000 to 60,000 feet (9 to 18 km) up. The two main jet streams in each hemisphere usually blow west to east over the warm subtropics and cold polar regions. The streams circle and recircle Earth in shifting, meandering paths, and sometimes merge into one. During the summer, a third jet-stream system springs up over India, Southeast Asia, and part of Africa. So there may be up to three jet streams operating in a hemisphere at once.

What causes these ribbons of fierce winds? Scientists say it has to do with the heating of the turning Earth by the Sun. Where warm air from the equator flows up to meet cold air coming down from the Poles, creating a huge difference in air pressure, high-speed jets of wind are spawned. Like high-altitude fences, jet streams mark the boundaries of cold and warm. And the bigger the difference between air temperatures, the stronger these high-level winds will be. (Which is why jet

streams are particularly strong in winter, when balmy winds from the equator

Like a strong ocean current running through the water near a beach, jet streams are narrow, rushing currents in the air high above Earth.

encounter the most frigid wind from the Poles.) Jet streams are the great equalizers, distributing heat away from the equator, helping make climate differences less drastic.

Weather forecasters talk about the jet stream because its daily wanderings and changes in intensity have a big influence on the weather, affecting the location of

high-pressure and low-pressure areas and storms. When the jet stream shifts far north or south from its normal position, the weather often turns unusual—drenchingly wet, bone-dry, frigidly cold, or oven-hot.

In some years, a warm Pacific Ocean current called El Niño is particularly large. As the water heats the air above it, the jet stream and storm clouds are forced north, which can mean heavy winter rains in the western United States.

There are jet streams on other planets, too; strong ones are found on nearby Mars. And recently, scientists discovered that there are jet streams on the Sun, too.

The jet streams on the Sun are rivers of hot, charged gas under our star's top layer. (Since the Sun is a ball of gas rather than solid like Earth, it's *all* atmosphere.) While tiny compared to the size of the Sun, each jet stream is wide enough to swallow two whole Earths.

What causes the different shapes of clouds?

AFTERNOON SNACK CLOUDS

Did you ever see a stallion running across the sky, its tail outstretched? Or a golden ladder, climbing toward the heavens? How about a wispy pen, writing with sunset-red "ink"? Clouds can take on fantastic shapes, created by water, air, and our vivid imaginations.

In 1803, a pharmacist and amateur weather-watcher from England named Luke Howard created categories for clouds based on their shapes. Billowy clouds were named "cumulus," from the Latin word for "heap." Flatter clouds that layered like blankets were named "stratus" ("layer"). High, icy, curlicue clouds were named "cirrus" ("tendril"). Today, meteorologists (weather scientists) still use Howard's cloud names.

The shape and position of clouds are constantly changing. Think of fat, fluffy cumulus clouds, the ones we often imagine in animal shapes. They grow when a parcel of warm, moist air rises—say, from a hot parking lot. When the warm air rises into

Hovering over mountain peaks, saucer-shaped clouds have been mistaken for UFOs.

higher, colder air, the cooling water vapor gloms on to dust or smoke particles, forming visible drops: a cloud. Rising moisture evaporates at the top of the cloud while new cloud forms at the bottom, creating round, cauliflower-shaped blossoms.

Wind makes cumulus clouds billow up, tilts them to one side, and pushes them

FAST FACT

Tall, anvil-shaped clouds usually mean a thunderstorm is on the way.

together into long lines across the sky. Strong winds blowing across a thunderhead cloud flatten the top, creating an anvil shape. Blowing air can also evaporate parts of clouds, leaving a line of frothy, "flocky" little clouds across the sky.

Above mountains, saucer-shaped clouds sometimes form. Water-heavy air is blown up mountainsides and encounters wind waves where air is passing over the peaks. The hilly shape of the airflow sculpts a saucer cloud. Hovering over mountain peaks, cloud saucers have often been mistaken for UFOs.

Sometimes, in a towering thunderhead, pockets of cold air will quickly sink through the cloud. The sunken air pockets make the bottom of the cloud bulge out in hanging pouches, called "mamma." Such pouches sometimes appear before tornadoes develop in a storm, and twist down to the ground. A tornado, of course, is one of the strangest cloud shapes of all.

The fantastically varying shapes of clouds are fertile ground for human imagination, which is very good at seeing patterns in things. At night, we see pictures in the stars, drawing lines between the stars to make pots (the Big and Little Dippers) or lions (Leo). Over eons, the positions of stars relative to Earth change, and people see different pictures in the night sky. (A million years ago, the Big Dipper looked like a broken spear.)

But because clouds change in minutes, not centuries, what we imagine we see constantly changes. An elephant head in a cumulus cloud may grow a longer trunk as the cloud stretches. A horse may transform into a big dog. In Shakespeare's play *Hamlet*, Hamlet and Polonius discuss a passing cloud that's changing shape by the second:

Hamlet: Do you see yonder cloud that's almost in shape of a camel?
Polonius: By the mass, and 'tis like a camel indeed.
Hamlet: Methinks it is like a weasel.
Polonius: It is backed like a weasel.
Hamlet: Or like a whale.
Polonius: Very like a whale.

Every kid will recognize this conversation: It's just like the one you have with your sister or brother, lying on your back and staring at the sky on a summer's day.

Why are rain clouds black in color? What happens to clouds after they form?

A horizon full of dark, menacing storm clouds can be a scary sight. But the reasons rain clouds are black aren't so scary.

First, some basic cloud facts. We sit under an ocean of air that presses down on each square inch of our bodies with nearly 15 pounds of force. Clouds form when moisture-laden air rises. As a clump of water-filled air climbs, it spreads out. (Why? Because high up, there is less air surrounding it, and so less air pressure.)

As the parcel of air expands, it cools like fudge spread on wax paper. When the air cools down to a temperature meteorologists call the "dew point," its water suddenly condenses from invisible vapor to billions of visible droplets, glommed on to stray bits of dust, dirt, or smoke in the air. A cloud hangs in the sky, where there wasn't one before.

In a storm cloud, rain occurs when these droplets bump into others, and become so heavy that they fall out of the cloud. Or when ice crystals in the cold peaks of the cloud fuse into snowflakes, which melt as they fall to Earth.

Such storm clouds appear gray for several reasons, according to scientists. Storm clouds are thicker than other clouds (some tower into the sky more than

6 miles), so not as much sunlight can pass through the cloud.

Second, water droplets in storm clouds have grown to larger sizes than those in

A big cloud's brief life span is determined mainly by the Sun.

white clouds or fog. Larger drops absorb more light than smaller drops, which tend to scatter sunlight out into the sky. So a cloud with larger drops will appear darker than a cloud with tinier drops.

Finally, not all dark clouds are storm clouds. Some clouds appear dark with glowing white borders, simply because they are lit from behind by the Sun, and light can't easily penetrate their huge, billowing middles.

Older clouds can take on a gray or purple tint, too. Why? As a cloud "ages," most of its small water droplets evaporate into the atmosphere. That leaves fewer drops, and larger ones, which, as we now know, don't scatter sunlight as well. So older clouds are darker than fresh, young clouds, which sparkle in the sun.

Like everything in nature, clouds are always changing—and quickly, too. Clouds spend their hours drifting in the wind, losing droplets and then gaining more as they float into moisture-laden air.

A big cloud's brief life span is determined mainly by the Sun. Clouds stay aloft because of warm air currents rising from Earth's surface. After the Sun sets for the day the earth cools, radiating heat into outer space. As air currents gradually cool, too, there is not as much hot air rising to keep clouds—especially puffy cumulus clouds—afloat. So billowy clouds begin dropping.

As a cloud sinks into the warmer air nearer our planet's surface, its droplets begin evaporating. Drop by disappearing drop, the cloud vanishes, never reaching the ground.

FAST FACT

Some clouds glow in the dark. Icy noctilucent clouds float about 50 miles up, and reflect light from the Sun even when it is far below the horizon.

What causes the sound of thunder?

Cracks, rumbles, and rolls: As you read this, some 2,000 thunderstorms are in booming progress around Earth, with lightning striking the ground about 100 times each second. It's no wonder so many cultures invented thunder gods to explain the terrible sounds.

In Europe there was red-bearded Thor, who wielded a mean hammer that returned like a boomerang. The Chinese had Lei Kung, a creature with a blue body, claws, and bat wings who beat out thunder with a mallet and drum. In ancient Sumeria it was Ninhar, the roaring bull (married to the much nicer Ninigara, the Lady of Butter and Cream). And North American Indians revered the mythical "thunderbird." Lightning flashed from the bird's beak; thunder was

the reverberation of its great beating wings.

In old England, thunder on Thursday meant your sheep were healthy, but thunder on Sunday foretold the death of judges and other "men of learning."

Today, we know that thunder is the sound lightning makes as it tears through air. Just as a tiny spark of electrons can jump across a rustling blanket in a dry room, a tremendous spark—a lightning bolt—can connect a storm cloud and the ground. And, like the little crackle you hear when sparks jump across a blanket, a clap of thunder shakes the earth.

Here's how it works. Out of the bottom of the cloud emerges a dimly glowing bolt, called a leader. It zigzags toward the ground in a fraction of a second, creating a channel through the air about 2 cm wide.

The bolt carries an electric current of about 200 amperes (normal household current is 15 or 20). When the bolt gets to within about 60 feet of the earth, a spark jumps out of the ground to join it. The two sparks connect, and the current races back up the channel to the cloud, increasing to more than 10,000 amps as it does.

Another leader snakes out and slams down the channel created by the upward stroke; another spark shoots back up to the cloud. Temperatures in the air channel quickly reach 50,000° F. These lightning strokes—firing back and forth many times in less than a second—are what we see as a single bolt.

In the channel, the superheated air expands violently, as air molecules get a tremendous burst of energy and fly apart. The air continues to expand outward in all directions from the lightning bolt at

Thunder is the sound lightning makes as it tears through air.

supersonic speed, forming traveling shock waves. A few feet away from the bolt, the waves slow to about 1,100 feet a second, the speed of an ordinary sound wave in air. When a wave reaches our ears, we hear a BOOM.

The boom, or thunder clap, comes from the main channel of lightning. The return stroke of the lightning flash actually makes the loudest sound, because it carries the most powerful current, heating and expanding the air most. The "crackling" sound we sometimes hear is made by lightning branching off the main trunk.

After the clap and roll, continuing rumbles are thunder's echoes from clouds, mountains, and buildings.

Why does a rainbow always form an arch?

When we think of rainbows, we picture dazzling colors, the sun coming out after a shower, and hidden pots of gold. But the fact that rainbows are curved has led many ancient cultures, from Africa to Europe, to compare them to—surprise—snakes, which likewise curve. In one African story, a rainbow is a giant snake that comes out to eat after the rain stops. The unlucky person that the

In one African story, a rainbow is a giant snake that comes out to eat after the rain stops.

rainbow falls on will be swallowed up, like a mouse by a boa constrictor.

In reality, a rainbow is a trick of light, rather than an object in the sky. A rainbow appears only when the circumstances are just right. Sunlight must be coming from behind you, and raindrops must be falling through the air in front of you. (Since you need bright sunlight for a rainbow to form, it usually means the shower is winding down or passing over in front of you.)

When light zips over your shoulders and head and pierces the outside of the raindrops, it bends, since water is more dense (closely packed) than air. White sunlight is actually made up of colors—red, orange, yellow, green, blue, indigo, and violet. The colors are simply light with different-length waves. A raindrop bends (refracts) each wavelength of light a little more or a little less as the light beam enters. That means the different wavelengths, or colors, go off in slightly different directions after they enter the drop. What was a neatly traveling-together white beam is now split apart into its true colors, each going its own way.

Within the raindrop, the colored rays collide with the raindrop's inside wall. Bent even more, they shoot back out of the raindrop through the side they originally entered. And you see a rainbow of colors spread in an arc across the sky.

Each raindrop refracts all the colors of the rainbow out into the sky. But from your fixed position on the ground, your eyes receive only certain colors from certain raindrops. Since raindrops bend red and orange most sharply, they are refracted down to your eyes from the highest drops. Blue and violet are less sharply bent, so you get them from lower drops. Yellow and green are what you can see from the drops in the middle. Put all the colors together, and you've got a rainbow.

Why are rainbows curved? Because the raindrops that make them are curved. Each raindrop is a little round ball, with sharply curving sides. So the light that emerges from inside echoes the curving circle of the ball. The rainbow arc you see is just part of this circle of light. (Sometimes, the arc will be a rather small slice of the circle, since rain may not cover the whole sky.)

If the wheel of color were complete, its center would be hidden at or below the horizon. Occasionally, from a hill overlooking a long, deep valley, and given a perfect rainfall, people have seen nearly full-circle rainbows.

What makes dew appear on grass?

Appearing seemingly from nowhere, and glistening on every blade of grass, leaf, and flower, people used to think dew was nectar from heaven. Rolling in dew was a favorite part of some ancient ceremonies, as was washing in it or drinking a bit for instant invigoration and good health.

But dew isn't confined to early-morning grass. A kind of dew appears on cold pipes in hot weather (we call it "sweating pipes"), and on the outside of ice-filled glasses in summer. Dew happens when water-filled air comes into contact with cooler surfaces—a blade of grass, a cold-water pipe, an ice-filled glass.

Air has what scientists call a "dew-point temperature." That simply means that at a particular temperature and pressure, a bunch of air is holding all the water vapor it possibly can. The air is saturated, like a washcloth full of water just before it begins to drip on your bathroom floor.

Whether dew is present in the morning depends on what happened the night before. After the sun goes down, the Earth's surface begins to lose the heat it stored up all day long. The moist air just above the ground loses heat, too. As long as the sky is clear, the heat simply radiates into space.

Dew appears not just on early-morning grass but also on cold pipes and ice-filled glasses in hot weather.

Cool air, which is more tightly packed, can't hold as much water vapor as warm air. So it quickly reaches its dew point, when it is as full of water as it can be without "spilling." If conditions remain calm—if no breeze springs up to mix in warm air from higher up—dew forms.

Here's how. The air, overfull of water vapor, touches a cool blade of grass. As the water vapor cools when it touches the grass, it turns into a liquid and drips onto the grass (rather like your dripping washcloth). Those droplets combine with water naturally evaporating from the plants. Soon, the whole lawn is covered with drops, which will glisten and shine when the Sun rises in the morning.

Dew forms most often at night when the sky is clear, since a clear sky means no clouds to prevent heat from radiating into space. So an old farmers' adage says that morning dew means no rain that day, whereas no dew means a storm is on the way.

Dew can have strange and wonderful effects on light. It can make a halo appear on the head of your shadow. If you happen to be on an evenly clipped lawn in early morning, just after the Sun has come up, you may see it. With your back to the Sun, look at the top of your long shadow on the wet grass. You may see a luminous halo surrounding your head.

You don't need to be a saint to wear the dew halo. Such halos form in a similar way to ordinary rainbows. Sunlight from behind the viewer strikes dewdrops in front of him, creating a little halo on the grass—much the same way a rainbow is created when you hold a spraying hose at just the right angle to the summer sunlight.

What is the cause of fog?

Fog is a cloud that hugs the ground. Usually, fogs are made of tiny droplets of water. The droplets sink and then rise again, carried by currents in the air. Sometimes they fall to the ground like rain, but new droplets appear to take their place.

Where do fogs come from? Fogs spring out of the air, where there are always water molecules zipping around. The water molecules jump into the air from oceans, rivers, lakes, and plants in a process called evaporation.

Warm air can hold a lot of water vapor. But as air cools, it reaches its saturation point and the water molecules condense into droplets. Water shapes itself into drops by attaching itself to particles of dirt or dust or pollutants in the air. A liquid droplet forms with the particle at its center like the pearl inside an oyster.

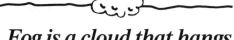

Fog is a cloud that hangs near the ground.

Droplets grow bigger as more and more water molecules collect together. As droplets grow and more droplets form, a light haze can thicken to a dense fog.

The kind of fog that forms at night and hangs around until morning is called a "radiation fog." After the sun goes down, the surface of Earth and the air above it cool, radiating away the heat stored during the day. If the air is moist or the cooling very great, a cloud of water droplets may form above the ground. (At night, riding down a dip in a country road, you may suddenly find yourself in a thick fog that your car headlights can't penetrate. That's because cold air tends to sink down the

FAST FACT

Occasionally, in places like the Arctic, ice fogs may form. Walk through an ice fog, and you will be surrounded by tiny, glittering ice crystals.

sides of hills and into valleys, carrying heavy fogs with it.)

A radiation fog becomes thickest in the morning, just after sunrise. Why? The first rays of the sun don't heat the air enough to burn off the fog. But the warming air becomes more turbulent. The cool air spreads, making a thicker layer of fog.

As the morning wears on, however, the air heats up. The water evaporates, the droplets splitting into molecules and whizzing off into the air. And the fog disappears.

Another kind of fog forms when warm rain from high clouds falls into a cooler layer of air near the ground. The cool air becomes saturated with water from evaporating raindrops, and fog forms. This fog is similar to the steam that rises from a tub of hot water into the cooler air of the bathroom.

Why do jet airplanes leave trails in the sky that look like clouds?

A jet climbing the vault of heaven can look like a comet streaking across the sky, trailed by a streaming, glowing tail. Watching the jet trail, you may have noticed its resemblance to those high, streaky clouds known as "cirrus." "Cirrus" means "curl" or "tendril." Icy cirrus clouds look like fluffy locks of hair.

The resemblance of a jet trail to a cirrus cloud is more than skin deep. In fact, a jet trail *is* a cirrus cloud, one produced by the engines of a jet airplane rather than by the sky itself.

Clouds form when water vapor collects in drops around floating particles of dirt, smoke, plant pollen, or salt in the sky. A jet's cloud is no exception. The water vapor comes from the jet's engines. And the particles come from the jet's exhaust, which spews out incompletely burned particles of sooty smoke.

Because jets fly so high—above 30,000 feet—the air around them is very cold. (When you are flying to visit a far-off relative, the air just outside the window next to your seat, no matter how sunny the day, may be 70° F. below zero.) In such cold temperatures, it takes just seconds for the water vapor from the engines to freeze around exhaust particles behind the jet, leaving a long, streaming, icy cloud. (This cloud is also called a "contrail," short for "exhaust condensation trail.") A jet is a flying cloud machine.

If the air around the jet is very dry, the contrail cloud will disappear almost as quickly as it forms, as the water dissipates into the cold air. That's why you sometimes see a jet with a short stubby trail, or no trail at all.

But if the air around a high-flying jet is already nicely moist, you will see the jet growing a longer and longer tail, streaming grandly across the sky from one end to the next. You'll notice the end of the trail, the oldest part, ballooning out. That's the cloud swelling as it slowly dissipates into the air. In moist air, a jet cloud can last for hours, drifting through the sky like any other wispy cirrus cloud.

In moist air, a jet cloud can last for hours, drifting through the sky until it looks like just another wispy cirrus cloud.

Glowing in the golden light of the setting sun, a jet trail may be one of the most beautiful clouds in the sky. Jet trails can even be used to predict the weather. If a passing jet leaves no trail or one that quickly disappears, then you know the air high up is dry. That usually means that the weather will be clear and dry, too. But jet clouds that last long enough to span the sky mean that the upper atmosphere is full of moisture, a good indication that rain or snow is on the way.

Why does the sky turn colors at sunset?

On a beautiful sunny day, the sky is blue, the clouds white, and the Sun a normal, if a bit boring, yellowish-white. But at sunset, white clouds and blue sky turn pink and orange and purple, and the Sun glows red. This stunning change is brought to you by whizzing gas molecules, floating dust particles, and other specks of this and that drifting in the sky.

Here's how it works. The light that is produced inside the Sun is white light. But white light contains within it many colors—all the colors of the rainbow. If you look at white light through a prism, you'll see this rainbow. The prism splits white light into its colors like a comb separating hair into its strands. White light enters the prism; bands of red, orange, yellow, green, blue, indigo, and violet light stream out the other side.

When sunlight enters Earth's atmosphere from space, some of the light slices cleanly through, reaching the ground untouched—staying white. But since Earth's air is made of gas molecules, such as nitrogen and oxygen, some of the light will run into these molecules on its way down.

At sunset, sunlight must travel through a thick blanket of air.

As sunlight passes into a gas molecule, such as oxygen, it is broken up into its true colors. The colors scatter out of the molecule in all directions. But the brightness of the emerging light depends on the color. Blue light shooting out of a gas molecule is eight times brighter than red light.

Intense blue light floods at us from billions of gas molecules in all directions in the sky—making the sky blue. (The sky isn't "pure" blue, because the other colors reach our eyes, too. But they are very faint.)

The sunbeam, having lost its blues, is yellowed, since the colors that are left in the beam are the warm colors. So the Sun looks more yellow to us than it actually is.

At sunset, an even more dramatic change occurs. The bottom layers of air are the thickest—more full of gas molecules and dust. So with the Sun low in the sky, sunlight must travel through an even thicker blanket of air than it does the rest of the day.

Why? When the Sun is overhead, its light passes through just the air above us—air that becomes thinner and thinner higher up, so much of the sunlight reaches our eyes unscathed.

But when the Sun is near the horizon, its light must pass through the heavier blanket of air near the ground, extending from the viewer to the horizon. As the light encounters many more air molecules, and more dust and pollutants, even more of the blue end of the spectrum is scattered out of the beam.

This leaves mostly orange and red light in the beam by the time it reaches our eyes. And so we see the Sun as a fiery orange ball rather than a pale yellow globe.

Particles of dust scatter the reddened light toward us, and clouds reflect the red light too, creating a tapestry of orange and red. Just after the Sun sets, purple patches may develop in the sky. Some scientists think the purple is a color overlap: intense red light from near the horizon, mixing with blue light from higher in the sky.

How is Earth like a magnet?

Stupid Science Experiment #1

Step ① Cover Earth with a sheet of paper...

Step ② Sprinkle with iron filings...

Step ③ Go to outer space to view pattern.

Have you ever seen a bar magnet, a rectangular piece of iron with a north and a south pole? If you cover the magnet with a sheet of paper and sprinkle iron filings or small iron nails on the paper, you will see the magnet's invisible force field. The bits of iron will line up in arcs around the magnet, the arcs ending at the magnet's poles.

The planet Earth acts as if it has a bar magnet lodged in its center. The north and south magnetic poles (near the actual North and South Poles) are like the two ends of a bar magnet. Arcing out from the poles is an invisible magnetic force field that extends thousands of miles into space above Earth's atmosphere.

All magnetic fields, whether emanating from a refrigerator door magnet or the Earth, are caused by electric currents—moving electrons. Electrons, which orbit the nucleus of atoms, have a negative electrical charge. A moving electron generates its own magnetic field, which loops out in a big arc around the electron's path. (For example, weak magnetic fields surround the current-carrying wire in a lamp cord when the lamp is switched on.)

Scientists think that electrical currents cause Earth's magnetism, too. The Earth's core is made mostly of iron. The very center of the core is solid; around the solid iron ball is hot liquid iron. As Earth rotates, the core rotates, too, and electrical currents are set up in the liquid metal. These electrical currents generate magnetic fields, turning our planet into one big magnet.

The Earth's magnetic field is too weak to make iron nails and frying pans stick to the ground. The field is strongest near the two poles. But even there, it is only a tiny fraction (perhaps 1/200th) of the strength of a red-tipped toy horseshoe magnet. (You can see how weak it is for yourself by holding a small magnet near a compass. The tiny magnet will pull the compass needle away from true north, demonstrating that your little magnet is stronger than Earth's.)

But Earth's magnetic field is strong enough to change the course of charged particles in space. We can see the visible effects of Earth's magnetism in a dazzling natural light show called an "aurora." Shimmering curtains of blue-green light, with patches of pink and red, may stretch 100 miles across the evening sky in the far north and far south. (The auroras are also

The Earth's magnetic field is much too weak to make iron nails and frying pans stick to the ground.

called the northern and southern lights.) If Earth's natural magnetism were some-how switched off, the auroras would disappear, too.

Here's why. Protons and electrons—bits and pieces of atoms—constantly stream out from the Sun in a flow called the solar wind.

As these electrically charged particles pass near Earth, they encounter our planet's magnetic force field.

The magnetic field attracts the particles, pulling them in. Pulled-in particles travel in "beams" along the magnetic force lines, which bend back to Earth near the North and South Poles. There they are dumped into the atmosphere.

Colliding with the particles high up in the air, nitrogen and oxygen atoms in our atmosphere give off photons of colored light. And we see the unearthly glow of the aurora.

FAST FACT

Scientists think birds can sense the magnetic field lines of the Earth, helping them navigate on long journeys.

Is it true draining water swirls in opposite directions north and south of the equator?

Perhaps you heard it from a friend, or even learned it in school: Bathtub water swirls clockwise in the Southern Hemisphere, counterclockwise in the Northern Hemisphere. What might make this happen? The Coriolis Effect.

No, the Coriolis Effect is not this summer's blockbuster movie. It's simply the effect that a turning planet—ours, in this case—has on moving bodies on or above the planet's surface. These can include bodies of water, weather systems, and even the paths of rockets.

The Effect was named after Gaspard-Gustave de Coriolis, a mathematician and engineer who lived in France in the 1800s. One of his fields of study was what happens to moving bodies when their frame of reference (such as the Earth) is rotating.

To get an idea of how the Effect works, put a piece of paper on a spinning turntable. Now, hold a ruler just above the turntable from the center to the edge and draw a straight line on the paper, following the edge of the ruler. When you look at the paper, you'll notice that the line you drew isn't straight, but curved—like a hurricane.

It's the Coriolis Effect that helps curve storm systems into spinning cyclones, spawning hurricanes on Earth and the Great Red Spot on Jupiter. Such storms on Earth rotate clockwise south of the equator, and counterclockwise north. And that's how the story about draining bathtubs—and flushing toilets—got started. People believed that if the Coriolis Effect did indeed influence everything, then vortexes of water must swirl in opposite directions in New York and Melbourne, Australia.

Unfortunately, they were wrong. While the Earth's spin does influence your bathwater, the effect is so slight as to be completely unnoticeable. See for yourself, using different drains in your house. (My bathroom sink in New York drains clockwise—the opposite of the predicted Coriolis Effect.)

The truth is, water goes down drains both clockwise and counterclockwise in the north and in the south. The difference depends only on the plumbing. The rotation rate of a tiny parcel of water in a sink can be 10,000 times faster than that of Earth (which, remember, takes 24 hours to rotate once). So the Coriolis Effect is too weak to make these little everyday vortexes behave.

To show the Coriolis Effect working as it really does in nature, on the scale of a hurricane, bathtubs would have to measure hundreds of miles across—fit for a race of giants.

Why do ships and planes disappear in the Bermuda Triangle?

Some call it the Bermuda Triangle. Others refer to it as the Devil's Triangle, or the Limbo of the Lost. "It" is a triangular area of the ocean off the coast of Bermuda, where at least 100 ships and planes and pleasure boats are supposed to have disappeared—or been mysteriously abandoned.

Usually, the triangle is said to be the area between three imaginary lines drawn from Melbourne, on the southeast coast of Florida, to Bermuda, to Puerto Rico, and back to Florida. However, the boundary lines vary according to who's writing about the triangle. Some say the triangle stretches from Florida to Bermuda to Virginia, for example. By drawing a bigger triangle, a writer can tally up more disappearances of boats and planes, making the area seem more mysterious.

Through the years, some TV shows and books have claimed that something funny is going on in that area of the ocean. Ships sail in and sink without a trace, they claim. Planes fly over and vanish forever. Their explanations range from monstrous waves churned up by undersea earthquakes to alien kidnappers from other worlds to time warps, sending the missing vessels into the past or the future. Or maybe a giant sea monster simply opens up its massive jaws and *chomp*, there goes another pleasure boat.

If all of this sounds a little wacky to you, you're not alone. Fortunately, we have a tool—scientific investigation—that can help us solve such mysteries. In the 1970s, Lawrence Kusche, a librarian and himself a pilot, set out to investigate the mysterious triangle. Eventually, he wrote a book about what he found out: *The Bermuda Triangle: Mystery Solved.*

As a pilot, Kusche was well aware of what could happen to planes in flight. And as a librarian, he knew how to search for old documents and records.

Kusche soon found that the goings-on in the so-called triangle did not need to be explained by the supernatural. First, he reasoned, it doesn't make sense to try to come up with *one* explanation for more than 100 separate incidents. You wouldn't believe it if someone told you that all the car accidents in New York were caused by drunk driving—or by drivers possessed by the devil. Likewise, accidents happen in the ocean for a variety of reasons: Bad weather. Broken equipment. Navigation errors.

Kusche combed through old newspaper clippings and reports and found that there were good explanations for most of the losses in the "triangle." An example is the disappearance of the Philadelphia yacht *La Dahama* in 1935.

Some writers reported that the yacht had sunk in a storm, its crew rescued at the last moment by a passing boat. Several days later, however, the yacht was found,

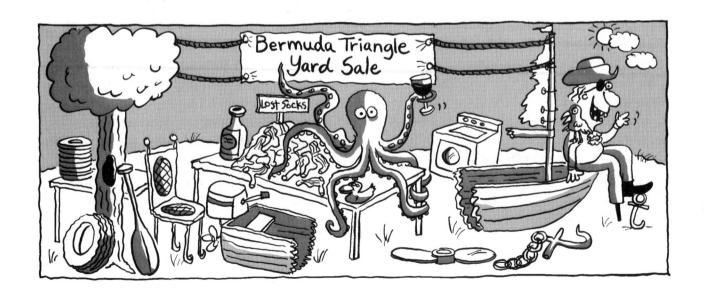

abandoned but full of food, in calm seas. Naturally, some writers dubbed it a "ghost ship."

Between 1850 and 1975, some 200 vessels disappeared or were abandoned between New England and Europe. But so far, no one's calling the Upper Atlantic the Devil's Rectangle.

The truth, Kusche found, was that there was no mystery about the reappearance of the boat—for there *was* no "reappearance." The crew of the departing rescue boat had reported the storm-damaged yacht was in "sinking condition" when they left the scene. They never said that the yacht had sunk. There was no ghost ship, and no mystery—and not even a very interesting story, certainly not one that would sell newspapers.

In case after case, Kusche found similar everyday, even boring, solutions. Lurid stories about the triangle were only half-truths; when the whole stories were told, the mysterious incidents became ordinary accidents. Rather than do the painstaking, unglamorous research Kusche undertook, others had found it easier, more fun—and more profitable—to concoct stories about ghost ships, time warps, and alien invaders.

A few disappearances, where physical evidence and eyewitnesses were lacking, couldn't be explained. But as Kusche pointed out, there are plenty of unexplained disappearances in other parts of the sea—they're just not as well publicized. The Earth's oceans are enormous. It's no wonder that some things get swallowed up without a trace.

For example, Kusche found that between 1850 and 1975, some 200 vessels disappeared or were abandoned between New England and Europe. But so far, no one's calling the Upper Atlantic the Devil's Rectangle.

Why do we seem to see a face in the Moon?

On nights with a bright, full, or mostly full moon, we see him: the Man in the Moon. Those big, hollow, almost sad eyes. That long nose. And a hint of a mouth. He seems to look down at us, an endless sentinel circling Earth.

We've named flowers after him (Man-in-the-Moon marigolds), mentioned him in songs and poems, and shown him grinning in cartoons and children's books. But he doesn't really exist, of course. The Man in the Moon is the creation of flowing lava, tricks of light, and human imagination.

But a man isn't the only thing people have seen in the Moon. Some cultures see a woman with a basket on her back, or a woman

weaving cloth. And all over the world, people have seen a rabbit in the Moon.

Where do the men, women, and bunnies come from? Billions of years ago, the moon wasn't the silent, gray world it is today. Like

The Man in the Moon is a creature of lava, light, and human imagination.

all rocky worlds, the Moon has a history of exploding volcanoes. Hot, glowing lava once flowed on the Moon's surface. In some areas, the lava cooled into solid, flat plains called "maria." There are 14 maria, all of them on the side of the Moon facing Earth. The hardened lava makes each mare appear as a dark-gray patch on the Moon. The maria are huge, and can easily be seen on a clear night.

Looking at the Moon, it's easy to see what the "Man" really is—maria form the "eyes," "nose," and "mouth" we imagine we see. *Imagine* is the key word. Human beings are pattern-makers. We tend to assemble unrelated features into patterns, or pictures. That's why we see animals in the billows of clouds, and all sorts of people and objects in the random arrangement of stars. This kind of intelligence serves us well in both art and science. And it means we also see a man (or a rabbit) in the Moon.

The Man in the Moon even has a cousin these days: the Face on Mars. First spotted in photographs taken by the Viking Orbiter in 1976, the "Face" measures a mile long and seems to protrude from the surface of Mars like the Great Sphinx of Egypt. Near the "Face" are features that some claim likewise resemble the Egyptian pyramids.

Some claim the Face on Mars is evidence that an intelligent civilization once thrived on the Red Planet—or at least visited it. But most scientists are skeptical. Astronomer Carl Sagan said that given how fond human beings are of seeing faces in nature, it's not too surprising that we should see the pattern of a face in the natural features of Mars. And isn't it interesting that it's always we humans, familiar animals, and our most prized possessions that show up regularly in the heavens?

However, NASA wants to lay the matter to rest. So a priority in ongoing missions to Mars will be to photograph the face close up—and perhaps settle, once and for all, whether it's a visual trick or authentic alien architecture.

Why does Earth have only one moon?

Mars has two cute ones. Neptune has eight. Saturn has eighteen. And then there's Earth, with one lonely one. Of course, it could be worse. Mercury and Venus are moonless (or "moonfree," if you actually prefer planets without them).

What's up with moons, anyway? Some planets get one or two. Others get a whole squadron. In the Great Moon Lottery, it might appear as though Earth were a loser planet.

On the other hand, our only moon is, it must be admitted, spectacular. Big and round and silvery, it's the stuff of songs and poems, tugging up great tides in the ocean of water covering our planet. What would we do without it?

But we did do without it, in the very earliest days of our planet, some 4.6 billion years ago. Just after Earth formed, the Moon was born. And surprise: It may have

If there were... ... Two moons!

You'd get a tan at night... ...Surf across the country at high tide... ...watch the man and ma'am in the moon!

had a twin sister moon, born at the same time, now long gone.

Here's how scientists think it might have worked. In the demolition derby that formed our solar system, debris circled round and round the baby Sun, causing numerous, violent collisions. New planets slammed into each other. Pieces broke off of some worlds. The chaos lasted millions of years. And when everything sorted itself out, there was a solar system. Orbiting the Sun were 9 planets,

Just after Earth formed, the Moon was born. And surprise: It may have had a twin sister moon, born at the same time, now long gone.

more than 50 moons, and thousands of asteroids, meteoroids, and comets.

Our moon may have had a particularly violent and dramatic birth. The very young Earth was still very hot—so hot that rock ran in lava rivers over the surface. Near Earth, scientists think, a smaller planet (Mars-sized or bigger) had formed. And the two new worlds were on a collision course.

Hurtling toward Earth at perhaps 25,000 mph, the smaller planet slammed into ours. The hot, liquid outsides of both planets blasted into space in a tremendous explosion.

Some material fell back to Earth, mixing in with the liquid rock. But most of the blasted-out material stayed in space, forming a lump of superhot rock orbiting Earth. Over thousands of years, the lump cooled and rounded into our familiar white-gray moon.

Recently, using computer programs to simulate the collision, scientists made a startling discovery. In 9 out of 27 scenarios they watched, two moons formed instead of one: a pair. There was the moon we call The Moon. And there was her unnamed sister, orbiting even closer to Earth.

As the scientists watched their computer screens, the inner moon's orbit became unstable, as Earth's gravity tugged and tugged. In less than 100 years, the moon crashed into Earth's surface, never to be seen again.

If theories are correct, you may be walking on bits and pieces of that Mars-sized alien world, as well as shards of a moon, our satellite's long-lost sister. Had it survived, we would have been forced to come up with a more creative name than "moon" for the second light in our night sky.

Ring Around the Moon

Have you ever gone out at night and seen a large, ghostly white ring around the Moon? Rings around the Moon can at first glance seem puzzling. We know that the ring does not really surround the Moon, which is traveling in the vacuum of space, some 250,000 miles from Earth. The ring is in our own skies. But why does the ring circle the Moon? And why does the ring appear only once in a while, rather than every night?

Look closely, and you'll discover that the ring isn't actually white. Rather, it resembles a faint round rainbow, light red on the inside and pale blue on the outside.

A moon ring, also known as an ice halo, appears when light is bent (refracted) by ice crystals in cold, high cirrus clouds. Each six-sided ice crystal in the clouds acts like a tiny prism. The crystal prisms bend the incoming moonlight, breaking the white light up into its rainbow of colors.

The altered moonlight appears in the shape of a ring because the crystals bend the light into a cone. (You, the observer, are positioned at the narrow end of the cone of light.) The ring usually appears to be about two fists' wide when you stretch both hands to arm's length. The ring's width depends on how much the moonlight is bent by the ice crystals. Most of the moonlight enters through the sides of the ice crystals and is bent exactly 22 degrees, creating an ordinary, smaller cone. But huge, 46-degree halos can also appear, just not as frequently. They are formed only when moonlight passes through the sharply bent points of the crystals.

A ring around the Moon is said to predict rain, and it often does, since a ring can only appear on a cloudy night.

How come Earth doesn't have any rings?

Until recently, the image of our solar system in the average person's mind was nine planets orbiting the Sun, one of them sporting a gorgeous girdle of rings. There was spectacular Saturn, and then there were the dowdy rest of us.

Times have changed. We learned that Jupiter, Uranus, and Neptune have rings too, although not as shiny and numerous as Saturn's. Although still beautiful, Saturn lost its uniqueness. And then, we discovered the most important ring fact of all: Planetary rings appear to be a temporary phenomenon—here today, gone 100 million years from now. And Earth may have had its very own ring, long, long ago.

The award for Most Elaborate Rings goes

to Saturn. Saturn's glittering rings look like solid bands. But each ring is actually made up of thousands of orbiting ice pieces and ice-covered rock. They range from crushed-ice size to snowballs to boulders to icebergs, all tumbling around Saturn at 45,000 mph.

How did the rings form? Scientists say that the rings could be all that's left of a moon that exploded when it was hit by an asteroid. Or perhaps a comet strayed too near Saturn and was ripped apart by the huge planet's gravity.

Jupiter wins the award for Loneliest Ring. Its single unshiny ring is probably made of sooty bits of rock and dust. Scientists think the particles are chipped off the planet's moonlets by tiny meteoroids, or spewed into space from volcanoes on Io, one of Jupiter's moons. Uranus has at least nine thin, dark rings, and Neptune wears at least four.

No matter what they are made of, or where they came from, a planet has rings because its gravity keeps the particles clutched around itself, orbiting in a perpetual loop instead of flying off into space. But gravity has a downside. Ring systems appear to be temporary, ephemeral constructions. Saturn's rings, as well as the rings around the other outer planets, have existed in their current form for no more than about 100 million years, scientists say.

How come? The gases that surround a planet—its atmosphere—thin out gradually into the emptiness of space. But even at the distance of rings, there are traces of gas. Tiny particles in the ring collide with the gas molecules, creating friction called atmospheric drag.

This slows orbiting ring particles, causing them to gradually spiral down toward their planet, pulled by gravity. Bits and pieces of the rings eventually tumble down into the skies of their home planets, just as satellites sometimes fall to Earth.

Ring systems appear to be temporary constructions.

And that brings us back to Earth. Scientists say Earth probably had a ring billions of years ago—instead of a moon. A collision between Earth and another nearby body, as the solar system was still forming, leaving an orbiting ring of debris around our planet. Instead of falling to Earth, most of the debris gradually coalesced, forming— you guessed it—the Moon.

Where does dust come from?

Have you ever sat near a sunny window and noticed that the beam of sunlight is full of floating, tumbling dust? Have you ever wiped off your dresser, only to find it covered with a powdery layer of something a day or two later? Do enormous dust bunnies live under your bed?

Perhaps there's a secret factory somewhere that spews clouds of the stuff into the air at night, recycled from the vacuum cleaner bags we put in the trash.

Most of the dust you push around with a feather duster is skin cells.

In reality, dust happens because Things Fall Apart. Most dust is made of tiny fragments broken off larger things. The world is always crumbling to dust, and much of it finds its way into our homes and up our noses. Gesundheit!

The stuff floating dreamily in a sunbeam could very well be the dirt you just tracked in from outdoors, bits of soil mixed with pulverized concrete worn off the sidewalk, with just a hint of rubber sole. Dust can be made of anything and everything. Imagine all the things on Earth that are constantly being worn down by erosion, burned up in incinerators, shaved off by band saws, and picked up by wind. (Not to mention filed off fingernails and shaken off powder puffs.)

In factories, dust comes from all the materials being drilled and ground. Factory workers must often wear face masks, to avoid breathing in tiny bits of metal, or teensy particles of glittering ground glass.

Plants dry up, crumble to bits, and blow around in the air. Your own dead skin cells are constantly flaking off. In fact, most of the dust you push around with a feather duster week after week may be coming from your and your family's shedding bodies: By weight, up to 70 percent of house dust can be skin cells. Making *you* the dust factory.

Volcanic ash is blown out of volcanoes and into the air, coating the surrounding countryside in gray powder. Such dust blocks sunlight and lowers temperatures, not to mention turning sunsets and moonrises blood-red.

The Moon is a plenty dusty place, too. Astronauts who stepped onto its surface stepped into a thick layer of dust, rock crushed by meteorites slamming in from space century after century. On Mars, our robot explorers plop down into rusty-orange dust. Even space itself, which looks so empty, is actually dusty, with floating molecules of this and that, from pulverized rock to exploded stars.

Dust never disappears, it just moves around, as anyone who's spent time cleaning knows. So some of the dust in your room right now may have come from a meteorite that once whizzed through space, or from an adobe house in an ancient desert, or from the dry bones of a long-gone dinosaur.

SAFARI

Earth was made for life. It happened like a shot in cosmic terms—the planet's first tiny life, an ancient cousin of blue-green algae, appeared at least 3.5 billion years ago. How did we get from algae to dinosaurs and porcupines and people? Evolution took care of that. Look around even your own small patch of Earth, or sit in a city park, and you'll have a window on the amazing variety of creatures alive today. Trilling songbirds (4,000 kinds). Bushy-tailed squirrels (260 kinds of those). Crawling, flying, buzzing insects (more than a million kinds). Giraffes with necks stretching 6 feet;

elephants with ears hanging 5 feet— all in all, more than 1,040,000 separate species of animal life on Earth. All adding up to billions and billions of individual animals, of all shapes and sizes. (Perhaps even more astounding, scientists say that some 2 billion *species* of animals and plants have lived on Earth—and that more than 90 percent of them have disappeared.)

Have you ever wondered *why* an elephant's ears are so outsized? Why so many animals have tails—but we don't? Why dogs bark, or why cats' eyes shine in the darkness? Take a safari into the heart of Earth's profusion of life—and find out.

How do fish breathe underwater?

Ever try to breathe underwater? Water goes up your nose, making you choke. Or you can hold your breath. Fill your lungs with air above the water, then dive under, holding the air in your lungs until you feel like you'll explode.

Now you know why snorkeling tubes were invented.

But fish don't need snorkeling tubes or oxygen tanks. While you are gasping for breath, they are swimming blithely by, with hardly a look in your direction.

However, take most fish out of water, and you'll see them flopping and gasping for air. Air, air everywhere, and not a drop to breathe, where most fish are concerned.

How come most fish can't breathe in the open air, but are apparently full of oxygen underwater? One word: gills.

Whales and dolphins, which are mammals like us, have lungs like ours, too. So they have to make frequent trips to the surface for a breath of fresh air—which they then store in their lungs, just as we hold our breath underwater.

But fish stay underwater—in fact, most must—because the water itself is the source of their oxygen.

The air that we walk through and breathe is about 21 percent oxygen. But the water a fish swims through is only about

A fish out of water isn't where it oughtta be...

They hate going out for walks ...

one-half of 1 percent dissolved oxygen. So a fish's body must concentrate the oxygen in order to get enough to survive. Not only that, but water is 1,000 times heavier than air and at least 50 times as viscous (syrupy). So it's quite a job getting the tiny amount of oxygen out.

That makes it all the more remarkable that although we humans can extract only 25 percent of the oxygen from the air we inhale, fish are able to extract up to *80 percent* of the oxygen in the water passing into their bodies. So fish are much better at getting oxygen out of water than we are at getting oxygen out of air.

Here's how it works. All fishes have gills inside their bodies, which are something like curtains hanging in folds. If the gills were unfolded, they would be 10 to 60 times as large as the body surface of the fish itself. Throughout the gills, the fish's blood circulates.

Water streams into the fish's mouth and through gill slits inside. Once it flows into the gills, the water and the fish's blood are separated only by an extremely thin membrane (less than 1/10,000th inch thick). This means that oxygen from the water needs to travel only this tiny distance to

Fish are much better at getting oxygen out of water than we are at getting oxygen out of air.

enter the fish's blood. Quickly, oxygen is absorbed through the thin membrane and into the blood. The oxygenated blood flows through arteries into the rest of the body, including the heart, supplying the fish with fresh oxygen.

At the same time blood is absorbing oxygen from the water in the gills, it is getting rid of carbon dioxide. (Our blood transfers carbon dioxide into the air through our lungs: We breathe it out.) In a

fish, carbon dioxide passes from the blood through the thin membrane into the water circulating in the gill.

Depleted of oxygen and carrying carbon dioxide, the water exits the fish through sets of gills on the outside of the fish's body. The fish has fueled up with oxygen and rid itself of carbon dioxide—without taking a single breath.

The gills' large surface area means that they can come into contact with a lot of water, and thus filter as much oxygen as possible into the fish's bloodstream. (Fish blood, by the way, is red like ours, tinted by the red blood cells that carry oxygen around the fish's body.)

Why do fish out of water usually gasp for oxygen? The typical gill collapses and dries out, cutting off the fish's oxygen supply. However, some fish have evolved gills that trap moisture, keeping gills wet even when exposed to air. And other fish absorb oxygen from air through tissues in their mouths, throats, or heads. Freshwater eels (eels are fish, too) have an especially clever design: They can breathe through their damp skin.

How come fish and dolphins don't sleep?

Parrot Fish Sleepover...

Who cares if they're asleep, there's mucus everywhere!

Nobody knows if fish sleep the way humans, cats, horses, and many other animals sleep. Human sleep has been studied for many years in laboratories. Scientists hook up their sleeping subjects to electroencephalographs (ECGs), which trace their brain waves. So they know that humans go through several stages of sleep each night, and exactly when they dream.

There doesn't seem to be as much interest in hooking fish up to ECGs to see if they really sleep or not. We do know some things, however. For example, fish whose skeletons are made of bone (like tuna, mackerel, and trout) don't have real eyelids, so they can't close their eyes. And all fish seem to remain at least somewhat aware of what's going on around them at all times. But at night, many bony fish do remain still for long stretches, resting on the sea floor or in caves.

You can see this for yourself if you have an aquarium. "Surprise" your fish in the middle of the night by flipping on a light. You should see your fishy friends resting on the bottom, caught in the act of what passes for sleep underwater.

Bony fish don't have real eyelids, so they can't close their eyes.

Scientists like to spy on resting fish, too. In David Feldman's book *When Do Fish Sleep?*, a scientist describes the nightly ritual of a tired parrotfish, which lives in reefs near shore. At night the parrotfish shoehorns himself into a crevice on the reef like a person crawling into a tiny bunk on a train. Settling in, the parrotfish begins oozing mucus, which forms a membrane over his body like a gauzy sleeping bag.

Once safely ensconced in his mucus comforter, the parrotfish nods off into what can only be described as a near-coma. His eyes are open but apparently unseeing, his body nearly frozen. If you approach very slowly, you can actually pick up a "sleeping" parrotfish without his awakening. (Scientists have pulled the same trick on hibernating squirrels.) But a dozing parrotfish isn't really dead to the world. Any sudden movements in the water nearby will send him darting off.

Sharks, which are not bony fish (their skeletons are made of flexible cartilage), are another story. Most kinds of shark swim constantly. But some species of shark do seem to sleep, motionless, in underwater caves or on the ocean bottom.

So much for fish—which brings us to the question of sleepy dolphins. Dolphins aren't fish at all; they're mammals like us. If dolphins slept like we do—eyes closed, most muscles paralyzed, unaware of most sounds—there soon wouldn't be any dolphins. Dolphins, after all, are one of a shark's favorite meals.

So to protect themselves, dolphins have evolved the half-snooze. Scientists say dolphins do sleep, and go through stages of sleep, from light to deep, like humans do. But unlike us, dolphins may sleep with only half their brains: While one side of the brain dozes, the other remains awake and aware, allowing the dolphin to swim, watch, and listen. (Even the sleeping part of the dolphin's brain is alert to sights and sounds.) No one knows what strange consciousness a dolphin is experiencing as she cruises the ocean in her half-alert, half-dreamy state.

Why do some sharks die if they stop swimming?

How is a shark like a jet plane? Keep reading, and you'll find out.

First, some basic shark facts: Sharks are fierce fishes that stalk and eat other sea creatures—including other sharks. When it comes to sharks, teeth 'r us: Their powerful jaws are studded with rows of jagged teeth, and their skin is made of converted teeth, too. And those teeth can really speed: Some sharks can accelerate to more than 40 mph when chasing prey. The smallest shark, the cigar shark, is only about 8 inches long. The largest, the whale shark, may grow to 50 feet—longer than a school bus.

Many of the 350 species of sharks must "move or die." Stop swimming, and their oxygen supply stops,

too. These sharks operate much like an airplane engine called a "ramjet."

A jet moves because a high-speed "jet" of gas from the rear of its engines pushes the plane forward. (Think of air jetting out of an out-of-control party balloon, and you'll get the picture.)

In a regular jet engine, air is squeezed by a compressor, then mixed with burning jet fuel. The hot gases stream out of the engine. But a ramjet uses its own forward motion to force air at high speed through a narrow opening in the engine's front. This squeezes the air automatically—no compressor required.

Now, back to sharks. A shark cruising silently through water is performing an aerobic activity—an activity that uses a lot of oxygen (like running). For a shark to keep moving, its respiratory system must process incoming oxygen, and its blood must deliver the oxygen to muscles and other organs that need it, right now.

Some sharks can accelerate to more than 40 mph when chasing prey.

Sharks, like other fish, get their oxygen from water instead of air. A shark has gills built in arches on the sides of its body. Behind the arches are slits. Water pours in, mainly through the shark's mouth, and flows over the gills, where oxygen is extracted. The oxygen passes into the shark's bloodstream. The used water streams back into the ocean through the gill slits. (For more

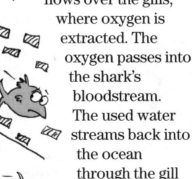

on gills, see page 80.)

Some kinds of sharks have very muscular gills that rhythmically pump water in and out. This pumps the shark full of oxygen, even when it's resting comfortably on the ocean floor. These sharks, such as wobbegongs, do not need to swim constantly to survive.

Then there are the sharks built like ramjets. As they glide through the ocean, their forward motion forces water through their mouths and gills. These sharks, such as the white and mako sharks, must keep moving to keep oxygen-rich water flowing through. Stop, and they slowly suffocate.

Other sharks use a handy combination method. The gray nurse shark switches from ramjet mode at cruising speed to muscular pumping when he stops for a rest.

For many sharks, it's also "sink or swim." Being denser than water, many sharks use constant swimming to stay afloat. Stop moving, and they sink gently down, down, down.

If whales can't walk, why do they have hips?

An ode to whale hips...

I think that I shall never see whale hips wiggling down the street toward me... Slipped into modish hiphugger jeans... Perched on long legs making the scene.

Imagine life beginning in water, billions of years ago. Over millions of years, it evolved from simple collections of cells to real creatures—fish and other ocean animals with brains and hearts and complicated lives.

But some 370 million years ago, something happened that would change the world forever. Animals that had evolved rudimentary feet began spending more time on land. They were still fishy-looking, but the die was cast. Land animals were evolving and coming into their own. As they branched out over millions and millions of years, Earth's solid ground was overrun by life.

Because of the way evolution worked, we tend to think of life as emerging from the ocean—as going in one direction, from wet to dry. But many animals that evolved into land creatures, such as the amphibians (frogs are one kind), ended up spending a good deal of their time in the water.

What happened with the whale, however, was a total change of direction. Whale ancestors came from the ocean, like all land animals. As land whales evolved further, they found the pickings better in the ocean, slid back into the sea—and stayed there.

How do we know? Some of today's whales have what scientists call "vestigial" hip and leg bones the size of human fingers. "Vestige" means remnant, so vestigial hips are like remnants of large, fully developed hip joints. Ancestors of the whales had the real thing—hips and legs, that is. And that must mean that they walked.

Scientists who study evolution are always on the lookout for fossils of transition animals, those whose shape and size show that they were the "halfway" point between modern animals and their more ancient ancestors. Some of the most distant ancestors of whales clearly walked on all fours. But until recently, scientists hadn't found the fossil of a "land whale" that was a missing link in the evolution of today's whales.

Then, in Pakistan in the early 1990s, diggers discovered the 50-million-year-old fossil of a whale with legs and feet. The animal was about 10 feet long and probably weighed 600 to 700 pounds. It had jagged teeth, short front legs, a long tail, and long, splayed-out back legs with enormous feet.

Along with other, younger fossils, the new find has helped scientists reconstruct what whales looked like as they evolved from land-lovers to ocean dwellers. These ancestors of today's whales were probably meat-eating, four-legged land mammals with a lumbering, sea lion–type walk. They may have swum like otters and eaten mainly fish.

Land whales found the pickings better in the ocean.

As the "land whales" evolved to forage in the oceans, their hind limbs became weaker. The evidence? The fossil of a 40-million-year-old whale had tinier, more useless hind legs than its 50-million-year-old ancestor. This whale probably spent all of its time in the water.

Today's whales began appearing about 30 million years ago. Broad tails had replaced useless, tiny legs, and whales had developed a hearing system specially adapted for underwater communication and navigation.

Do whales really sing?

Life in the ocean is different than life on dry land. Dive underwater and try to smell an orange, or see more than a matter of feet in any direction. Animals that spend their time in the water had to evolve different ways of sensing their world than through smell or sight. One of these ways was sound.

Whales have a whole repertoire of sounds that they use both to communicate and to find their way through the cloudy depths. But only certain whales "sing." Whales are divided into two groups, according to how they feed them-selves: toothed whales and baleen whales.

Toothed whales are more aggressive. They include sperm whales and orcas. Toothed whales feed like big jungle cats, by

For my first number...

hunting and catching prey, from small fish to octopus and sea lions. Then they swallow their catches—whole.

The gentler-seeming baleens are known as "filter feeders." Baleen whales include, among others, the humongous blue whales and the singing humpbacks. Baleens feed by skimming along the surface, their mouths agape, trapping tiny plants and animals in bristly strainers inside.

The sea is murky even during the daytime, and many toothed whales travel and hunt at night. How do they do it? Like a bat swooping through a dark barn at midnight, some whales send out blips of sound and then listen for the echoes. The noises they make sound like clicks or pings. When the sound wave hits something in the water—say, a rock or a fish—it bounces back.

Ordinary ears don't work well underwater. Sound waves that are vibrations of air make mainly the eardrums vibrate. But

Whales also make sounds by snapping their jaws and slapping their flukes.

a wave carried by water sets the whole skull vibrating. So as whales evolved in the oceans, their mostly useless ear

channels shrank to tiny pinholes. Whales still have eardrums, however. It's just that sound takes a different route to reach them, traveling from the jawbone or forehead through a layer of oil to the eardrums.

In addition to clicks (which may come in a long, creaky-door series), toothed whales communicate through whistles and trills. (One toothed whale, the beluga or white whale, trills so much that it is known as the "sea canary.") Whales also make sounds by snapping their jaws shut and slapping their flukes (those twin flaps on a whale tail). Some whale sounds are as deafening as a jackhammer breaking up a sidewalk.

Baleens click, chirp, and whistle like the tootheds. But they also emit low-frequency moans. Among male humpback whales, these haunting moans can take the form of "songs" that may last more than an hour. Scientists call them "songs" because they have rhythm, structure, and repeating phrases (like choruses or refrains), and only humpbacks "sing."

Scientists who've recorded and analyzed the songs say that if the songs could be converted into a language made up of varying tones, some would have the amount of information contained in a short book. Some of the sounds are too low for us to hear; others must be played at extra-slow speed for humans to make out what is actually being sung. Whales swimming in one part of the ocean sing the same song, but individuals vary the number of phrases.

The whales remember and change their songs as the seasons change.

No one knows why the whales sing or what the "songs" mean. Some say they help the males establish their watery territories, or are a part of the mating ritual. But those may just be human interpretations of a whale world we haven't begun to understand.

FAST FACT

Humpback whales sing the most during their mating season. The songs can be heard by other whales from 100 miles away.

Why are electric eels electrical?

First, true eels want you to know the facts: An electric eel is not really an eel. A true eel is a long fish that looks a lot like a snake with fins. An electric eel is a different kind of fish, shaped like an eel (like a blimp is shaped like a football). And unlike the more harmless true eels, electric eels can give you a nasty shock.

Electric eels are one of some 500 separate species of electric fish. Among these are electric catfish, electric skates, and, appropriately, electric rays.

What good is electricity? Imagine you're an electric eel. (If you're a big one, you may be a slinky 9 feet long and weigh nearly 50 pounds.) The water you live in is cloudy,

Electric Eels at Home

Zap your sister once more and I'll turn you into an EXTENSION CORD!

filled with a lot of floating debris. So even during the daytime it's hard to see.

How do you find your way through the dark, murky water? Different animals have evolved different methods for finding their way through the dark. Bats navigate the darkness by sending out blips of sound, listening for the echoes bouncing off objects in their way. Similarly, electric eels find their way through dark waters (and compensate for their poor eyesight) by using electric fields produced by their own bodies.

The eel swims along, its electric field pulsing out around it. The field shape changes when it encounters an object that conducts electricity differently than the water—say, another fish, or a plant, or a rock. Then special skin cells on the eel's body will detect that something has disturbed its field. So even in the dark, the eel will sense the objects around itself.

This extra sense gives electric fish like the eel an advantage over animals that must rely on senses like touch, taste, hearing, smell, and sight. For example, without touching it or seeing it, one kind of electric fish can detect a thin glass rod one-twelfth of an inch across hidden inside a pot underwater—simply by sensing disturbances in its own electric field as the field sweeps through the pot.

An electric eel has a special set of electric organs stretching the length of its tail. (Four-fifths of an eel's length is tail, or about 3 to 7 feet). These organs are made from modified muscles. Ordinary muscles, like your biceps, contract by means of tiny electrical currents. The electric organs in an eel are made from

An irritated eel may build up a charge of 500 volts, enough to knock a human being unconscious and light up a room full of lightbulbs.

muscle fibers originally evolved for swimming in the fish world. Over the centuries, evolution modified these fibers in electric eels to give shocks.

These muscle fibers can't contract like our muscles or regular fish swimming muscles, but they can still produce electricity. Instead of being long, like familiar muscle cells, these "electroplaques" are shaped like dinner plates. The electroplaques have neurons on one end, like the knobs on batteries. And they are stacked in rows, like batteries placed one after another in a series—about 700,000 in one eel tail. Even when an eel is resting, it continuously gives off one to five low-voltage electrical pulses a second. Get the eel excited, and the pulses will start coming faster—20 to 50 times a second.

Why did the electric organs evolve? Besides letting eels sense unseen objects in the water around them, the electric organs act like stun guns. The eel uses strong discharges to knock out or kill prey, such as other tasty fish that swim into range of the electrical field. The electrical organs also act like an electrical fence, letting the eel zap predatory animals that make the mistake of eyeing an eel as a meal. An irritated eel may build up a charge of more than 500 volts at 1 ampere of current, enough to knock a human being unconscious and briefly light up a room full of lightbulbs.

FAST FACT

When two electric eels meet, each stops generating electricity and then both change frequencies. That way, their electrical fields won't interfere.

How does a chameleon change its color?

Imagine your mother is calling you to come in for lunch on a cool fall afternoon. You are playing in a pile of leaves—red, gold, green, and brown scraps of color, crackling and shifting. You don't want to stop. As your annoyed mother comes into the backyard to look for you, you relax and sink into the leaves. You idly watch as the skin on your hands and arms quickly begins to change color, from its normal flesh tone to mottled, red, gold, green, and brown. As you lie quietly, perfectly matching the leaves, your mother passes nearby, muttering to herself. "When I find him . . ."

Your now-orange lips suppress a smile. Fooled her again.

Being a chameleon for a day sounds like fun. But what's a real chameleon's life like? You're probably familiar with the pet shop chameleon, small and green. But chameleons come in 84 more varieties. Many live on Madagascar, a huge island off

Professional Chameleons...

Pickpockets...

the east coast of Africa. Others skitter around the African mainland, India and Pakistan, and the south of Spain. Some kinds are less than an inch long; others measure 2 feet or more. Their long, darting tongues make it easy to catch insects, as

Professional Chameleons...

Undercover police ...

well as spiders and scorpions. Some of the bigger chameleons even eat birds and small mammals.

Each chameleon comes equipped with special skin cells called chromatophores, which contain an array of pigments that allow chameleons to change their body colors—totally or in part. The chameleon's body secretes hormones that trigger the chromatophores to redistribute pigment.

This means that a chameleon has the extraordinary ability to blend in perfectly with its surroundings—to take on the exact green shade of a sheltering leaf, or to fade to brown against a bare tree trunk. A

scuttling scorpion might not notice its enemy until it's too late to escape. Likewise, a branch-leaping lemur might continue on its way, unaware that a chameleon dinner is within easy reach.

Ever see a mood ring? Popular in the late 1960s, mood rings changed color with body heat, supposedly reflecting the wearer's emotions. Well, chameleons are nature's mood rings—or, rather, mood lizards. Madagascar's panther chameleons shift from an ordinary green to an array of neon colors before they do battle, like British redcoats in the American Revolutionary War. The angrier these male chameleons are, the brighter their colors—an

A chameleon has the extraordinary ability to blend in perfectly with its surroundings.

intimidating display to a potential rival. (When some chameleons feel threatened, their skin actually develops a menacing-looking arrowhead pattern.)

At mating time, chameleons change color to attract or repel potential suitors.

An ordinary brownish female may turn bright orange, signaling she is available to mate. After hooking up with the male of her choice, she turns Halloween colors—black with orange splotches. This tells other interested males that this lovely chameleon is, unfortunately, taken.

Changing temperature can cause a color change, too. Chameleons can use color to regulate their body temperature. By turning a darker color, they will absorb more heat and warm up. A shift to a lighter color will reflect more heat, helping the chameleon cool down. (We use the same principle when we wear white rather than black T-shirts in the hot summer sun.)

If you were a human chameleon, you would probably soon grow tired of displaying your every emotion in living color. It's bad enough to blush in the presence of someone you have a crush on; imagine turning bright orange all over, like an international distress signal. Given the choice, most people would probably leave the color-shifting to the lizards.

Professional Chameleons... ...Hungry lizards!

How can a hummingbird fly both forward and backward?

Hummingbirds are probably a little tired of being called "nature's helicopters," but that's what they are. Or, rather, since hummingbirds came first, helicopters are technology's hummingbirds.

Just as a helicopter can perform feats that put ordinary planes to shame, so hummingbirds can fly rings around other birds—forward, backward, and even upside down!

First, for those who've never seen a hummingbird, here are some quick hummingbird facts. There are more than 300 kinds (species) of hummingbirds. Most live in the tropics of South America. But hummingbirds buzz around Central and North America, too, as far north as Alaska.

The tiniest is the bee hummingbird, at about 2 inches long; the biggest is the "giant" hummingbird, whose body, at about 8½ inches long, is only the size of a large sparrow's. Each hummingbird is partly covered with iridescent feathers. When the

A person whose body burned energy like a hummingbird's would have to eat about 155,000 calories a day. That's the equivalent of 1,550 bananas.

light is just right, the feathers shimmer like the rainbow colors in a oil slick.

Hummingbirds are famous for their long bills, which, straight or curved, are needle-slim. The longest belongs to the sword-billed

FAST FACT

The tiny rufous hummingbird, weighing only one-tenth of an ounce, migrates yearly between Alaska and central Mexico. Measured in body lengths, it's the longest round-trip of any bird.

hummingbird, whose bill, at 4 inches, is as long as her body. The shortest, at a minuscule five-sixteenth inch, is wielded by the tiny purple-backed thornbill.

Hummingbirds use their slim bills to nose deep into flowers for the sweet nectar hidden there. Then they rapidly flick their snaky forked tongues to lap up the nectar. For protein, hummingbirds swallow tiny insects lurking in the flowers' fragrant depths, or snatch some bugs caught in the nearest spiderweb.

Hummingbirds use enormous amounts of energy simply being themselves. When a hummingbird is sitting quietly, its heart beats a staccato 550 times a minute. When a bird is engaged in its aerial acrobatics, its heart can speed up to 1,200 beats a minute. A person whose body burned energy at the rate of a hummingbird's would have to eat about

155,000 calories a day. That's the equivalent of 1,550 bananas.

A hummingbird's wings beat fast, too—18 to 80 times a second. (Compare that to a vulture's once-a-second flap.) In fact, the humming sound coming from the little bird is the sound of those tiny wings beating.

An ordinary bird flies only by flapping, moving its wings forward and downward with great force. The upstroke muscles are weak, weighing only 5 to 10 percent as much as the powerful downstroke muscles.

The hummingbird difference? First, its flight muscles (pecs) make up nearly a third of its body weight, compared to 15 to 20 percent for other birds. Second, its upstroke muscles are as big and powerful as the downstrokes. Like a regular bird, a hummingbird flaps its wings to fly forward. But a hummingbird's wings rotate at its flexible shoulders nearly 180 degrees. By slanting the angle of its wings and using its powerful chest muscles, a hummingbird can tip up and fly backward.

By spreading its tail and doing a quick backward somersault, a hummingbird can also fly upside down (a position in which its powerful upstroke—now a downstroke— may become important).

Finally, a hummingbird can hover. It does so with its body nearly straight up and down, moving its wings forward and backward in a figure-eight pattern. This allows it to suspend its body weight over a delicate flower, while it sips the flower's nectar. In addition, like a helicopter, a hummingbird can lift straight up into the air. This comes in handy for doing a quick turnaround in a nest.

Alas, all the fancy flying feats come at a price. Try as they might, hummingbirds cannot soar, surely one of the high points of possessing the ability to fly. So the next time you see a sparrow soaring into a deep blue sky, don't feel sorry for it because it can't fly backward.

FAST FACT

Pound for pound, the hummingbird has the most powerful muscles of any animal. The muscles powering a hovering hummer's wings "burn" 133 watts of power per kilogram of weight. Compare that to a marathon runner's leg muscles, which use about 15 watts per kilogram.

How do birds know where south is?

Imagine you're on a long car trip. It's night, and you take a wrong turn onto a dark country road. With a sinking feeling, you realize that you have no idea where you are.

Then you glance up at the sky, and the answer is written in light: a glowing compass face, with north, south, east, and west at the four points, and a big needle pointing at north. What a relief! You turn your car around and head in the right direction, guided by the sky.

What happened on this nighttime migration down a country road is just a fantasy, of course. But for migrating birds, finding their way over long distances through the darkest nights is second nature.

Feathered Friends Find Vacation Land...

Travel Agents...? Tourist Info..? Word of Mouth..?

How about the Maui Hilton?

Flight Plans

Turn left at Savemore and fly till your wings fall off.

We thought Venezuela was overrated...

And they do it by reading directions in the sky—directions written by light and magnetism.

As summer wanes, many birds prepare to fly south. They don't pack suitcases or lunches, but they do join others of their species in huge flocks. The flocks take brief, swooping flights and perch on telephone lines, seemingly waiting for just the right moment to leave.

But when migrating birds fly south, they are not going on vacation. When they appear in their southern homes on a fall or winter day, the local residents see them as "their" birds, just as we see them as "ours."

No one knows exactly why some birds migrate when others don't. Food gets scarcer in winter in cold lands, but other birds manage to survive. Some birds migrate only if food begins to run out. Others do so no matter how plentiful the food or mild the winter.

Some migrating birds don't go very far, making the short hop from a mountain home to the warmer valley below. Others, however, make truly epic journeys.

Prompted by the change in seasons, blackpoll warblers soar into the sky over Maine and fly more than 2,000 miles to Venezuela in South America. They fly without stopping, not even for a drink of water. (And they weigh less than half an ounce, feathers and all.)

How do birds who go long distances find their way, year after year? Not all the answers are in, but scientists say birds use three main ways to find their way to their winter or summer homes: Looking for navigational markers, like the constellations on a starry night. Using sunlight to determine the exact direction of the Sun in the sky. And sensing Earth's

When birds appear in their southern homes, residents there see them as "their" birds, just as we see them as "ours."

magnetic field patterns, like flocks of flying compasses.

A bevy of birds, winging silently across the sky on a clear moonless night, are like sailors on a boat in the middle of the sea. Although they might be unable to see familiar landmarks in the dark, they can check the stars. Scientists say that birds probably use constellations like the Big Dipper to determine directions like north and south, just as we humans do. Since most birds migrate mainly at night, they have learned to be very good astronomers.

Of course, some nights are cloudy, hiding the stars from view. What's a traveling bird to do? Simple (at least for them). The Earth is a giant magnet, with magnetic field lines looping out from near the North and South Poles. Birds apparently can sense or even see this force field, and, along with other clues, make sure they are traveling in the right direction.

What are the other clues? In recent years, scientists have discovered that during the daytime migrating birds use sunlight to tell where they are going. How? Incoming

FAST FACT

Birds travel routes scientists call "flyways," nearly as regular as the routes cars take on a drive south. There are several big flyways crossing North America, including one down each coast of the United States.

sunlight is "polarized" by gas molecules in the atmosphere. (Polarized means that the light vibrates in only one direction, in a flat plane.) Birds can see this polarized light as a band across the sky if the day is bright and clear. When the Sun is due west, the band is north-south. So departing birds apparently glance at this band in the sky to orient themselves before winging their way home.

Winter Vacations

About two-thirds of bird species that nest in eastern U.S. forests go far south for the winter, to places like Mexico or South America. Their final stop is usually a tropical rain forest. But each year they find less and less forest standing as trees are cut down for lumber or to make room for cattle ranches and resorts. Mexico, for example, cleared 1.5 million acres of forest each year in the 1980s.

It's very difficult to count birds and figure out how many are surviving year to year, but around the world the number of migrating birds seems to be going down by about 1 percent a year. (That means that for every 1,000 birds last year there are 10 fewer this year.) Among those in danger are the whippoorwill, the wood thrush, the northern oriole, and the scarlet tanager—along with 53 other kinds of North American birds.

Saving the tropical rain forests is crucial for many reasons—not the least of which is that trees clear the air of carbon dioxide and supply the air with oxygen. Most of the world's remaining trees live in the rain forests. If too much carbon dioxide accumulates in the atmosphere, more heat is trapped on Earth, creating a "greenhouse effect." The rise in temperatures may disrupt weather systems and melt the polar glaciers, with flooding in some places, droughts and famines in others.

The greenhouse effect sometimes seems too complicated to imagine, but it's not hard to imagine tired, hungry birds—those that survived the flight south, because many do not—finding their winter homes a smoking ruin. Saving the rain forests will ensure we have no birdless "silent springs" in the north.

Why are butterfly wings so colorful?

I love the color down the center, but the Bermudas are frightening!

Compare a butterfly to the average dog, and the insect seems impossibly exotic. Butterfly wings come in a painter's palette. The wings are often iridescent, rainbow-shimmering like a pool of oil-topped water on a road. Sea-blue wings with lines of white polka dots and splotches of orange; mosaic wings of brown, lemon, and turquoise; wings striped black and bright yellow like a bumblebee. If you can imagine it, there's probably a butterfly already wearing it.

That's because there are more than 12,000 different kinds of butterflies fluttering around on Earth. Butterflies and moths make up a single bigger group of insects called "lepidoptera." All together, there are more than 100,000 kinds of lepidoptera.

(And incidentally, while we think of moths as dull gray or brown, many are just as colorful as butterflies.) Butterflies and moths make tasty meals for thousands of other animals, from birds and lizards to bats and monkeys.

Why are so many butterflies so colorful? Besides being beautiful, colors and patterns in nature help living things survive. Colorful wings and coats make potential mates take notice. So more babies are born. And body patterns allow animals to hide from predators, or scare

Colorful wings and coats make potential mates take notice. So more babies are born.

them off. The colors and patterns on butterfly wings help the insect protect itself from other hungry animals, such as birds, by creating confusion.

How? Many writers have noted that highly colored butterflies look like "flying flowers." So when they alight, they may look like just another flower to some predators. In addition, the patterns on moving butterfly wings may confuse predators, as does the

changing outline of a moving striped zebra. Unlike the clean outline of a solid-colored animal, patterns draw the eye away from the cookie-cutter animal and into a puzzling moving display.

Many butterflies also have what scientists call "eye spots" on their wings. These dark spots may perplex or even scare other animals; when they look at a butterfly upside down, they face what appears to be another set of eyes staring at them.

The dyes (or pigments) for future wings are manufactured in a future butterfly's body when the insect is still a "pupa," the in-between resting stage between a caterpillar and an adult butterfly. The pigments are made from flavonoids, chemicals found in the plants that caterpillars dine on during their brief life.

But pigments are only part of the story. The color of an adult butterfly's wings also depends on how the wings are constructed: their overlapping scales, hairs, and the oily film on top of them. When light strikes these structures it is refracted, creating shades of blue and green, metallic silvers, and iridescent rainbow colors.

Like the skull and crossbones on a bottle of poison, the particular colors and patterns of a butterfly may also signal a predatory animal to keep away. A good example is the orange-and-black monarch butterfly.

Female monarchs lay their eggs on milkweed plants, which contain a toxin that other animals avoid. The butterfly babies ("larvae") eat the milkweed leaves. When the larvae later become adult butterflies, their bodies contain poison made from the milkweed.

A hungry bird that swoops down on a monarch gets a nasty surprise, vomiting violently after its poison butterfly dinner. So the next time it sees the familiar orange and black wings, it will probably fly on. Because the monarch is so distinctive-looking (not just a muddy brown or gray, like many creatures), it is easily identified as a bad meal. And that helps it survive.

Some nontoxic butterflies have coloring that mimics that of the poisonous kinds. So even though they don't have a built-in poison to protect their species, animals avoid them because they look just like the ones that do. When it comes to eating a butterfly, the average bird reasons, it's better to be safe than sorry.

Migration of the Mighty Monarchs

The Halloween-colored monarchs that flit around your garden have a secret: Each year, they take an incredible journey, flying up to 5,000 miles round-trip to spend the winter in a warmer, safer place. Proving, once and for all, that small can be stronger and faster than big could ever dream of.

In the summer months, monarch butterflies can be found as far north as Canada, and across the United States. But starting in August, they begin a long flight south. Monarchs don't just fly until they reach tropical havens, some butterflies going here, others going there. All monarchs spend northern winters in one secluded

continued on next page

continued from previous page

area: the high sierra mountains of Mexico, about 80 miles west of Mexico City.

Each year, as northern summer winds down, hundreds of millions of monarch butterflies take off into the skies for their marathon flight. Catching a breeze streaming south, a flock of monarchs, flapping tiny wings, may reach a top speed of 35 mph. One monarch, marked by scientists, was found to have traveled 265 miles in a single day—much farther than the best ultramarathon runner. On average, monarchs make the trip south in about 40 days.

The butterflies that survive the journey—and many don't—descend into a Mexican Shangri-la, more than 10,000 feet up, thick with fir trees, dark and cool and hidden from prying eyes. There, some 300 million butterflies alight on tree trunks and branches, settling in for a winter of watchful resting. The few who have stumbled upon the monarchs in their resort home—which wasn't discovered until 1975—report that the trees appear festooned, crown to roots, with orange flowers.

In the spring, it's time for the monarchs to hit the road again. Starting in March the butterflies rise into the sky above the mountains of central Mexico and head north. However, like an extended outer-space trip, it's not those who set out, but their descendants who will actually arrive. Butterflies leaving Mexico will lay eggs in places like Texas and Louisiana. And it's the offspring who, transformed from caterpillars, will take off in an orange-and-black blur to fly on, as far north as Canada.

How come moths eat wool?

We've all had the experience: You open the closet to take out a favorite shirt or your winter coat, only to discover it is studded with small, raggedy holes. The little holes in your coat were made by hungry moths—moths you may never have even glimpsed in the dark of your closet.

Think "moth" and you might picture a swarm of bumbly gray insects banging into the porch light on a summer night. But all moths are not alike, and the kind on your porch are not the kind hidden in your closet.

In fact, there are tens of thousands of different kinds (species) of moth in the world. Each species, in turn, has millions of members. (It's a very moth-y world we live in.) The story of the amazing ways they have evolved to avoid being eaten by other animals could fill many paragraphs. (One moth tricks hungry birds by sitting quietly on a tree branch, disguised as a heap of white-and-black bird droppings. Another

moth secretes a chemical that makes it smell like vomit.)

With all those moths competing with other creatures and with each other for dinner, it's not surprising that each moth species has evolved to prefer different kinds of food. Some moths in their caterpillar stage may feast on leaves and

One moth makes a breakfast of cow tears.

fruit. One Southeast Asian species is a vampire, sucking animal blood. Another moth makes a breakfast of cow tears.

The sort of moths that like meals of wool are known as clothes moths. Such moths are brown-and-tan-colored and quite

small—only a quarter inch long. Outdoors, so-called clothes moths eat animal hair, stray sheep wool, feathers, dead insects, and flower pollen. But a dark, warm closet indoors is a clothes moth's idea of paradise.

Before a moth can fly, it's a caterpillar. And it's the caterpillars rather than the winged moths that actually chomp on clothes (and blankets, and carpet—anything made with a little wool). Some caterpillars spin a silk case over themselves so they can feed in peace. Hidden underneath is the steadily growing hole in your coat.

Female clothes moths lay 100 to 300 soft white eggs in clothing, which take a week or two to hatch. The tiny caterpillars, or larvae, immediately begin feeding on the fabric, and gradually grow into winged moths. Clothes moths dislike light, and

Moths are especially attracted to clothes spattered with food and sweat; wool isn't always the main taste treat.

crawl or fly off into the dark recesses of your closet when the clothing they perch on is moved. Adult moths live 1 to 4 weeks.

Like butterflies, many moths drink flower nectar when winged and full-grown.

One way to keep moths away is to keep your clothes very clean. Moths are especially attracted to clothes spattered with food and sweat; wool isn't always the main taste treat. To repel moths, many people use moth balls, those smelly white balls saturated with chemicals such as naphthalene. The problem is, moth balls are very toxic. Inhaling their vapors may damage eyes, kidneys, and bladder.

But there are more pleasant, nontoxic ways to keep moths out of your hair. Highly scented cedar wood sends moths flapping in the other direction, which is why cedar chests are good places for storing clothes. And small cloth bags stuffed with dried herbs, including lavender and eucalyptus, may also send moths flying.

FAST FACT

Moths often get the blame for holes in clothes made by other insects—the notorious carpet beetles.

Where do bugs go in cold weather, reappearing like magic when it warms up?

Unfortunately, many insects don't survive the freezing cold of winter. Others, however, have come up with clever schemes to hang on until spring.

For example, cluster flies sometimes hide out in the nooks and crannies of a warm house or barn over the winter, venturing out to fly around only on milder winter afternoons.

Mosquitoes, like bears, hibernate through the winter cold. Adult mosquitoes look for dark, damp, hiding places—like your basement—to spend their winter vacation. In spring, the females slowly become active, flying around looking for food (fresh blood). Once they've had their blood meal, they're ready to lay eggs, and hatch a new crop to plague us during the summer.

Some mosquito species do things differently. In summer they lay their eggs. The adults die off. But all through fall and winter the eggs lie still, actually freezing when the weather turns nasty. When the warm rains of spring finally come pelting down, the eggs thaw and hatch.

Some water-dwelling insects burrow into lake and river bottoms for the winter, and some beetles hibernate in tree bark. Certain honeybees cram together into a ball, using their wing muscles to generate heat and keep the temperature above freezing in their hive.

Other insects harden themselves to the cold by changing their body chemistry. For example, some caterpillars in the far north produce a substance similar to car antifreeze and can survive even when the temperature drops below minus 100° F.

Like birds, some insects migrate in the fall, escaping the cold for warmer places. Locusts are migrators. So are some species of butterflies, moths, dragonflies, ants, termites, bees, wasps, and ladybugs.

The monarch butterfly, the beautiful orange-and-black insect seen in North America in the summer, is one of the most famous migrators. (For more on monarch migration, see page 107.) For many years scientists knew that the butterflies took off for the south in cool weather, but no one knew where they spent the winter.

Mosquitoes, like bears, hibernate through the winter cold.

An entomologist named Fred Urquhart spent more than 40 years trying to solve the mystery of migrating monarchs. Urquhart devised a way to tag individual butterflies

Winter Survival Guide for Insects...

Create a bug beach in the basement...

Fly with friends to a secret hideaway....

Have a hive party and dance till spring!

Get down!

... with your bad bug self!

by attaching lightweight adhesive strips to their wings. He convinced hundreds of people to help him look for the butterflies on their flights. Finally, he was able to narrow the search for their winter resort to the Sierra Madre Mountains in central Mexico.

In January of 1975, when snow covered the northern homes of the monarchs, one of Urquhart's friends hiked into a 20-acre area of the mountains and was flabbergasted by what he saw: More than 1,000 trees were covered from top to bottom with a living carpet of half-asleep monarch butterflies.

There were so many butterflies piled onto the trees that limbs sometimes broke under their weight. The mystery of the missing monarchs was solved.

FAST FACT

Honeybees may eat up to 30 pounds of the honey stored in their hives over a long winter.

How many eyes does a fly have?

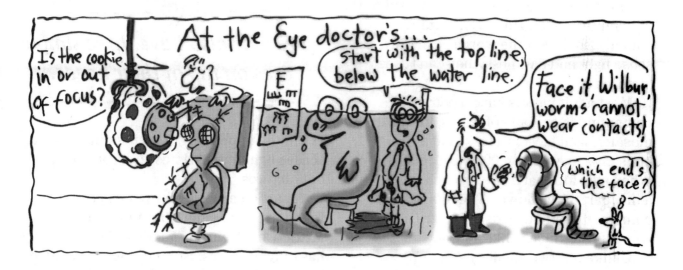

L ife on Earth depends on the Sun, which shines with the light of 4 trillion trillion lightbulbs. So it's not surprising that nearly all animals can sense light, in a world flooded with it. However, not all animals have two eyes like ours. In fact, visual organs are as different as snowflakes.

But animals that can sense light do have something in common: All have light-sensing cells called photoreceptors somewhere on their bodies. Certain worms, for example, sense light through their skin, using a nerve cell with a specialized, light-sensitive ending.

Other animals, including humans, have entire specialized organs—eyes—devoted not only to sensing light but to regulating it. For example, in the human eye, a little opening called the pupil changes size to let more or less light in, just like the aperture in a camera. In addition, there's an open-and-shut lid that can slam down like a shade when the light's too bright.

The eyes of most vertebrates (animals with backbones), most arthropods (like spiders and crabs), some mollusks (like octopus and squid), and a few worms allow the animal to see a picture of the world full of definite images. However, certain animals, such as some worms, can only sense light and darkness; they can't "see" pictures.

Most adult insects have a pair of compound eyes made of facets, like a mosaic. Each facet is a lens, and a housefly's eyes have 4,000 facets each. When a fly looks at a flower, each facet sees a tiny part of the flower. The fly's brain combines the thousands of images into one whole flower image, like a jigsaw puzzle.

Unlike our two small eyes, a fly's compound eyes cover a large portion of its head. In many male flies, the two compound eyes are so huge that they actually meet in the middle of the fly's forehead. If that weren't enough, flies usually also have three simple eyes mounted on top of their heads.

With a compound eye, objects can be seen most clearly when they are very, very close. If you hold a cookie too close to *your* eyes, it gets out of focus. But if you were a fly, your sharpest focus on the cookie would occur when you were crawling around on its surface.

Lizards have unusual eyes, too. In addition to two eyes especially suited for distance vision, some lizards have a third

Flies may also have three simple eyes on top of their heads.

eye in the upper part of their skulls, which senses light and darkness but can't make out pictures.

A particularly clever eye design can be found in the so-called "four-eyed fish" of Mexico and Central America. The fish really has only two eyes. But the eyes are divided horizontally by a band of tissue. The upper halves of the eyes are adapted for seeing in the clear air above water. The lower halves of the eyes are good at seeing underwater objects. So a four-eyed fish swimming just below the surface holds its upper eyes above water, like twin periscopes.

How do you get lice, and how do you get rid of them?

Lice are parasites: freeloading animals that suck the blood or munch the leavings of other living creatures, like vampires. Just as one mice is a mouse, one lice is a louse. Judging from language alone, people aren't too fond of lice. We have "lousy" days and to "louse up" means to spoil something.

Head lice, the kind kids usually get, are flat bugs the size of sesame seeds that sport tiny claws and roam among the hairs on your head like animals in a jungle. They make your scalp itch, and the idea of bugs in your hair can make anyone queasy. (People can also get body lice, otherwise known as cooties. Remember the game Cootie, in which you put together a plastic cootie? Real cooties come fully assembled, and like to live in underwear.)

Lice are as happy in squeaky-clean hair as they are in hair that hasn't been washed for a week. Head and body lice are blood-sucking insects. They aren't looking for food crumbs; they're looking to pierce the scalp and draw some blood. Like mosquitoes, they use their sharp mouthparts to cut a hole in the skin to slurp out their blood meal, leaving an itchy bump behind.

A female head louse actually glues her tiny eggs (called "nits") to the hair she lives in. The waxy white eggs can be found attached to hair strands near the roots. How do you get lice? Lice are creepy-crawlers that clamber among hair strands using leg claws. They spread by climbing from the head they're living on to an uninfected head of hair.

This happens when kids share combs, brushes, and hats; when hats and coats hang against each other in crowded coatrooms; and when kids bump heads, use the same headphones, or sleep in the same beds. The best way to avoid lice is to avoid doing these things.

A female head louse actually glues her tiny white eggs to the hair she lives in.

Humans aren't the only ones who get lice. There are more than 400 kinds of sucking lice on earth, and they like the blood of animals from cows and pigs to horses and dogs.

There are also some 3,000 kinds of chewing lice, who, as their name indicates, munch rather than suck. Chewing lice make a delightful meal of loose fur, dried blood, and flaked-off skin cells from their victims, which include cows, dogs, and rats. Some chewing lice live on birds (like pigeons and chickens), hiding among their feathers. One louse makes a snug home in the throat pouches of pelicans.

Even though they live underwater, fish get lice, too—more than 120 different kinds. One fish louse can measure more than an inch long. Fish lice have compound eyes and eight handy swimming limbs. Some fish lice are Olympic-class swimmers. Others like to somersault through the water on their way to their next fishy victim.

There are even book lice and tree-bark lice. And plagues of lice occasionally devour grapevines, ruining vineyards.

Given what a louse-y world it is, it's not surprising that kids get lice as often as they do. Faced with lice, adults must pitch in for a good round of nit-picking—just like baboons and monkeys do. First, use a special lice-killing shampoo you can buy at the drugstore. Choose a product containing permethrin; it's the man-made form of a chemical found in chrysanthemum flowers. Follow the directions on the bottle. (Shampoos containing Lindane, a powerful pesticide, may be harmful, and studies show they don't work as well.)

FAST FACT

Contrary to popular belief, head lice can't jump or fly. They can only crawl on their six hair-grasping legs.

After using lice-killing treatments, it's important to remove any leftover eggs before they hatch. A parent should do the nit-picking, using a fine-tooth comb and a strong light. Here's how it's done: Part the hair every inch, looking for tiny white eggs glued to strands, and scrape them out with the comb. Some hair strands may have to be snipped out if eggs won't budge. Don't worry, they'll grow back.

Then it's on to soaking combs and brushes in alcohol, and washing clothes and bedding in soap and the hottest water possible. Finally, thoroughly vacuum furniture. And bid bye-bye to bugs.

Why do elephants have such big ears?

When you see a big, wrinkly gray elephant, what's the first thing you notice? Probably its long, curling trunk, like an animated water hose in place of a nose. The second thing you notice is probably those enormous, flapping ears. No wonder Dumbo could fly.

But the truly giant, Dumbo-esque ears only belong to one kind of elephant—the African elephant. There are also Indian (Asian) elephants. And the ears of Indian elephants aren't nearly so outsized.

Whatever their ear size, elephants are the largest mammal outside the oceans. If it weren't for certain whales, elephants would be the largest animals on the planet.

Elephants live in places like Africa, India, and Ceylon, as well as other regions in Asia.

Do your ears hang low?
Do they wobble to and fro?

Can you tie them in a knot?
Can you tie them in a bow?

Can you throw them over your shoulder, like a continental soldier...

Do your ears hang low?

Their large heads give a hint of their enormous intelligence and highly emotional makeup. Preferring to live in groups of 25 or more, elephants are nomads, traveling hundreds of miles to forage for food—grasses, leaves, fruits, and nuts. Every 18 hours, an elephant must chow down on about 600 to 700 pounds of food, leaf by leaf, nut by nut. She washes down all that roughage with 20 to 40 gallons (75 to 150 liters) of water a day.

Besides ear size, there are other differences between elephants. The African elephant's skin is rumpled and wrinkled, while the Indian elephant's skin is smoother. The African elephant has two "fingers" on the end of its trunk, like our thumb and forefinger, and can use its "fingers" to grasp objects. Indian elephants have only one "finger," requiring a neat curl of the trunk to pick an object up.

Which brings us back to ears. The African's ears are huge and shaped much like the continent of Africa. Each ear can weigh up to 110 pounds. The Indian's ears are smaller, but still impressive.

Sporting such huge ears, an elephant can hear a pin drop, right? Wrong. According to scientists, an elephant's hearing isn't all that great.

So what's with the big ears? Turns out they're an elephant's version of air-conditioning.

Elephants don't have sweat glands, so they can't sweat to cool down on hot days. Instead, they flap their ears. It's not that they're fanning themselves, however. Elephant ears contain a network of large

African elephant ears can measure 6 feet long and weigh up to 110 pounds.

blood vessels that swell in hot weather and shrink in cold. On sweltering days, elephants gently flap their ears to pass cool air over their enlarged ear veins, cooling the blood flowing through them.

Since a single ear can measure up to 6 feet long, a lot of blood can get cooled as it passes through the road map of blood vessels on the ear's surface. This cooler blood then flows back through the elephant's body, helping it chill out.

How can camels survive with little or no water?

Camels, unlike people, fit into dry lands like a hand into a glove.

Two-humped camels (Bactrians) endure long cold winters and short hot summers in the Gobi desert in Central Asia. The one-humped camel (dromedary) plods on through the endless heat of the deserts of North Africa and Arabia. Camels first made their appearance, surprisingly, in the deserts of southwestern North America. Over millions of years, they evolved to be the dry-living experts they are today.

But water is essential to all life on earth, and camels can't survive without it. Blood is 91 percent water. If water is lost—through sweating and urination, for example—and not replaced, the blood thickens. Instead of streaming through blood vessels, it moves like molasses.

How do Camels Survive without water?...

No Swimming...

Iceless drinks...

That's dangerous, because quickly flowing blood helps cool the body. How? As the body converts food into energy, heat is produced. Blood heats up from these reactions deep in the body, carrying this heat as it streams up to and through the skin. Presto: The skin radiates the heat into the air. Result: The body stays cool. But honey-thick,

Camels can survive for up to 17 days between drinks of water.

dehydrated blood can't get to the skin fast enough. Heat builds up; death may follow.

Even in the coolest weather, human beings can live only a few days without water. Camels, however, can survive for up to 17 days between drinks. No, the humps aren't sloshy coolers, as some think, trickling stored-up water into the camel's bloodstream. Camel humps are actually filled with fat.

But camels do use their humps (and the rest of their bodies) in a unique strategy for dry life. First, the camel's body temperature fluctuates with the air temperature. It falls to about 93° F. at night, then may rise to 106° during the day (when Sahara temperatures can reach 135°). With the difference between body and air temperature lessened, the air doesn't heat a camel's body as much as it would a cooler body (like ours).

Second, the camel's metabolism—the speed at which its body burns food—slows during hot weather, making for less body heat. Third, a camel can actually recycle some water from its kidneys to one of its four (!) stomachs and back into its blood, rather than lose it all through urination.

Finally, the camel's hump acts as a protective hood. Baking in the summer sun, the mound of fat absorbs and holds heat, slowing its descent to the camel's internal organs. What body heat does build up inside is quickly radiated into the air from the camel's spindly legs.

Camels can lose 25 to 40 pounds of water for every 100 pounds they weigh, without getting sick. (The water is lost mostly from tissues other than the blood.) But no one said camels enjoy living this way. After surviving mainly off its own recycled water for days, a thirsty camel may swallow 100 liters of water in 5 minutes.

They brush their teeth with orange juice!

Why does a porcupine have quills? How do they work?

Pining Away...

I love those strong, silent types!

Porcupines may look odd, but their quills are part of a long tradition of animal defenses. Animals don't walk around with knives and guns to protect themselves, like some humans. But each animal has evolved its own unique safeguards. Skunks spray. Electric eels jolt. Porcupines jab. While the porcupine is unique among animals, its defenses are very similar to a plant we all know and love—the cactus. (In fact, the porcupine has been called a "walking cactus.")

Some fast facts: There are 43 different kinds of porcupines. Porcupines live in North and South America, Asia, Africa, and southern Europe. They hang out in trees or on the ground, foraging nightly for everything from twigs and bark to apples and dandelions.

A porcupine has about 30,000 quills.

A porcupine can weigh up to 25 pounds. They don't move very fast; they waddle.

But what it lacks in speed a porcupine makes up for in armor: about 30,000 quills, ranging from the very short, very sharp quills on a porcupine's tail to the 4-inch quills on its back and flanks. The quills are actually hairs, but hard as shards of clear plastic. And quills are barbed rather than smooth, so they'll catch and lodge in their victim's skin.

Before a porcupine resorts to quills, however, she gives fair warning—gnashing her teeth, rattling her quills, lashing her tail, and even, skunklike, giving off a foul odor. But when push comes to shove, a porcupine doesn't send her quills zinging through the air like darts, as we've seen in countless cartoons. How

it really works: A threatened or angry porcupine uses muscles in her skin to makes her quills bristle all over. The quills fit so loosely in the porcupine's hide that when touched, they easily dislodge and jab into the victim. Of course, the porcupine may speed the process by rushing at an intruder or smartly slapping him with her tail, releasing many quills into his skin or clothing.

Once lodged painfully in the skin, a quill will work its way further in, often disappearing under the surface. Sometimes, the quill will pierce an organ inside the body, even causing death. More often, quills are very painful but cause no lasting harm. Quills can be slowly pulled out, and they often work themselves out on their own. For example, one man watched a quill stuck in his upper arm retreat under the surface, slowly travel under his skin, and finally exit near the wrist two days later.

Quills may keep porcupines safe in more ways than one. Biologist Uldis Roze of New York City's Queens College discovered that hidden in the greasy coating of each quill is a natural antibiotic. Roze was jabbed with a quill. When the quill came out—two days later—he discovered that the wound, unlike a splinter puncture, was clean and uninfected.

Analyzing the fats found in quill grease, Roze discovered that they could kill six kinds of bacteria, including staph and strep.

Quills fit so loosely in the porcupine's hide that when touched, they will easily dislodge and jab into the victim.

Why would porcupine quills be coated with bacteria-killing substances? Porcupines can sometimes impale themselves or other porcupines by accident. Antibiotics can prevent such injuries from becoming serious, helping the porcupine and his kind survive.

Porcupines may look fearsome, but they are actually like most animals—if they get to know and like you, they'll take care not to hurt you. Another biologist, Richard Earle, found this out when he raised a male porcupine from babyhood. He named it Tubby.

Tubby liked to play a sly game with Earle. Tubby would start to spin around and around. Then he would stop abruptly and slap his tail against Earle's leg. The idea, apparently, was that Earle would know the slap was coming but would be caught by surprise by exactly when it occurred—rather like the game musical chairs.

What added excitement, of course, was that a slap of a tail is exactly how one gets a legful of quills. But when Tubby walloped Earle, he would make sure he twisted his tail so that only the soft underside slapped the biologist's leg.

Why do raccoons have black masks?

With their black masks and their convict-striped tails, raccoons can look like bandits—or like guests at a masquerade party. Raccoons also have short, stubby legs; pointy noses; small, stand-up ears; and a waddling walk. From the end of its nose to the tip of its bushy tail, a raccoon may measure nearly 3 feet (90 cm) long, and weigh about 22 pounds (10 kg).

Raccoons make their homes from Canada to South America, often building snug nests in hollow trees. But they can also camp out in a dugout in the ground, snooze in an old barn or shed, or curl up in the crawl space under a porch.

Usually, about three or four baby raccoons (called "kits") are born at a time. Little raccoons make a twittering sound when they are upset, rather like baby birds. Kits depend on their moms for milk for about 10 weeks, when they begin sampling solid food.

What do raccoons eat? Anything and everything. Raccoons, like bears, are omnivorous—they take what food they can get, depending on the time of year and where they happen to be camped out. On the menu any given day might be some tasty crayfish, a crunchy cricket, a sloppy raw egg, a handful of sweet blackberries, and an ear of yellow corn. Raccoons do much of their foraging at night. That's when you might catch a raccoon in the beam of your flashlight, looking like a masked robber going through your garbage can.

Raccoons have five toes on their feet and five fingers on their front paws, including a "thumb." And raccoons use their "hands" in much the same way we do— picking up and turning over

Cool stuff in here!

Raccoon Body Language Unmasked...

objects and prying open lids (especially trash can lids) to get at what's inside.

Anyone who has been around raccoons knows that they are very smart and very curious. Raccoons, like little kids, are attracted to bright, shiny objects like mirrors. And they've been known to open back doors to get into well-stocked kitchens.

Raccoons sometimes appear to wash their food before they eat it, dunking it in water until it's nice and wet. But according to scientists, getting the food clean may not be the point. A raccoon may douse his food, they say, because it reminds him of the pleasures of eating out of a lake or river. After all, a raccoon's favorite foods—crayfish, frogs, and crabs—are water creatures.

Kits sport their little black masks by 2 weeks of age. Raccoons use their faces (as we do) to communicate with other animals, of their own and other species. They also use their ears and tails.

According to scientist Dorcas MacClintock, the mask and other markings make certain behaviors, such as being

Thanks for leaving the door open!

Raccoon Body Language Unmasked...

threatening or showing meekness, more obvious to other animals. How? It's easy to see exactly what a face, tail, and ears are doing when they're colored so distinctively. In addition, the mask, rings, and other markings help raccoons identify one another (much as you might identify an approaching friend by his red baseball cap).

But there is another reason black masks may make good evolutionary sense. Like

Raccoon Body Language Unmasked..

Mom?

The black masks and other markings help raccoons identify one another.

the black smeared under the eyes of a football player to reduce the sun's glare, a raccoon's black mask may cut the glare of light from water—sunlight during the day, moonlight at night.

Do flying squirrels really exist?

Bullwinkle the moose would be shocked. If flying squirrels don't exist, who's that character with the leather hat and goggles who's been his (smarter) sidekick all these years?

Okay, Rocky the flying squirrel doesn't really exist. But real ones definitely do. Real flying squirrels don't wear World War 1 flying-ace helmets, but some of their "flights" are truly remarkable, carrying them thousands of feet through the air—with no net.

Flying squirrels are rodents. Other rodents in the squirrel family include

chipmunks, prairie dogs, and woodchucks. Plus, there are some 230 kinds of tree and ground squirrels, like the gray squirrels we see in the park, eastern fox squirrels, European red squirrels, and tassle-eared squirrels.

Flying squirrels have their very own group in the squirrel family. Far from being rare, there are actually 43 kinds sailing

Flying squirrels do most of their traveling after dark.

around Europe, Asia, and North America. They range in size from the toylike pygmy flying squirrel, less than 3 inches long, to the giant flying squirrel, which can measure 4 feet from nose to tail tip. (The average is about 17 inches.)

Flying squirrels do most of their traveling at night. As darkness falls, they go looking for dinner, which might include an appetizer of acorns, a main dish of spider, and a lovely fruit dessert. Flying squirrels are also partial to flower buds, insects, birds' eggs, and, alas, baby birds.

Do flying squirrels really fly? No, but they do glide. And as anyone knows who's seen a

hang glider or a glider airplane pass overhead, gliding can be even better, more effortless, than true flying (which involves flapping or engines).

A flying squirrel has a flap of loose skin folded against his body on each side, connected from wrists to ankles like a furry tarp. When the squirrel stretches out all four legs, his body looks like a kite, complete with tail, ready to rise on a current of air.

When a flying squirrel wants to take off for a far tree, he spreads his legs and jumps from the highest branches of the one he's on. Gliding through the air on a slightly downward arc, he uses his body and tail to tilt up and brake as he lands, as gently as a parachutist, at the base of the new tree. Scampering up the trunk, the squirrel will fling himself into the sky again, making swift progress through the woods.

A flying squirrel can even use his side flaps to execute banking curves like an airplane, or to make a sharp right or left turn in midair. The distance he glides depends on the height he jumped from, and the direction and strength of the wind carrying him. Like a swimmer pushing off from the side of a pool, a squirrel uses his powerful hind legs to push off a branch into a forceful glide. The longest flight ever recorded was a trip taken by a giant flying squirrel, who sailed along for 2.5 miles before drifting down.

How do cows digest their food?

Have you ever turned an experience over and over in your head, like when someone made a mean remark, and you didn't think of a good response? It's called "ruminating," and it's what cows do when they eat—chewing and rechewing their food, just like you did with your thoughts.

Cows are ruminants; so are sheep, goats, buffalo, deer, antelopes, camels, and even giraffes. All have unique stomachs to digest the grasses and leaves they eat.

Cows have perfect mouths for grinding: big, flat teeth in the back, on both upper and lower jaws. But a cow has front teeth on her bottom gum only. The top gum is toothless in front, just a thick pad of cartilage. (So cows asked to smile take very strange pictures.) Reaching down with her head, a cow wraps her tongue around a clump of grass stems and breaks them off between the bottom teeth and the fleshy top gum.

Chew and swallow; cough up and chew some more. That's ruminating, and the average cow spends up to 8 hours a day doing it.

Cows have four stomachs: rumen, reticulum, omasum, abomasum. Each one is a specialty stomach, taking on a different part of processing the wads of grass and hay that squeeze down a cow's throat.

Cows chew their grass or hay just enough to moisten it and get it swallowed. Down the esophagus it goes, and into the rumen and reticulum. Like mixmasters, the first stomachs get to work on the food, blending and softening it. Millions of bacteria and other microorganisms that live in the stomachs start to feast, beginning to break down the tough cellulose fiber in the stems and leaves.

Now, here's the gross part. After a while, the cow coughs up balls of the partially-digested food—and chews it some more. The balls are called cud. So if you happen to see a cow, thoughtfully chewing, you know that what's in her mouth isn't gum—it's something much more disgusting.

Chew and swallow; cough up and chew some more. The cud goes up and down, up and down. That's ruminating, and the average cow spends up to 8 hours a day doing it.

Eventually the cud passes through the first two stomachs and into the second set, where the food breaks down still more and then passes on into the intestines. And the cud is officially digested.

FAST FACT

Cows are part of the animal family called "Bovidae," which includes sheep, goats, buffaloes, and antelopes.

Why do dogs bark?

Sound familiar? Every evening, it's the same story. A dog begins barking. The same dog. In the same rhythm, night after night. Woof woof. Pause. Woof woof. Pause. Woof woof. Pause. Minute after minute, sometimes hour after hour, the rhythm and the time between woofs never varying. The impression given by your doggy neighbor is that he's not playing with a full deck.

But we all know that dogs are intelligent creatures. So why do they sometimes bark so mindlessly? And for that matter, how did they come to use barking when they really had something to say—for example, that a burglar is attempting to crawl through your porch window?

Scientists studying animal communication have found many examples of vocalizations full of meaning. For example, take the sounds made by prairie dogs. Prairie dogs apparently yip to tell other prairie dogs when someone is approaching, and even what that someone looks like.

But prairie "dogs" aren't really dogs at all—they're rodents (as in rats), members of the squirrel family. So we can't look at prairie dog behavior to tell us the story behind real dogs, and why they bark.

To figure out the barking habits of *dog* dogs, we need to look at wolves, their closest relative in the wild. (The fox is a close second.) Scientists have found that adult wolves rarely bark, and when they do, the barks are brief and isolated. But wolf puppies bark quite a lot.

If a wolflike animal was the ancestor of today's dogs, then how come dogs bark so much, often for no apparent reason? Some think the answer lies in how dogs came to spend time with people.

Scientists think that more docile wolf-dogs hung out on the outskirts of human settlements, scavenging for food. Over time, these dogs naturally bred with each other, producing tamer and tamer dogs—dogs that could be brought into the settlement and used for human ends.

Scientists doing experiments with wild foxes found they could breed more docile foxes. Over 20 years, they produced tame foxes, friendly to people. But there were some strange side effects in the foxes. One of these was floppy, doggy ears. And

another was that the foxes' vocalizations sounded more and more like domestic dogs.

We all know that baby animals, from wolf pups to lion kits, are more docile and friendly than their adult counterparts. So breeding animals to make them more docile

As dogs evolved to be docile, they essentially became overgrown, yappy puppies.

tends to make them more cublike and babyish, too. That's what happened to the foxes. And that's what scientists think happened naturally to the wolf-dogs. As dogs evolved to be docile, they essentially became overgrown puppies. And what does a puppy, even a wolf puppy, do? Bark.

So even in the absence of danger, dogs may bark for no reason at all—just for the puppylike thrill of it. One cocker spaniel was counted to bark 907 times in 10 minutes.

So when a yapping dog is driving you crazy, think "toddler." Think permanent "terrible twos." Blame it on evolution. And try this: "Oh, grow up!"

How do cats purr?

No one knows for sure how or why cats purr. But from watching cats and listening closely to their sounds, researchers who study animal behavior have a good theory.

In the past, some scientists suggested that the sound of the cat's blood swirling through its chest is making all the racket. The blood, they said, becomes turbulent, like water in river rapids. This happens, they argued, when more blood suddenly flows to the cat's heart, as when a cat arches her back, or her emotions suddenly change.

What a sweet kitty!

Purvvvvv*

* How 'bout some chow?

They went on to argue that the rushing, tumbling blood is loud enough for us to hear because its sound is amplified by the cat's diaphragm. (That's the thin, muscular sheet between the lungs and abdomen that helps cats—and people—breathe and communicate.)

However, this theory has been rejected by most scientists in recent times. If you listen to purring through a stethoscope, said the anthropologist Desmond Morris, you'll discover that it doesn't sound anything like rushing blood. Instead, it sounds like something is vibrating. And the vibration seems strongest in the cat's throat, not the chest.

So what's vibrating? Most researchers now think it's the cat's false vocal cords in the voice box (larynx). Just like a person, a cat has ordinary vocal cords that let it meow and yowl and wail. But cats also have a second set, called false cords, which can start vibrating as air rushes by. These vocal cords seem to be the source of the sound we call purring. Some scientists think the cat's diaphragm is vibrating during purring, too. That would explain why, when you touch a purring cat, the purring can be felt both in the throat and near the stomach.

Purrrrrr*

You are the cutest!

* I haven't eaten for 3 days, I'm starving!

A cat can purr continuously for many minutes, rather like a person humming along to a tune. Purring is a very soothing sound. Why do cats do it? Morris thought that purring is a close relative to our own smiling.

The idea behind purring seems to be reassurance: "Don't worry—I won't hurt you."

We smile for many reasons, he pointed out—to reassure other people, for example, or to appear friendly. It's the same with purring, he believed. Purring is a cat's way of saying, "Don't worry—I won't hurt you. Come closer."

Mother cats purr when they trot over to their kittens. Kittens purr when they scamper up to an adult cat, wanting to play. The idea behind purring seems to be reassurance.

Something similar may be going on when a cat purrs near a more aggressive cat. The purr may be saying, "Look, I'm not here to make trouble, so please don't start anything."

Cats also seem to purr when they're content and satisfied. When a mother cat is feeding her kittens, the whole boxful is purring.

Purring started out as a way cats communicate with cats. But cats also adapt some of their signals to their human pals. A purring cat is usually showing friendliness; it may want to be petted, or to jump into your lap

Like a smiling person, a purring cat may not always be happy. Even sick or dying animals may purr. But it's usually a signal that the cat wants to be close to you. In a way, it's a cat's form of a compliment.

Why do cats' eyes shine in the dark?

I hate it when they leave their beams on high.

Have you ever seen a cat pass by in an alleyway or darkened hallway? As it turns toward the light to look at you, its eyes gleam for a moment before it slinks off.

Shining eyes are a side effect of a cat's excellent night vision. Domestic cats evolved to do much of their hunting at night. Today

that may mean nothing more than locating the bowl of cat chow in a dark kitchen. Still, it's a handy ability to have—in a power failure, a cat could navigate near-darkness much better than you or I.

First, a little about how eyes work: When light bounces off an object it zooms into the cornea, the clear shield covering the eye, getting focused as it does. The light zips on into the "iris," the colored part of the eye, through a black area called the "pupil."

The little black pupil gets bigger in the dark to let more light in, and tiny in bright sunlight. (Watch your pupils do a rapid shrink by standing in the dark in front of a mirror, and then flicking a light on.) Muscles in the iris push and tug on the pupil to make it behave.

Light that is allowed through the pupil passes into the lens, a rubbery membrane that focuses the light once more. Then, as the light streams through the eye's dark inner chamber, it hits a screen called the retina. The retina's nerve cells, called rods and cones, send signals to the brain through the optic nerve, and the brain registers an image. You see something. And it all happens in a split second.

Cat eyes work like human eyes, with a difference: Cats have a special layer of cells in the rear of their eyes, called the "tapetum lucidim" (Latin for "bright carpet"). This carpet of cells reflects light like a mirror back to the cells in the retina. So in near darkness, a cat's eyes collect and magnify every bit of light that enters them. This

Cats have a special layer of cells in the rear of their eyes that reflects light like a mirror to the cells in the retina.

means that cats have excellent night vision, and can see objects in near darkness that we would miss. And it's also why cats' eyes shine so brightly in reflected light at night.

Cats can't see in absolute darkness, however. Shut up in a windowless room in pitch blackness, a cat would find its cautious way by sniffing everything around it and listening carefully. As it crept through the room, its sensitive whiskers would brush against darkened objects, telling it how much space it had to navigate in.

Because her eyes work so well in dim light, capturing every bit of light, you might expect that very bright sunlight would hurt a

FAST FACT

The biggest cats of all—tigers—can see six times better in the dark than we do.

cat's sensitive eyes and make it hard for her to see. The round pupils in our eyes react to bright light by shrinking to let in less. The special pupils in cats' eyes, however, narrow to a long slit in bright light. This lets cats' eyes control the light exactly.

How? If we humans begin to close our eyelids in bright light, we soon cut off all light entering the tiny, round, pinpoint pupils. But in cats, the pupils become narrow, vertical slits—up and down, rather than side to side. So cats can use their eyelids to hide more or less of the slit, like a shade partially pulled down over a window. This gives them more precise control over the amount of light entering their eyes than nearly any other animal. On a blindingly bright day, cats can avoid letting in too much light, while still being able to see perfectly well.

How do animals communicate without language?

Animals (not to mention we humans) have evolved an astonishing list of ways to communicate. Why do animals communicate at all? To captivate and charm other members of their own species—or to warn others to keep their distance. To make sure their own little groups, from prides of lions to hills of ants, survive and prosper. And, some say, to simply express emotions, from sadness to glee.

Animals have so many different ways of communicating with each other (and with us) that to list them would fill several books. However, even a few examples show that other animals' communication styles are as surprising and peculiar as our own winks, grins, grimaces, and love letters.

A smiling human who holds out her hand to be shaken is communicating without words. So is the bee who whirls her body in dance, giving her hivemates directions to the flowers she's discovered. However, in this case, it is the bee who is communicating the more complicated message.

Many animals signal each other not by gestures, but by using body chemicals. Ants frightened by an intruder emit chemical alarms that other ants can smell. Everyone then takes cover or gears up for attack. (If you accidentally kick over an army-ant nest, you may notice a lemony smell—the telltale scent of 500,000 panicking ants.)

Some animals (including 500 species of fish) use electricity to communicate. A banded knifefish can scare a rival by flashing his electrical signal on and off—the fishy version of a human's angry words.

Of course, animals also make sounds. Dogs bark and growl; cats purr and yowl. Geese squawk and honk to keep everyone together in the flock. Whales chirp and click and "sing" complex songs that can last up to an hour. (For more on whale songs, see page 89.)

Animals also use their voices to warn off animals of other species—a dog barks fiercely at an approaching mailman; a cat hisses at a dog. Animals and humans who live together work out their own system of communication: A cat meows in a particular way when he's hungry and wants his human to open a can of cat food; a dog makes a distinctive sighing/whining noise when she needs to go outside.

Frightened ants emit chemical alarms that other ants can smell.

In formal experiments, some researchers have communicated with chimpanzees using simple sign language or symbols on a computer keyboard. But science has only scratched the surface when it comes to animal communication. The first task is to decipher what animals are saying to each other. Until relatively recently, it was assumed that animals didn't communicate—they simply "vocalized."

What's the difference? Imagine you are wandering around your house at night and your brother suddenly jumps out from behind a door. You scream. That's vocalizing.

But if you go on to complain to your mother, "Billy jumped out and scared me," that's a complicated form of communicating, containing a lot of information.

Scientists thought that when an animal warned another about approaching danger, the sound it made was more like a scream than one that conveyed any real information.

However, when scientists at the University of Arizona took the time to really listen to one animal—the prairie dog—they discovered that we may be missing out on a whole world of animal communication.

Scientists recorded the high-pitched "barks" of prairie dogs when scary predators approached. The researchers found that when the threatening animal was flying through the air, the prairie dogs barked differently than when the predator was creeping in over land.

Next, they noticed that the barks seemed to vary depending on what kind of animal was approaching on land—a human or big cat, for example. At first, the researchers thought that each prairie dog might simply have a different style of barking out the idea "land animal approaching."

So they set up an experiment: They had a person walk through several prairie dog colonies. Next, they sent a pet dog.

What they found: All the prairie dogs used the same sound to warn of the threatening human—but a completely different sound to alert their friends of the approaching dog. In other words, prairie dogs were communicating something like, "Watch out—it's a human." Or "Watch out—it's a dog."

But the researchers made an even more surprising discovery. One by one, they walked through the prairie dog colonies, recording the little rodents' reactions. To their astonishment, they found that the prairie dogs' warning barks were different for different people. Instead of "Watch out—it's a human," they seemed to be saying, "Watch out for the tall guy in the red jacket." Or "Look out for the short fat guy with the droopy jeans."

FAST FACT

Prairie dogs convey information by varying tones in their barks. In some human languages, such as Chinese, the same word may mean different things depending on how it is inflected. For prairie dogs, the pitch of the bark, rising and falling in a particular way, tells the story.

How come so many animals have tails (and we don't)?

Where did tails come from? We could imagine some ancient cosmic game of Pin the Tail on the Donkey (and the elephant, and the crocodile, and so on). But the fact is, tails came from the sea.

Scientists believe life started in the oceans. Long before there were any land animals, there were primitive fish. Fish evolved with tails because tails allowed them to move easily through the water.

A flipping tail provides a nice forward thrust, as anyone who's worn flippers in a swimming pool knows. Later, lizards evolved from fish, and mammals evolved from lizards.

Incidentally, what is a tail? In animals with backbones, such as cats, tails are just more of the spine, projecting into space. Over time, tails specialized to do different things in different animals. Meanwhile, creatures like us that had no use for tails evolved tailless.

> ### *Tree-dwellers like squirrels use their tails for balancing on limbs, and as a rudder for leaping through the air from branch to branch.*

But before we are born, each human embryo repeats some of our evolutionary history. Tiny embryos start out with gill slits like fishes, our most distant ancestors. And by their fourth week of development, human embryos have little tails, remnants of their mammal ancestors. The tiny tails grow for about 2 weeks before gradually disappearing. All that's left of the tail is a fused-together lump of bone at the end of the spine called the "coccyx."

Burrowing animals tend to have very short tails; longer ones would just get in the way. But animals that climb trees or run along the ground often have long tails—think monkeys, squirrels, tigers, wolves.

Tree-dwellers like squirrels use their tails for balancing on limbs, and as a kind of rudder when leaping through the air from branch to branch. In some animals, such as chameleons and spider monkeys, the tail is "prehensile," meaning that it functions like a spare hand. A spider monkey can grasp a branch with her tail, wrap the tail around it like a rope, and hang on for dear life.

Lizard tails come in handy to distract predators like snakes, especially when the lizard is halfway down a hole, tail waving above him. When caught by a predator, many lizards drop their tails, as you would drop your wallet in front of a mugger. As the tail wriggles on the ground, the predator is momentarily confused, and the lizard escapes. Later, he'll simply grow a new one.

Porcupines use their tails as weapons, positioning them to release a raft of sharp quills into a threatening animal's nose.

(See page 124.) Some dinosaurs used their heavy, spine-studded tails like armored clubs.

Tails can also be used—just as we use body language—to communicate. Like a little kid jumping up and down, a dog crazily wagging his tail indicates excitement. A tail held up high can say "I'm top dog," like a man pulling himself up to full height in an attempt to intimidate. Likewise, tucking a tail under and cowering communicates, "Okay, you win. You're the boss, and I'm afraid of you."

On the other hand, a cat whips her tail back and forth when she's annoyed or angry. A cat may also lash his tail from side to side when he spots prey, like a tasty bird hopping blithely by in the near distance.

Surprise! The animal with the longest tail—up to 8 feet!—is the male giraffe. Giraffes also have the longest necks in the animal world.

How did dinosaurs get their long and difficult names?

Their names are tongue twisters: Archaeornithoides. Dachongosaurus. Megacervixosaurus. But it seems fitting, somehow, that long, weird names should belong to the biggest, weirdest creatures ever to walk or fly over planet Earth: the dinosaurs.

Jurassic Inventus...

Bibliotops...

That's Book face to you!

It all starts with the word *dinosaur* itself. A scientist named Sir Richard Owen coined the word *dinosauria* in 1841. He combined two Greek words, *deinos* and *sauros*. *Deinos* means "terrible"; *sauros* means "lizard." And some (though not most) dinosaurs were terrible lizards indeed.

One of the most terrible was the familiar Tyrannosaurus. This big-headed, long-toothed, 39-foot dinosaur is a favorite movie monster. The Tyrannosaurs, armed with heavy claws and massive jaws, attacked and ate other animals, including other dinosaurs. Their name fits them well: Tyrannosaurus means "tyrant lizard."

It has been scientists—mainly biologists—who have named the dinosaurs whose bones have been unearthed over the years. Each name has its own story.

... Hors d'oeuvre-o-saurus...

Watch out at cocktail parties!

Some names refer to how scientists believe the animal behaved, as with ferocious Tyrannosaurus. Take Oviraptor ("egg stealer"); scientists who named it thought it snatched and ate other dinosaurs'

A scientist combined two Greek words, deinos *(terrible)* and sauros *(lizard), to make the word* dinosaur.

---

eggs. Then there's Segnosaurus ("slow lizard"), whose long thighs, short shins, and short feet probably made it one of the pokier dinosaurs.

Some names refer to a dinosaur's physical features, especially those that set it apart from other kinds of dinosaurs. For example, Triceratops means "three-horned face." Triceratops had a long horn mounted above each eye and a short, stubby horn atop its nose. And Deinonychus ("terrible claw") had large fangs and claws, including two longer claws shaped like scythes.

Other names identify where the dinosaur was found. Minmi was an armored dinosaur named after Minmi Crossing, a place in Australia near where its first skeleton was discovered. Danubiosaurus ("Danube lizard") was first found in Austria, where the Danube River runs.

And a few dinosaurs are named after people, some of them scientists, some of

... Autoraptor...

I love stick shifts!

them not. Herrerasaurus ("Herrera's lizard") was a 10-foot-long flesh-eater. It was named after Victorino Herrera, a goat farmer who found the skeleton in the Andes Mountains of South America.

While the average person may have heard of a handful of dinosaurs, hundreds of kinds of dinosaurs have been identified and named. These include Abrictosaurus ("awake lizard"), Anatotitan ("giant duck"), Barapasaurus ("big-leg lizard"), Chindesaurus ("ghost lizard"), Daspletosaurus ("frightful lizard"), Fulgurotherium ("lightning beast"), Phaedrolosaurus ("gleaming lizard"), Seismosaurus ("earth-shaking lizard"), and Vulcanodon ("volcano tooth").

Here's an idea: Why not create, describe, and name your own dinosaur?

FAST FACT

The dinosaur with the longest name—micropachycephalosaurus—was one of the smallest dinosaurs, a mere 20 inches long. (Its name means "small, thick-headed lizard.")

Why do animals become extinct?

We know that individual animals and people live and then die. Likewise, scientists say that over time, each species lives and finally dies out, too. Over the billions of years life has existed on Earth, millions and millions of species have suffered this fate.

Fossils tell us about some of these lost animals. Saber-toothed tigers. Dodo birds. Dinosaurs. Miniature horses. Woolly mammoths. Giant sloths. New England sea minks. The intelligent-as-we human beings known as the Neanderthals. There are the many lost species we know about, and the many more we don't.

Even today, scientists are still discovering species of life they didn't know existed, only to find that they're in danger of extinction.

And the extinction list gets longer every day.

Extinction of a species of animal begins when more animals are dying than are being born. Gradually, numbers dwindle, until the few remaining animals die off. What causes extinctions? Scientists say that the disappearance of whole species is inevitable, a fact of nature: Species tend to naturally disappear over time. Usually, it's because another species is more successful at finding food and shelter in the local environment. Later, that species may die out, too, replaced by another upstart species.

For example, take horses. Sixty million years ago, the horses we know today didn't exist. What there were instead were dawn horses, only 15 inches high and with four toes rather than one on each front foot. Over time, the dawn horse species died out, replaced by a somewhat larger species of horse with bigger brains and fewer toes.

Much of evolution works by natural selection. There's only so much food and shelter to go around in one area. The more "successful" animals—those that are well suited to the conditions of life in their locale—will get the lion's share of the food. Those who aren't so well fitted will tend to die out over time.

Take the case of horses. Animals who were, by natural variation, born bigger and smarter tended to survive to have more offspring. Over time—hundreds of thousands of years—a new species of horse had evolved to replace the old one. By 25 million years ago, the horse species that existed on Earth stood more than 3 feet high, and had three toes, rather than four, on their front feet.

Huge sloths, tiny horses, and a different species of human being—all vanished.

As the eons passed, horses became larger and larger, and their number of toes fewer, until only one remained on each foot. Early horses had teeth suited to grab and chew up leaves. Millions of years later, modern horses had a cheekful of large, flat teeth best suited to grinding grass. (Which is why, today, we see horses nibbling at the ground, not at the bushes.)

But most species now gone didn't die out because a competitor was a better fit to the conditions of life in their small locale.

Instead, they disappeared in what scientists call "mass extinctions"—thousands or millions of species disappearing around the same time, all over the world. The first scientist to discover that such a cataclysmic event had ever happened was a French paleontologist named Georges Cuvier. Early in the 1800s, Cuvier was examining layers of rocks and noting the animal fossils he found.

Lower layers of rock are older; higher layers more recent. Tracing fossils from one layer to the next, Cuvier noticed that the fossils of certain species common in one layer would totally disappear in the next higher layer. That indicated that many different animals that had flourished in one past time period had vanished from Earth by more recent times.

In this century, scientists have noted that some mass extinctions seem to take place like clockwork. About every 26 to 30 million years, animals (and plants) start dying. What could cause this? A planet-wide disaster that strikes Earth every 30 million years suggests the culprit may be the long-term movements of Earth and other bodies through space.

Here's one scenario scientists have come up with. Scientists think that there is a huge field of

FAST FACT

Out-of-control fires started by early humans may have caused the extinction of many species.

comets surrounding our solar system called the "Oort Cloud." As our solar system is carried around the Milky Way galaxy, we may pass familiar landmarks, such as dense clouds of gas and dust, on each round-trip. So the Oort Cloud may be disturbed every 30 million years or so by a patch of interstellar smog, sending comets flying in every direction.

Some of those comets may rain down on Earth, their impacts hurling debris into the air and drastically changing Earth's climate. A chain of events of plants and animals dying then begins. About 250 million years ago, for example, more than 90 percent of all ocean species simply vanished in a catastrophe scientists call "The Great Dying." (For another view of what might have caused this mass extinction, see page 15.)

About 65 million years ago, the dinosaurs began disappearing. Today, many scientists think that another impact from space—a comet or asteroid—may have started a similar chain of disastrous changes in the climate. Not only dinosaurs, but many other reptile and fish species died off, too.

Human beings wield so much destructive power that we may be setting in motion the next mass extinction.

Impacts from space are factors we can't control. But there are those we can, like our behavior. Many animals, such as the saber-toothed tiger, the quagga (a kind of zebra), and the Carolina parakeet became extinct because human beings deliberately killed them or the animals they preyed on, hunting them into oblivion for food, pelts, or sport.

Today, scientists say that humans wield so much destructive power that we ourselves (rather than an impact from space) may be setting in motion the next mass extinction. Half of the 5 to 10 million species of animals and plants on Earth live in the tropical rain forests, and we are methodically chopping and burning the forests down. Also, as trees disappear, carbon dioxide builds up in the air. This traps heat, leading to global warming and enormous climate changes—and perhaps more extinctions.

Modern humans—homo sapiens sapiens—have only existed for about 40,000 years. Who knows if we'll make it another 40,000? If we manage to survive, avoiding environmental destruction and nuclear war, it may be because we'll have become not simply an older species, but a wiser one.

BODY WORKS

AH-AH-AH

Human beings were late arrivals on Earth. Other animal species swam the oceans and roamed the planet for hundreds of millions of years before we showed up. Modern Homo sapiens have been leaving footprints in the soil—first barefoot, then sandals, boots, shoes, and high-tech sneakers—for only about 40,000 years. (On a 500-inch timeline representing the years from the birth of Earth until now, modern human beings would occupy only the last tiny half-inch.)

Stare at yourself in a mirror, and after a moment, you'll have the unsettling sense that *we* are the aliens. Those long, dangly arms.

The little round ears, so close-set to the head. The expanses of hairless skin. We humans are as peculiar-looking as any creature that ever walked, swam, or crawled across this planet.

Inside, our bodies work feverishly, around the clock, with no breaks—manufacturing sweat that seeps from our skin; thrusting hair out of holes in our head; pumping 1,800 gallons of blood a day through hundreds of miles of arteries and veins strung through our bodies. All that and much more is going on, while we're busy doing other things. Take a trip through the bodyworks, and find out how it all happens.

Why do fingers get wrinkled after soaking in water for a long time?

Washing dishes. Washing your dog. Taking a long bath. You pull your hands out of the water and there it is: the heartbreak of pruny fingers. Wrinkled beyond recognition, with high ridges, deep valleys. And they feel funny, too.

Imagine if you eased into the bathtub for a long, hot soak, and when you emerged half an hour later, your skin was pleated from head to toe. A wrinkled, science-fiction face of a 250-year-old. Skin on arms and legs pulled into peaks and valleys. A stomach like armadillo armor.

If this were the way skin worked, few people would risk jumping in the pool for a summer swim, only to lie out in the sun afterwards as crimped, ancient-looking versions of themselves. Thankfully, we have only wrinkly fingers (and toes) to deal with. It all comes down to how skin responds to moisture.

The outer, thin layer of the skin—the part you can see covering your body—is called the epidermis. In the epidermis live the melanocytes, the special cells that give skin its color.

Sufferers of ...
The Heartbreak of Prune Hands
Transatlantic swimmers...
your hands are a mess!

Dishwashers...

Underneath the epidermis is a thicker layer called the dermis. The dermis is where hair is rooted, sweat glands make sweat, blood vessels carry blood, and fat cells lie around being their plump selves, giving the skin a soft, spongy feel. The epidermis is attached to the dermis, but there is some "give" between the two.

The wrinkling of fingers (and toes too) happens in the epidermis, the outer layer of skin.

Under the skin is the skeleton, and under the skeleton, our vital organs. So the body has several layers of defense from the outside world. Our fat and skin keep us warm; our skin cools us in summer by sweating; and our skin is a barrier against everything that brushes against us or splashes us.

But skin isn't waterproof. Skin is nourished and plumped by water. Skin absorbs water from the air, and when we immerse our bodies in water, skin soaks some up.

Wrinkly fingers are the result of skin's water-loving ways. On hands and feet, skin is quite thick, so it soaks up more water than skin elsewhere.

Submerge your hands, and the protein of the epidermis will slowly soak up 6 to 10 times its own weight in water—just like the paper towels in those annoying commercials.

As the epidermis swells and swells, it pulls away from the dermis and folds up into ridges and furrows.

However, the palms of your hands and the soles of your feet stay relatively smooth. Why? On palms and soles, the outer layer of skin is so tightly anchored to the inner layer

Lovers of very long baths...

yuk!

that it can't pull up into silly little ridges, as much as it might like to.

You can see this for yourself. Tug on the skin above your left index finger with your right hand. See how easy it is to pull it up into a ridge? Now try the same thing with the skin on your left palm. Good luck.

After a long soak, wrinkly skin quickly smooths out again once you are out of the water. Cleansing your skin in soapy water rubs off the natural oils that cover the skin and keep water from escaping. The skin, stripped of its protective coating by its bath, is suddenly exposed to the air. So excess water quickly evaporates, just as water evaporates from your wet hair when blown by a hair dryer. The warmer and drier the air your skin is exposed to, the faster it will dry out, losing its prunelike appearance.

In fact, skin dries out so efficiently after a bath that it may contain less water than it started out with. For those with normal skin, there's no problem. But people with very dry skin might end up with a flaky, scaly outer layer. If you have very dry skin, it's a good idea to put on a moisturizing lotion after a bath—especially on hands in cold, dry weather, so skin won't chap.

Why do people get goose bumps?

Recipe for goose bumps: Take one dark room. Place one sister or brother behind a half-closed door. Wait for other sister or brother to enter. Jump out. Voilà: instant goose bumps, accompanied by screaming, followed by shouting (possibly of parent).

In Great Britain, goose bumps are called "goose flesh." People have been using "goose" words for temporarily bumpy skin since at least the early 1800s. What do the bumps have to do with geese? People used to eat a lot more goose than they do now, especially on holidays. After a goose has

THE FACES OF GOOSE FLESH...

been plucked of its feathers, its body is covered with little bumps where the feathers once sprouted. So when little bumps rose on someone's arms, people thought their skin looked like goose flesh or goose bumps.

What causes goose bumps? Goose bumps spring up when small muscles around hair follicles suddenly contract. This pushes up a bit of skin and hair, making a bump. Have you ever seen your cat's tail puff out suddenly, or a porcupine's quills suddenly spring up? These are forms of goose bumps, too.

Animals, us included, get goose bumps when they are startled or threatened. Scientists say goose bumps are part of the "flight-or-fight" response. A surge of stress hormones makes muscles contract. In a cat, this causes hair to stand on end, and may make the cat look big and scary to another animal threatening it. Our goose bumps are an echo of this evolved response; our ancestors had more hair, and goose bumps made good evolutionary sense for them.

Goose bumps also break out when we get an abrupt chill. Why? Because our distant ancestors had fur. And for animals, fur fluffing up in the cold provides better insulation.

When porcupine quills stand up, that's goose bumps, too.

Goose bumps can break out in any thrilling circumstance, not just frightening ones. Hearing your country's anthem play at the Olympics, learning of a strange and wonderful coincidence, or witnessing a selfless act of courage may make the hairs on your arm rise. Even the memory of a thrilling event or encounter may bring on a rash of goose bumps. In such cases, our bodies may not be threatened, but our spirits are deeply moved.

Why do we get bruises? And why are they black and blue?

Cuts are red, but bruises come in a rainbow of colors. When you get cut, blood seeps from the body and out through the wound until clotting seals the cut dry. But a bruise is an injury in which the blood is going nowhere fast. Bump your leg, and tiny injured capillaries spring leaks and spurt blood under the skin. The spilled blood collects at the spot where you were hurt. Meanwhile, the blood's clotting agents, such as platelets, work to stem the tiny hemorrhages before too much damage is done.

Why does the bruise turn colors? The red you see in the bruise is simply the hemoglobin, the red pigment in red blood cells that have pooled under the skin. The darker colors—the nearly blacks, purples, and blues—are a kind of optical trick. Light striking the red hemoglobin is reflected and refracted in many thin layers of skin, making it appear more "bluish" than it really is.

As the hemoglobin disintegrates over a week or so, it loses its bright red color, turning brownish. So the light that strikes it reflects more yellow tones, and the bruise appears green, yellow, and brown as it fades. Some bruises may take 2 weeks or more to heal and disappear completely.

There is very little cushioning fat around the eyes, which is why a jab in the eye makes such a dramatic black-and-blue "shiner."

Saying people are "thin-skinned" means they are especially sensitive to others' remarks about them. But the truly thin-skinned do bruise more easily than other people. Women, for example, bruise more than men. That's probably because each layer of skin in a man is thicker than the same layer of a woman's skin. Also, the older we get, the

thinner and weaker our skin becomes, which is why many elderly people can get terrible bruises from even minor injuries.

Male or female, old or young, all of us have "thin skin" over certain parts of our bodies. There is very little cushioning fat around the eyes, for example, or between the shinbone or knee and the skin above them. That's why a jab in the eye makes a dramatic black-and-blue "shiner," and a fall off a bike can leave knees and shins a colorful mess.

But here's a simple way to stop bruises before they start—and it really works. Say you're walking by that sharp-edged coffee table and hit your leg. Immediately put the heel of your hand over the spot that hurts—and press. Keep pressing for several minutes. That alone may be enough to keep an ugly bruise from forming. You can also apply ice after pressing. Or, if you are near

FAST FACT

Bruises to the legs usually take the longest to heal, since higher blood pressure in the legs means more bleeding.

the kitchen when you get hurt, you can kill two birds with one stone by pressing a box of frozen vegetables to your leg.

These methods work because pressure puts an immediate stop to bleeding, and ice constricts the blood vessels so that further bleeding and swelling are reduced.

If you do get a bruise and want to get rid of it faster, wait about 48 hours until the bruise reaches its peak, and then apply heat, such as a warm washcloth. This will bring fresh blood to the bruise, which will absorb and carry away damaged cells.

What you eat can also help prevent bruising. Citrus fruits (like oranges), tomatoes, broccoli, and other foods with lots of vitamin C can help. Vitamin C strengthens capillaries throughout the body. Many doctors recommend taking 1,000 mg of vitamin C a day—500 mg in the morning, and 500 mg in the evening—if you bruise easily.

How does blood stop flowing out of a cut?

It's a hot summer day, and you've turned on the hose to play in the water. After a few minutes, you leave it lying on the ground. Water is pouring out into the yard. "Stop wasting water!" your mother calls out the window.

Suddenly, before you can even turn off the faucet, the hose begins to shrink before your very eyes, becoming skinnier. The flow of water begins to slow. Then, minerals in the water begin collecting at the open end of the hose, blocking some of the water from exiting. Finally, a sticky web grows over the hose end, and the water is trapped inside. The hose has sealed itself!

Hoses can't shut themselves down, of course, even if ordered to by an angry parent. But blood vessels can, and do. When you cut your finger, your body acts quickly to stop blood from dripping out through the cut vessel. Blood, after all, is what carries oxygen and nutrients to all our organs, from brain to liver to heart. Without it, the body quickly dies.

First, all by itself, the blood vessel shrinks a little so that the blood has a harder time getting through. Meanwhile, platelets in the flowing blood begin sticking themselves to the rough edges of the cut vessel. (Platelets are small, round, colorless blood cells; scientists think they are fragments of giant bone marrow cells.) Clumps of platelets build up, getting in the way of the outrushing blood—making it still harder for the blood to pour through the hole.

As the platelets team up at the cut end of the vessel, they also begin releasing a chemical called serotonin. When serotonin touches the walls of the blood vessel, it makes them contract even more.

With the narrowing of the vessel and the clumping of platelets, the passage of blood has been slowed, but has not entirely stopped. The blood still needs a good clot to seal off the exit entirely. For that, two special proteins in the blood swing into action.

The first protein, called "prothrombin," is immediately converted to a substance called "thrombin." How? Various factors in the blood change into enzymes, one after the another in a kind of cascade, converting the protein in a matter of seconds.

Once thrombin forms, it helps a second protein, called "fibrinogen" (already floating in the blood), to form "fibrin." Just like it

Fibers trap outrushing blood cells like a spiderweb traps insects, creating a reddish clot.

sounds, fibrin is a network of fibers. These fibers trap outrushing blood cells like a spiderweb traps insects. A reddish clot made of the fibers and trapped blood cells builds up. This clot neatly plugs up the torn blood vessel—and blood finally stops welling out.

Blood can make clots, but it can also destroy them. An enzyme in the blood called "plasmin" neatly dissolves the threads in a clot. Plasmin also destroys the substances around the threads that help blood to clot, such as the clotting factors. This helps the blood clear tiny clots that might be clogging the capillaries, the body's smallest vessels. It also destroys blood clots that have formed in body tissue after blood leaks in—for example, under the skin of the jaw after dental surgery.

Some people are born missing one of the factors needed to make blood clot. They may have a condition called "hemophilia," in which even a small cut or bruise can start uncontrollable bleeding. Sometimes, bleeding inside the body can even start on its own. So occasionally, especially after an injury, people lacking clotting factors will need a blood transfusion containing the missing factors.

 # Sleepy Limbs

You've been sitting on the floor watching TV for an hour, and when you get up, wham!, your leg buckles under you and feels numb. What's going on? The culprit is pressure on nerves and blood vessels. If you sit in one position for a long time, the pressure of your leg against the chair or floor may compress or stretch the nerves that carry messages from your spine through your legs. You may also be stopping some of the blood flow to those nerves. The result? Your leg "falls asleep," meaning it feels numb and heavy. Touch a pin to your skin, and the tip feels dull rather than sharp.

However, the numb condition is only temporary. When you stand up (carefully, since your leg will feel like a heavy stone block), you release the compressed nerves and blood vessels. With the nerves springing back into action, your leg at first tingles violently as feeling returns. After a few seconds, it is back to normal. To avoid numb legs and arms, change position frequently when sitting, and try not to sleep on your arm.

What makes your nose bleed?

Nasal Prospectors of the Wild West

Mining for Gold by day...

Picking their noses at night...

Gunfights and nose bleeds in between.

Anyone who is now a kid, or ever was one, has probably had a nosebleed or two. Nosebleeds can start for no apparent reason—and just as quickly stop.

Crisscrossing the lining inside the nose are tiny blood vessels called "capillaries." These vessels are just under the lining, close to its surface.

Blood trickling from your nose usually means that some vessels have been hurt and have sprung a leak. Nearly always, these broken vessels are on the center wall that separates the two nostrils. Although it sometimes seems as if you are losing a lot of blood, it is usually only a tiny amount.

What injures a blood vessel? Well, among kids, it's a gross but true fact: Picking your nose is the number one culprit.

However, since noses are sensitive little things, there can be as many causes as there are nosebleeds. You're slammed in the nose by a softball. You're fooling around with a friend, and he hits you in the nose. You have a bad cold, blow your stuffed-up nose—hard—and your Kleenex comes away bloody. Or your nose is unbearably itchy, you scratch it, and—oh, no, not again—it bleeds!

Sometimes, nosebleeds happen when you are just sitting there, minding your own business, your hands folded quietly in your lap. When the air is very dry, such as in an overheated room in winter, the lining of your nose dries out. Robbed of water, the lining shrinks from plump to thin. So tiny vessels are even less protected, and at the slightest provocation, blood trickles out.

Some kids get nosebleeds only once in a while. Others seem to get them a lot. But, happily, we seem to grow out of nosebleeds—they don't happen as often in teenagers and adults.

Nosebleeds are usually harmless. And they usually stop by themselves, as blood vessels form clots and close off. (See page 163 for how clots form.) Sometimes, however, a nosebleed can be stopped faster if you or someone else squeezes the nose at the bottom between your thumb and index finger for about 3 minutes. That way, the chemicals in the blood that help it clot won't be wasted by flowing out of your nose. And the blood will clot nicely.

But don't scratch, bump, or blow your nose once the bleeding stops, because clots are easy to break. If the bleeding just won't stop, you need to see a doctor, who can use medicine to shrink the blood vessels.

A gross but true fact: Picking your nose is the number one cause of nosebleeds among kids.

How to prevent nosebleeds in the first place: Don't pick your nose. Blow your nose gently, not hard, when you have a cold. Use a vaporizer in your room at night in winter, to keep the lining of your nose moist.

Occasionally, and especially in an adult, a nosebleed may mean something more serious. High blood pressure can make the nose bleed easily, as can growths in the nose, such as polyps and warts. Allergies can irritate the lining. Also, a nosebleed after a head injury may mean that the skull is fractured; only an X-ray can tell for sure. Good advice for everyone: If your nose seems to be bleeding frequently, see a doctor.

How does hair grow?

Have you ever thought about how a grassy lawn looks like a thick head of hair? The lawn is made up of thousands of individual blades of grass, together making one grassy expanse. Likewise, the hair on our heads is made up of thousands of individual strands, which together make one hairy cap.

Pull up a blade of grass, and you'll see that the green blade has roots at the bottom. Through this little tangle of roots the blade draws water and nutrients out of the soil, to keep itself alive.

There is something similar about the way hair is attached to our heads. Hair doesn't extend very far into the body. There is no central hair factory, deep within the body, from which hair emerges in a profusion of foot-long spaghetti strands. Instead, the skin is the hair's shallow soil; hair is rooted in the skin.

Pull a hair out of your head and take a good look at it (preferably under a magnifying glass). Like spaghetti, hair is a long tube. But instead of being made of flour, hair is a tube of keratin, a tough protein that also makes fingernails and toenails.

Although the hair tube looks smooth, it is really covered with scales, like a fish. This layer of keratin scales is called the "cuticle." You can see the scales under a microscope. They get ruffled up when hair is dry and damaged—by overbrushing, hot blow-drying, and harsh hair coloring. For hair to be shiny—to reflect light—the scales must lie flat, like the surface of a mirror.

Inside the hair tube is a spongy core. The sponginess makes the hair flexible, so that it can bend without breaking. Fine, wispy hair sometimes has no spongy center.

Like spaghetti, hair is a long tube. Although the hair tube looks smooth, it is really covered with scales, like a fish.

Follow a hair down into the skin, and you'll eventually find its root. Under the skin, each hair is encased in a slim tube called the "follicle." The follicle's bulb-shaped end is rooted in the dermis, the lower layer of skin, like a tulip bulb is embedded in the ground.

Near the top of the follicle, just under the skin's surface, sebaceous glands secrete oils that build up on the hair if they are not washed away.

Here's how hair grows: At the bottom of each follicle bulb is a ring of cells, supplied with nutrients and oxygen by a tangle of blood vessels. These cells divide, forming new cells, in the same way that new cells are made all through the body. The newly made cells pile up in a tube and push up through the follicle. Cells on the inside of the tube die and harden into hair. Cells in the outer layer of the tube also die, and harden into a covering, or sheath.

As they are pushed up through the follicle toward the surface of the skin, the hair and its sheath are firmly stuck together. But near the skin surface, chemicals secreted by the follicle walls eat away the sheath, uncovering the hair beneath. This hair, naked except for its layer of scales, is lubricated by oil from the sebaceous glands. Then it thrusts up through the skin and out into the air. A hair.

That's why, no matter how often you cut it or shave it, hair will continue to grow, anywhere from one-half to 1 inch a month—or 1/100,000th to 2/100,000th of an inch each minute.

Why does hair grow mostly on our heads?

Hair—from the glossy, silky strands in shampoo ads to the coarse hair on a German shepherd—is a signature of being a mammal. Human beings and dogs are mammals, as are our other hairy friends—cats and cows, giraffes and gerbils. Mammals are warm-blooded, and they nurse their young with milk made in their own bodies.

Hair can come in strange forms and unlikely places. The biggest mammal, a whale, has a stubble of hair only around its enormous mouth. And the porcupine's razor-sharp quills are actually very stiff hairs.

Reptiles, which evolved on Earth before mammals, had no hair—still don't. So why did hair evolve along with other mammal features? Scientists think that animals born

by accident with some hair (mutations) survived to have babies with hair.

Over many generations, hair proved to be a survival advantage. Hair insulates like a natural coat over the skin, holding in body heat and helping warm-blooded animals maintain their body temperature at around 99 degrees in cold climates. In hot climates, a thin coat of hair on animals like chimpanzees shields them from the burning rays of the Sun. So furry animals could look for food in colder as well as warmer places, giving them an edge over animals who couldn't venture out of the heat. Those that evolved the heaviest coats of fur, such as bears and wolves, flourished in cold northern areas, yet another niche in which to settle and expand.

Over time, patches of hair on the body became specialized, to serve particular functions. Eyebrows keep sweat from running into the eyes, so that we can see well even when working hard in hot weather. Hair in the nose and ears traps dust before it can enter the body.

When something gets too close to one of our sensitive eyes, it brushes against the hairs on the lid, the lashes. When the hairs move, the nerves in the surrounding skin send a message to the brain to close the eye. Likewise, the whiskers on a cat brush against the objects around its head, helping it feel its way through the dark.

On most humans, the hair growing on the head is the thickest hair on the body. Some men have hair on their chest and back, but many don't. And virtually everyone starts out

The biggest mammal, a whale, has a stubble of hair only around its enormous mouth.

with a full head of hair in childhood, even if they lose it later.

Why? It makes sense that humans kept their head hair, even while losing much of the hair on the rest of their bodies as they evolved. The body loses extra heat in cold weather through the head, since the brain consumes so much energy to keep us alive and thinking. Head hair helps holds heat in winter, and protects the head from burning in the summer sun.

Head hair has another survival advantage: It is attractive to other people. Which is why many of us spend so much time worrying about how our hair looks. Displaying a beautiful head of hair—despite the occasional Yul Brynner or Sinead O'Connor—is part of attracting a mate in many cultures.

Why do men seem to lose their hair more often than women do?

Pick your Pattern Baldness...

Paisley—classic style, goes great with evening wear...

Pinstripe—for office or sporty occasions...

Greek Meander—a natural for toga parties or just hanging out reading the "Iliad."

The map of a bald head—no hair, or a few sprigs, on top; a fringe of hair on the sides and back—is called "male pattern baldness." It's the pattern of how men lose hair as they get older. But surprise: so-called male pattern baldness afflicts women, too. Women begin losing their hair later than men, and usually less noticeably. But when they do lose hair, it's in the same pattern—mainly from the top.

Did you ever notice the strands of hair that seem to slip out when you wash your hair, getting caught between your fingers? This hair loss is normal—everyone, even

Everyone, even those with thick, luxurious hair, loses about 50 to 100 strands a day.

those with thick, luxurious hair, loses about 50 to 100 strands a day. Luckily for most of us, when old hairs fall out, brand-new strands sprout in their places.

Here's how it works. Like a growing plant, each strand of hair goes through phases. The anagen phase is the growing phase, which lasts for 5 or more years. (A strand will grow 30 or more inches if you let it.) Then for 2 or 3 weeks the strand is in transition (the catagen phase), gradually winding down. Finally, the hair enters the telogen or resting phase. The strand has stopped growing and is just waiting to fall out. It can take several months for a newborn hair to push the old,

resting hair out of its follicle. But that's where those 50 to 100 hairs a day in your hairbrush and tub drain come from.

Disease and stress can disrupt this normal process in the skin, causing hair loss all over the head and body. So can radiation and many drugs, such as those used to fight cancer. When a person is severely deprived of vitamins—because he or she isn't getting enough food to eat, or the right kind—hair can also begin falling out everywhere it grows.

But pattern baldness on the head occurs naturally as we get older. In fact, scientists say you can figure out the number of men who have some pattern baldness by their age. So 25 percent of 25-year-old men have thinning hair on top. And 80 percent of 80-year-olds are partially bald.

How come? The very hormones that make a boy a boy play a part in making a man a bald man. After a boy reaches young adulthood, certain genes, which he inherited from his family, switch on and tell the hair follicles to make extra batches of a particular enzyme. This enzyme converts the hormone testosterone into one called "DHT."

Too much DHT seems to make hair follicles gradually shrink. Scientists think this occurs because DHT somehow signals the immune system to attack its own hair, as if each hair follicle had become a foreign body. So each strand gets thinner, while its growth phase gets briefer. Eventually, there are patches of thin, short fuzz where strong strands once sprouted. This fuzz easily falls out from daily wear and tear. The result? A growing bald spot.

Women's bodies also produce small amounts of male hormones. So if they inherit the baldness genes, their hair can thin, too. However, because their levels of male hormones are lower, fewer women have pattern baldness—and it usually isn't nearly as obvious.

FAST FACT

Contrary to popular belief, shaving hair off doesn't make it grow back thicker or faster.

Why do we get pimples?

Pimples seem to appear at the worst times. Like the morning you're supposed to give a presentation to the class. Or the day your school picture (a close-up, for the yearbook) will be taken. And of course, there's the ever-popular date zit, the biggest, reddest, ugliest pimple of all, complete with a charming white center, which pops out just hours before a school dance or party or concert—making an already nervous situation a potential total disaster.

Just when we are about to become teenagers—at ages 11 to 13—just when life takes a turn for the overwhelming, pimples appear, to add to the fun. It isn't fair, but there it is. (There are the lucky few who will never

My First Pimple...

Was a voodoo curse...

see a pimple mar their perfect skin. We hate them. Just kidding.)

The tendency to get pimples, it turns out, is inherited. So just as you can thank mom or dad for your thick, glossy hair, you can blame them for the angry red outcropping on the side of your nose.

Did you ever wonder why you never get pimples on the palms of your hands or soles of your feet? Clue: There's no hair growing there, either. Pimples crop up at the base of hair follicles. And there are hair follicles all over your face, back, and chest, even if the hairs are too downy-fine to see or have fallen out.

People used to blame skin breakouts on things we eat, like chocolate or pizza. But the the real cause of pimples is hormones—the kind we start

My second pimple was inherited...

making like crazy when we're about to become teenagers.

The scoop: Both boys' and girls' bodies, as they approach teenagehood, start making more hormones called "androgens." (Boys' bodies make more androgens than girls'; that's why androgens are called "male hormones," and why boys tend to have more pimples than girls). Androgens trigger the sebaceous glands at the roots of hair follicles to make more waxy, oily "sebum," which seeps out of skin pores. Or plugs them up, in the case of pimples.

Underneath the tiny plug, dead skin cells and more sebum build up, trapped. As the plug gets bigger, it pushes up into an ugly bump. A small, whitish bump is called a "whitehead." A bump more exposed to air and light darkens; it's called a "blackhead."

Bacteria living on the skin can turn blackheads and whiteheads into big, red, inflamed pimples—the kind you desperately try to cover up with skin-colored pimple cream. How it works: As the bacteria chow down on dead skin cells and other tasty gunk in the follicle, white blood cells rush to the rescue. Soon, you have a nasty inflammation, swelling, and a pus-filled sac, as your body fights the bacterial infection. If you squeeze a pimple (and we know you do), you may spread the infection to skin around it— seeding a whole new crop of zits.

Washing your skin too much can actually worsen acne. Cleaning skin once or twice a day with a mild soap is best. Scrubbing it with a rough washcloth or sponge as if your face were a crusted frying pan will only make your pimples much, much worse.

While no one particular food has been proven to worsen acne, a high-fat diet can make the skin produce more oil. So eating less fat and more fruits and vegetables may make your skin drier, if not clearer.

My third pimple, the largest of all, was from blind-date stress.

What causes warts?

The skin bumps we call warts seem to appear out of nowhere. Warts are caused by a meddlesome group of about 50 viruses called "papilloma." These viruses thrive in the cells of our skin and mucus membranes.

Cleverly, the virus scrambles the usual growing instructions inside skin cells. Skin cells begin to multiply abnormally, building up into the yucky raised bump we call a wart. A wart can range in size from a nearly invisible pinhead to a pea. Fingers, palms, and forearms are favorite wart homes. By themselves, most warts are painless, but plantar warts on the bottom of feet can make walking hurt.

Since they are caused by viruses, warts are contagious—they can spread from person to person or multiply across your skin. But unlike other viral diseases like chicken pox, warts are only mildly contagious. So warts on the hand may make more warts on the hand, but they don't usually spread to the feet. Likewise,

Witch's Wart Cream Recipe...

Boil one banana, one roll duct tape, one rusty screen door...

...soak...

Cool!

...and enjoy.

touching plantar warts on the feet probably won't make warts appear on your fingers. Kids get more warts than adults, probably because adult immune systems have had more practice at fighting them off.

Kids get more warts than adults, probably because adult immune systems have had more practice at fighting them off.

If you ignore a wart, it will usually go quietly away on its own. Half disappear after a year; 85 percent are history after 3 years. But if you want to get rid of yours immediately, you may be in for a battle. Because they are caused by viruses, warts are tenacious little bumps. There are dozens of treatments for warts, which indicates that there isn't any one treatment that is really effective.

At the drugstore, you'll find salicylic acid preparations like Compound W. Applied to a wart, the acid erodes the upper layer of skin; skin falls off, taking most or all of the wart with it. However, the wart often reappears in the same or a nearby spot.

Doctors can use frigid liquid nitrogen to freeze off warts and lasers to zap them. But once again, the warts often pop back in weeks (probably grinning ear to ear).

Home remedies for warts include applying vitamin E or A oil and then covering with a Band-Aid, taping a piece of banana peel to the wart, or covering the wart in duct tape. The simple act of keeping a wart tightly covered, some doctors say, may speed its departure.

But strengthen your immune system, and it may take care of warts for you. Eat lots of fruits and vegetables and reduce stress. Most importantly, get ample sleep. Studies show that sleep is one of the main requirements for the body to keep bacteria and viruses in check.

Finally, consider this: In many cases, people report that their warts vanished in days when they decided to do something drastic to them, such as have them surgically removed. Faced with a trip to the doctor's office, the body quickly cleaned up its act. Our bodies seem to know how to get rid of warts better than medical science does; we just need to figure out how to trick them into doing so.

What causes freckles?

Some people are virtually covered with freckles. Others have a few around their noses or on top of their shoulders—places where they probably got sunburns in the past.

What causes the spots? The color of freckles, as well as the color of the skin around them, depends on a chemical called "melanin." The more melanin in our skin, the darker we appear. When a light-skinned person sits in the sun for too long, his skin produces more melanin. In other words, he gets a tan—or freckles.

Making more melanin is the skin's way of defending itself against ultraviolet radiation from the sun, which causes skin cancer. Melanin absorbs ultraviolet radiation, which helps to protect the skin against further damage.

Melanin is made by special cells in the skin called "melanocytes." (One out of every 10 skin cells is a melanocyte.) A melanocyte is shaped funny; instead of being round, it looks like an octopus.

Inside the melanocyte, chemical reactions transform amino acids, which come from the proteins we eat, into the pigment melanin. The melanin travels out into the cell's "tentacles." These tentacles jut up against the wall of surrounding skin cells. Using the tentacles like feeding tubes, the skin cells absorb some of the melanin, giving skin its color. The more melanin, the darker the skin—or the deeper the tan.

Freckles are places on the skin where a lot of melanin pigment is concentrated. Unlike moles, which may be slightly raised, freckles are flat and brown or golden.

People with fairer skin freckle most easily. Redheads, who usually have light skin and a hard time tanning, have the most freckles. Along with skin and hair color, the tendency to freckle is inherited from your parents.

Think of freckles as a tan broken up into spots rather than spread across the skin. Freckles usually appear when we are children, cropping up on expanses of skin exposed to sunlight, such as the face and arms. Contrary to what might be expected, there are actually fewer melanocytes in an area that forms a freckle than in the surrounding skin. However, the melanocytes are bigger and more active—churning out loads of dark melanin to color just that one spot.

Freckles hatched in the summer tend to fade over the winter. And if you have only a sprinkling of freckles, they will often disappear completely over time. So a girl who tended to get summer freckles in elementary school may grow up to find herself a freckle-less adult. If you don't want any more freckles, keep your skin shaded from the strong summer sun with hats and long-sleeved shirts.

People who freckle usually have skin that sunburns easily. That means an increased risk of skin cancer. So they should be especially careful to limit their exposure to strong sunlight, either by covering up or using sunscreens.

Think of freckles as a tan broken up into spots rather than spread across the skin.

A light sprinkling of unwanted freckles can often be faded without the use of drugstore chemicals. After washing, simply moisten a cotton ball with lemon juice and apply to the spots once a day. Over a period of months, they may gradually fade. But freckles will quickly reappear if you indulge in a day or two of unprotected sunbathing—a bad idea in any case.

Why does the sun make our skin darker, but our hair lighter?

When I was young, my friends and I would comb lemon juice through our hair and then lie in the sun. The idea was that at the end of the day, we'd have bronze skin and blonde hair. That old miracle worker, the salon in the sky otherwise known as the Sun, would grant us our summer dreams.

What usually happened instead was that our skin burned to a flaming lobster-red, and our hair dried out to straw. The dark-haired among us did not become blonde. However, by the end of the summer, our skin had darkened by a shade or two, and our hair had lightened perceptibly.

Today we know that sunbathing can bring you skin cancer along with your tan. But the Sun still works its paradoxical wonders: darker skin, lighter hair.

You might think that hair would darken along with skin, so that by the end of each summer, blondes would have golden-brown hair to match their golden-brown skin, and dark heads of hair would all turn raven-black. However, skin and hair are made of different stuff, and undergo different chemical reactions when hit with a bundle of rays.

Skin is a living organ covering the body, stretched neatly over muscle and bone, keeping things like heart and stomach inside and sheltered from the cruel world. The skin is made of layer upon layer of living cells. Tiny blood vessels run through the skin; sweat glands push water through the skin so it can evaporate into the air.

Mixed among the ordinary skin cells are octopus-shaped cells called "melanocytes."

These make the pigment (coloring) called melanin, which gives our skin its color. Who our parents are determines the skin color we are born with. The darker their skin, the darker ours. But our skin will darken further when exposed to the Sun.

Here's why. Light from the Sun comes in all frequencies, from low to high. The kind of light we can see, visible light, is medium-frequency. Higher-frequency light is invisible. It includes ultraviolet (UV) light, and UV light is mainly what makes our skin darken.

Skin darkens to protect the body against the damaging effects of UV radiation. First, dead surface skin cells absorb some of the UV. Then, melanocytes start producing extra melanin, which soaks up more UV. (Even a good tan only stops about half of UV light from penetrating the skin, however.)

Skin darkens to protect the body against the damaging effects of UV radiation.

So the more UV light we encounter, the more melanin piles up, making our skin darker and darker.

Hair is a different story. Hair is made of keratin, the protein that makes fingernails, toenails, and animal horns. Hair isn't really living tissue. Instead, hair is thrust out of living skin. Hair gets its color from the melanin made in melanocytes in the skin at its roots. Hair doesn't make new melanin; only skin can do that.

Think of each hair as a very thin, colored horn, like the horn on a rhinoceros. When hair sits in strong sunlight, it tends to bleach out, like bones in the desert. UV radiation causes a chemical reaction in the hair that destroys the melanin previously deposited there by the scalp skin. So hair gets lighter and lighter as the rest of the body gets darker and darker.

Why and how do we get fevers?

Finally a game the whole family can play!

A. I'm sitting on a radiator, in a wool suit, drinking coffee. What's my temperature?

B. I'm in an ice cave, eating Häagen-Dazs, in a wet bathing suit. What's my temperature?

C. I'm sick (big surprise) with a high fever, but I've taken two aspirins. What's my temperature?

Answers:
A. 98.6°
B. 98.6°
C. 101.3°
if I stand in bed.

Everyone knows what it feels like: Maybe you've got a cold, with runny nose and scratchy throat. And your skin is burning hot to the touch. You're like a toaster with the lever pushed down. Yet you have the shivering chills, and no matter how many blankets you pile on, you still feel cold. You've got a fever.

Nearly all vertebrates (animals with backbones) get fevers occasionally. But despite the fact that animals everywhere get hotter to the touch when they are ill, fever remains something of a mystery. How a body gets the message to suddenly heat up all over hasn't been completely figured out, but scientists have a pretty good idea.

Normally, our body temperature stays between 98 and 99 degrees F. (The old standard 98.6 doesn't hold true for most people.) Our temperature is usually lowest when we wake up in the morning and higher in the late afternoon and early evening, but it

A *fever seems to make macrophages better at killing bacteria.*

doesn't vary much. Scientists think that the body's thermostat is the hypothalamus gland, which sits in the center of the brain, keeping our inner temperature steady as the temperature plunges or soars outside.

When we get sick, however, the "thermostat" can be reset, the heat turned up to fight the infection.

When disease-causing microorganisms overwhelm the body, its defenses swing into response. Macrophages—scavenger cells of the immune system—become activated during an infection. They float through the blood, targeting bacteria and virus cells.

These macrophages in turn produce special proteins called "cytokines." Floating through the bloodstream, the cytokines come in contact with nerve cells around the outside of the brain. These nerve cells in turn send messages to the hypothalamus and brain stem. Then certain hormones are produced, and others decreased, creating all the effects of fever.

Normally, we lose the heat produced by the workings of our body through the skin, as blood flows just underneath. But the hormone changes of a fever make blood tend to flow away from the skin to deeper layers in the body, minimizing the amount of heat lost. Sweating dwindles to a minimum (which is why when a fever "breaks," you sweat profusely). Quickly, the body's temperature may rise 2 to 7 degrees.

What does the extra heat do? First, it seems to make macrophages better at killing bacteria. Second, it makes it harder for the invading microorganisms to copy themselves.

How? When the temperature rises, the body

switches from burning sugar (which bacteria love) for energy to burning mainly protein and fat. So there is less sugar available for bacteria to chow down on. Someone with a fever also loses their appetite, which further reduces sugar levels. And they become lethargic, so their inactive muscles don't require much sugary fuel.

The overall effect is to give the "host" body an edge over the invading microorganisms. A fever is the body's own defense against being overwhelmed by nasty microbes. So it may be best to let a few-degree fever do its job rather than run for the aspirin or Tylenol.

However, a too-high fever (above 104 or so) can be as dangerous as any disease. Very high temperatures damage the central nervous system, make the heart beat irregularly, and cause brain damage. To bring a temperature down, doctors advise using cool compresses and acetaminophen or, in an adult, aspirin. Extremely high temperatures call for a trip to the emergency room.

FAST FACT

The bodies of snakes, fish, lizards, and insects stay about the same temperature as the air around them. These so-called "cold-blooded" animals can get hot hot hot, especially on a broiling day in the desert.

Why do our ears pop when we fly on a plane or drive in the mountains?

The Pressures of Travel... An ear-ie experience

Rubber chicken, teeny seats...

It's a pain in the eustachian tube!

Imagine you are the passenger in a car going up and down steep mountain roads. At some point, your ears may seem to fill up with an invisible substance. Noises may sound muffled. Or perhaps you don't notice any change in your ears until you feel them "pop." Then, all of a sudden, all the sounds around you—the chirping of birds in the woods, the irritating whine of your little brother—become clearer and louder.

Ears pop when the pressure of air on them changes dramatically.

The same thing happens in a plane—your ears seem to close up. The noise of the jet engines is muffled and far away; voices in the cabin are low. Then, suddenly, your ears pop open. The engines drone loudly again; the hustle and bustle in the plane rises. Your hearing has returned to normal as mysteriously as it left.

Why do ears care whether we go up and down? The answer has to do with air pressure. Ears are very sensitive to changes in pressure. They must be, since ears hear because they react to fluctuating waves in the air (sound waves), pressing against eardrums and then releasing.

Ears pop when the pressure of air on them changes dramatically. Imagine the air surrounding Earth as a blanket of gas molecules. The closer we are to Earth, the more air there is above our heads. So a

maximum amount of air presses on us when we are standing on flat ground.

But the higher we rise, the less air presses on us. High up, air gets thinner and thinner, until it fades into the airless vacuum of space. That's why air pressure is lower on top of a mountain—or around a high-flying plane.

Although a passenger jet may fly 35,000 feet above Earth, where the air is very thin, cabin air pressure is kept higher, so that passengers can breathe easily. Even so, as you climb into the sky, the pressure changes from that at ground level to what you would find on top of a mountain 5,000 to 8,000 feet high.

This is a quick and dramatic change for your ears. As air pressure lessens, the air normally in your middle ear, freed from some pressure, relaxes and spreads out. Some of this air may escape into the eustachian tube, which is the tunnel connecting your ear to your nose. This can cause that "popping" feeling.

When the plane begins to descend, pressure once again increases. Air in the middle ear is squeezed smartly back into place. There may even be a partial vacuum created in your ear—a place where there is no air at all, since the bloodstream tends to absorb stray gases.

If there is a tiny airless space in your ear, air should flow up the nose and through the eustachian tube to fill it. But if the tube is closed by mucus—as it may be when you have a cold or allergy—air can't flow through. Did you ever hear the phrase "Nature abhors a vacuum"? If there's no air available, fluid may begin to fill the empty space in the ear instead. That can cause a stuffed-up feeling in your ears, which can last for hours, or even days.

You won't be able to hear well until the fluid drains away. If the clogged condition lasts too long, the eardrum may be damaged.

FAST FACT

Just before ears pop, your hearing will be muffled. That's because if air pressure isn't equal on both sides of the eardrum, it can't vibrate freely.

That's why doctors may tell you not to fly if your nose is very stuffed up.

However, for temporarily clogged ears on a plane or in a car, try one or all of these: Swallow hard, take a big yawn, or chew gum as you are descending. This can help clear the eustachian tube and equalize the air pressure.

Why do people sneeze?

All together now: Ahhhhh-choo! There, don't you feel better? Sneezing can be very satisfying, especially if your nose begins tickling and twitching uncontrollably, like the nose of a rabbit overly interested in a carrot.

Sneezes have any number of causes, but each sneeze works pretty much the same way. Sneezing is a reflex. And surprise—it's not a reflex centered in the nose! Instead, a sneeze is a spasm of the pharynx (a cone-shaped tube at the back of the mouth, connected to both the esophagus and the nasal passage) and of the chest.

Here's how a sneeze works: Nerve cells in the lining of the nose get excited and send impulses to the brain stem, the part of the brain just above the spinal cord that controls involuntary actions like breathing. (Involuntary actions are those we don't think about—they just happen.)

The brain stem then speeds signals to chest muscles. The chest muscles go into a spasm, squeezing the lungs. The muscles in the pharynx snap shut, too, preventing most of the air that is being squeezed out of the lungs from entering the mouth.

Where does the air go? You guessed it. Straight out the nose, in what we call a sneeze.

Contrary to the suggestion at the beginning of this article, we can't really sneeze on command. And although we can, with great effort, partially suppress a sneeze, it's a very bad idea to try.

Why? Air jetting out of your nose during a sneeze can reach speeds of up to 100 mph. So sealing your lips shut, pinching your nose, or holding your breath during a sneeze can create tremendous air pressure in your nose and throat. This pressure can force bacteria from your nose back into the mucus-lined sinus cavities in the bones of your face, or even into your ears. A nasty infection can be the result.

Tears, sniffles, runaway boogers... I'm ready!

Raised to be **strong**, brave, and courageous

But why do we sneeze in the first place? The nose is the body's air purifier. As air enters the nose, it is warmed, humidified, and cleansed of particles and bacteria, so that the lungs get as fresh, warm, and moist a supply as possible.

Air jetting out of your nose during a sneeze can reach speeds of up to 100 mph.

Sometimes, however, the self-cleaning nose gets overwhelmed—as, for example, when a cloud of dust blows into your face. Nerve endings become irritated. And you expel the dust particles out of your nostrils like a snorting horse.

We also sneeze to get rid of bacteria and viruses, when they multiply out of control in the nose, such as during a

Nothing can prepare one...

cold. Sneezing is just another of the body's ways of trying to rid itself of substances it would prefer not get inside, using a blast of air to sweep the nose clean. (Unfortunately, those in the path of our sneezing may inhale the virus that's making us sick, and get sick themselves.)

Sneezing is often also an important part of allergic reactions. For example, many people sneeze in hay fever season, when ragweed pollen blows through the air and is drawn into the nose.

Finally, a surprising number of people start sneezing—sometimes violently—when they first walk outdoors into very bright sunlight, especially in the summer. Scientists think this sun-triggered sneezing is a reaction by cells in the nose to the ultraviolet radiation that is part of sunlight. So when sunlight first hits the face, your nose gets that tickly feeling—and you begin sneezing.

...for those 100 mph gale-force winds!

What makes us allergic to things?

Nose running—or clogged solid? Eyes watering, itching uncontrollably? Sneezing? Yucky stuff in the back of your throat, causing you to make annoying snarking sounds?

If all this sounds familiar to you, you may have an allergy. That's the strange syndrome in which the body, for no apparent reason, declares war on a tiny grain of flower pollen, a helpless peanut, or the dust bunnies minding their own business under your bed.

Is the body just a big bully? Scientists say no. We have these odd reactions, they say, because the human body evolved mechanisms to fight invading parasites.

Common Kid Allergy Attacks

Green Veggie Attack... Characterized by hives, blurry vision, and dislike of broccoli.

Unwanted Kisses Attack... Characterized by fainting, weakness, and lipstick all over you.

Can't clean up room Attack... Characterized by numbness and plans to go to the movies.

(Parasites are organisms that would like to live inside us, sapping our energy.)

An allergic reaction occurs when these immune system mechanisms get out of hand. Instead of battling a parasite, your body may react as if it's under attack from your purring kitten's saliva—or your plate of scrambled eggs.

Scientists who study allergies say there are two kinds of cells—mast cells and eosinophils—that lead the charge. Both are made in bone marrow. But the blood can carry them everywhere—to nose, throat, and lungs, and to stomach and intestines.

Imagine you are allergic to tree pollen. (You may not have to imagine!) It's a beautiful spring day; trees are budding and flowering. You breathe in some pollen from the elm tree in your yard. And your body goes on red alert.

Antibodies—special proteins that are part of your body's defense system—called "IgE" fit themselves into receptors on the surface of nearby mast cells, like keys into locks. Then, the whole assemblage binds to the intruding pollen like a magnet. When it does, there is a miniature explosion, with the mast cells (and nearby eosinophils) spurting out histamines and other substances. The histamines have an immediate, powerful effect on your body. Blood vessels swell. Air passages shrink. Mucus is pumped out, clogging your nose and/or lungs. Your eyes itch and water.

Allergies run in families. If one or both of your parents have hay fever (an allergy to late-summer plants like ragweed), then you probably do, too.

One of the worst allergic reactions is asthma, in which the lungs' airways swell nearly shut and clog with mucus. Each wheezing breath is an effort; it's as if you're drowning.

Recently, scientists have discovered that many people's asthma is often triggered by a simple household pest—the cockroach. Cockroach droppings, which look like tiny poppy seeds, can hide in ovens, cupboards, and floorboards. Kids and adults can develop severe asthma in a cockroach-infested home, especially when a hot oven vaporizes the droppings into the air. Getting rid of roaches by using bait traps or other means may ease or eliminate breathing problems, too.

What causes an itch, and how come it feels better when you scratch it?

Ever get an itchy spot on your back that you can barely reach? Now that's torture. You manage to scratch it, and it feels better. Then a moment later it is itching again, just as badly as before you scratched it.

In fact, you may begin to feel itchy reading this. Itching shares this quality with yawning: just hearing about it may make you experience it. Itching, after all, involves the brain. And the brain, like a hypnotized audience member in a magic show, is very suggestible.

Pain and itching are both sensations carried by our nerves, but they are clearly very different. Pain has been studied for many years by many researchers: what causes it, what it can be a symptom of, and how it can be reduced.

But itching, doctors say, is an "orphan symptom." Surprisingly little is known about it, and surprisingly little can be done about many cases of itching. It is not a big area of research in universities or in the labs of drug companies, so it's not like something new is learned about itching every day.

According to *The New England Journal of Medicine*, many researchers have assumed that what they have learned about pain can be applied to itching. Both sensations are transmitted as electrical impulses by nerve cells (neurons).

A neuron has fibers extending from itself, like a starfish has arms. There are three basic kinds of nerve fibers—A, B, and C. The sensation of pain and the sensation of itchiness both travel through the C fibers, which are the smallest of the three. (The C fibers also conduct electrical impulses the most slowly.)

However, scientists think there may be "itch" neurons distinct from "pain" neurons, each making use of the C fibers to send their irritating impulses.

There are many clues that pain and itching go their own ways. For example, when you're in pain, the central nervous system makes natural opiates that act like codeine or other painkillers. But these same opiates may actually increase itchiness, scientists say. In fact, a drug that blocks opiates can also relieve some uncontrollable itching.

Like pain, itching has a zillion causes, ranging from the ordinary to the serious: bug bites, poison ivy, sunburn, dry skin, hives, lice, mites, chicken pox, measles, reactions to medicines, allergies, skin infections, athlete's foot, anemia, psoriasis, diabetes, hepatitis, cancer. Any one of these can trigger itch nerves to swing into action.

How? Take bug bites. When you get a mosquito bite, for example, your body produces histamine because it is allergic to mosquito's saliva left behind in the wound. Histamine starts the itching sensation

traveling along the nerves. (Histamine is what makes our eyes itch during pollen season; antihistamines block histamine and make us feel better.)

Scratching stimulates itch nerves to fire more and more, making you even itchier.

Why does scratching help? Although scientists don't know the whole story, they say scratching the skin stimulates certain nerves that help regulate the travel of itching impulses through cells. So scratching temporarily short-circuits the itching impulse somewhere along its trip.

However satisfying it may be, scratching can ultimately make the itch much worse. You've set into motion the dreaded "itch-scratch" cycle in which, like clothes in the spin cycle, what goes around comes around. Your scratching stimulates itch nerves to fire more and more. Pretty soon, you can't stop scratching—and you may even infect your own skin.

So what's the best way to stop an itch? Try a wet, cool washcloth; a bath with baking soda or oatmeal added; calamine lotion or aloe vera gel. Home remedies are usually best for minor itches, especially since scientists admit they've barely scratched the surface when it comes to understanding itching.

How does the nose smell things?

You are walking down the street one day and notice a certain faint smell in the air—perhaps a combination of moist earth, cut grass, and ozone, signaling approaching rain. Suddenly, your brain fires off a memory of you standing sheltered in your open garage while rain pelts the driveway on a summer day, the smell of rain, soil, and grass all around you.

Author Helen Keller, who could neither hear nor see, wrote about this power of smell to recall the past. "Smell is a potent wizard who transports us across thousands of miles and all the years we have lived . . . odors, instantaneous and fleeting, cause my heart to dilate joyously or contract with remembered grief." More than any other sense, smells are linked to memory and emotion. Seeing a photograph of yourself standing in the garage watching the rain, or feeling rain on your hand, or hearing rain patter on your roof won't evoke the memory of what it felt like a tenth as well as smelling the smell of that long-lost day.

Compare smell to taste: A tongue can mainly distinguish only sweet, sour, salty, and bitter. But a human nose can discern more than 10,000 separate odors, from the aroma of fresh-ground coffee to the waxy smell of a new box of crayons. (Hold your nose, and an apple tastes no different than a carrot.) We live awash in odors, new ones arriving with each breath.

The sense of smell is so powerful that it plays a central role in survival. Smell enables animals to find mates—and, most important, food. A newborn animal searches for its mother's milk through the sense of smell, since its eyes aren't yet sharp enough to see the nipple. Human babies do this, too. On the flip side, spoiled food usually smells bad—rotten or moldy or otherwise stinky—so smell helps us avoid getting sick.

Scientists are only now beginning to unravel the mysteries of how we smell what we smell. Behind each nose are about 1,000 separate odor receptors, nestled in a little patch of tissue the size of half a penny. Made of protein, the receptors stud the surface of the tissue, which is a bundle of nerve cells.

A human nose can discern more than 10,000 separate odors, from the aroma of fresh-gound coffee to the waxy smell of a new box of crayons.

These nerve cells are connected by tendrils to the olfactory bulbs, whose nerve fibers project directly into the brain. And the part of the brain they extend into, the limbic system, just happens to be the seat of our emotions.

Some odor molecules, such as those given off by flowers, float right up our nose and lodge in the odor receptors. Odor molecules from food we are eating take a different route, wafting up from the back of the throat.

Odor molecules come in various shapes—wedges, spheres, rods, discs. When a molecule makes contact with an odor receptor, the receptor changes shape—like a lock altering to fit an intruding key. This shape-changing prompts a nerve cell to fire off a signal, which travels through the olfactory bulbs and into the brain. The brain interprets the signal as a particular smell—say, "wet dog."

Scientists think there are "families" of odors and that each family's molecules have similar shapes. There are seven families, or categories of odors: minty, floral, musky, resinous (like turpentine), acrid (like vinegar), foul (like rotten eggs), and ethereal (like the smell of a fresh pear).

Different receptors seem to pick up on different components of an incoming smell. For example, many different components go into the smell the brain labels "popcorn." Change the components, and receptors will cause the brain to report back "corn on the cob" instead.

Many objects around us—like those made of glass—don't smell, because they don't evaporate and send off odor molecules at ordinary temperatures.

How come chopping onions makes you cry?

Onions are a unique vegetable: They seem to make us sad. Within seconds of cutting into an onion, tears may begin to stream down your cheeks uncontrollably. The fact that onions make people cry has made them a favorite prop in comedies, and an annoyance to anyone blinded by onion tears when they are trying to cook.

For years, scientists were curious about this property of onions. As they studied onions, they found that a similar chemical process takes place in onions and garlic—with different end results.

It's hard to believe, but both onions and garlic are members of the lily family—the group of flowering plants that includes the Easter lily, with its tall, showy, trumpet-

shaped blooms. Onions and garlic are the bulb part of the plant. Pull up a wild green onion in your yard, with its long, grasslike top, and you'll see the tiny onion bulb that was hidden under the soil.

For as long as there were humans, we have used onions and garlic to season food. And for thousands of years, people have used these pungent bulbs as medicine, too. An Egyptian medical book from around 1550 B.C. mentions garlic in 22 of 800 medical formulas for use against headaches, animal bites, intestinal worms, tumors, and heart disease. In China, onion tea has been used to treat headaches, fever, and deadly infectious diseases like cholera and dysentery.

Today, scientists know that ancient healers weren't off the mark. Garlic oil kills bacteria, in some cases more effectively than penicillin. It also acts to stop blood from clotting so quickly, which may be why people who eat a lot of garlic tend to have fewer heart attacks.

FAST FACT

For drier eyes, chill onions before chopping; cold weakens the lacrimatory factor.

What does all this have to do with crying while chopping onions? When you cut or crush a bulb of garlic, a special enzyme comes into contact with another chemical in the garlic. The enzyme transforms the chemical into allicin. Allicin is the substance that gives garlic the pungent smell that clings to your fingers (and your breath). Allicin is also the chemical that kills bacteria and keeps your blood free-flowing.

Likewise, when you cut into an onion, an enzyme nearly identical to the one that makes allicin in garlic swings into action. The enzyme reacts with a chemical in the onion to make a chemical called "lacrimatory factor." Droplets of lacrimatory factor fly up into your eyes when you chop onions, making them sting and water. (Scientists named the chemical after the tear glands, which are called the "lacrimal glands.")

Scientists have speculated as to why garlic would make allicin and onions the lacrimatory factor. Allicin kills not only bacteria but also fungus. So it may protect the garlic plant against decay of its bulb. And lacrimatory factor may keep curious animals from eating up growing onions, after they take that first fateful, stinging bite.

What gives foods their different tastes?

You may think that the answer lies in the taste buds on your tongue. But try this: Pinch your nose shut while you chew and swallow a bite of food. Most of the food's flavor will mysteriously disappear. With your nose shut, your favorite brand of ice cream will no longer have any special advantage over the brand you hate.

Taste and smell must work hand in hand if we are to experience what we call "flavors" in foods. Even before we bite into an orange, we smell that citrusy, orangy aroma. That's because odor molecules from the orange float through the air and up our nose. Different odor molecules come in different shapes, like baby blocks. The shapes fit into different-shaped slots in the nose called odor receptors.

When we actually bite into the orange, more odor molecules are released. These molecules waft back into your throat and up into the back of your nose.

But smell is only part of flavor; the rest is due to the little bumps in the mouth called "taste papillae." Bunched on the tongue, but also scattered throughout the mouth (including the roof), the papillae contain nerve fibers wrapped around taste buds. The nerve fibers sense the feel of food, its temperature, and whether it is painfully irritating, like hot peppers. Receptors in the taste buds sense its saltiness, sourness, sweetness, and bitterness.

With the mouth recognizing four basic tastes, plus texture, temperature, and spiciness, and the nose able to identify thousands of separate odors, we're in the flavor business. The combination of messages sent by the nose and the mouth to the brain lets us know whether we are eating a cold bowl of chocolate ice cream or hot and spicy chicken.

Some people are "nontasters," born with only 15 taste buds in each square centimeter of tongue. Others are "supertasters," with

more than 1,000 in each little square. Most of us are in between. Supertasters taste in extremes—foods can taste too sweet, too salty, too bitter. Nontasters may pile on the salt and still insist a dish is bland. But smell levels the playing field, since aroma is the key to true flavor.

Eating fruit from the West African miracle plant can make a taste mysteriously change into its opposite. Take a bite and some of the fruit's protein will linger near the sweetness receptors in your taste buds. Then taste a food that contains sour acid, like lemon. The acid changes the shape of the leftover fruit protein, enabling it to slip right in to the sweet receptor. So you get a rush of sweetness—your lemon tastes like candy.

FAST FACT

Insects and other animals without backbones have taste receptors in special hairs on their legs, feet, and other body parts. So a fly landing on a sugar cube will realize it has stumbled onto a treat from the instant rush of sweetness in its feet and legs.

Why do our faces flush, eyes water, and noses run when we eat hot, spicy food?

At this moment, hundreds of millions of people all around the planet are biting into food that bites back. Hot peppers are so popular that every space shuttle is equipped with packets of hot sauce before it blasts into orbit. There's even an old hot-pepper weather forecast: Chili today, hot tamale.

Botanists (plant scientists) say hot peppers got their start in the "New World"—North America, Central America, South America, and the Caribbean islands. Explorers from Europe saw people eating chili peppers and tried the hot foods themselves. They liked the tasty bite so much that they packed up plants and seeds and carted them home on the return voyage. Soon, the popular peppers were growing around the world.

Peppers, both mild green bell peppers and hot chili peppers, are members of the Solanaceae, or nightshade family. You might be surprised to learn who else is a part of this talented, tasty, and sometimes scary clan: potatoes, eggplants, tomatoes, and tobacco, as well as the very poisonous belladonna ("deadly nightshade") and jimsonweed.

Pepper plants are bushy, and most bloom with small white flowers. Inside each flower a berry grows: a hot or mild pepper, depending on the species. Peppers have fleshy walls and are filled with little seeds.

Peppers come in all sizes (from an inch to a foot long), colors (green, red, yellow, orange), and flavors (from sweet to screamingly hot). Why do hot peppers make our tongues burn, faces flush, and noses run? The answer is capsaicin, a crystalline protein.

When capsaicin touches the nerve endings in the mouth and tongue, it's like a fire alarm goes off in the brain. Given a jolt of adrenalin, the heart speeds up. Meanwhile, blood vessels widen, making the face redden, the nose run, and the eyes water.

> *When capsaicin touches the nerve endings in the mouth and tongue, it's like a fire alarm goes off in the brain.*

Meanwhile, capsaicin binds with the taste receptor cells in the mouth, actually making them more sensitive to flavor. So it's

Jalapeño Hook and Ladder Brigade

ONE Alarm... Jalapeño cookies. Two Alarm... ...Orange habanero pancakes... Three Alarm... ...Red savina soup!

not your imagination—hot peppers really do make foods taste better.

The brain, sensing pain and possible injury, releases endorphins, the body's natural painkillers. (They are also secreted during hard exercise.) Endorphins create a pleasant, floaty feeling, which may be why your head sometimes swims when you eat very hot food.

Hot peppers even have their own rating system, a scale created by pharmacist Wilbur Scoville back in 1912. A sweet green bell pepper rates 0 Scoville units, not hot at all. But a jalapeño jumps to 4,000 units. Tabasco burns in at 40,000 units. A fiery orange habanero can pack a blistering 300,000 units. One Red Savina habanero was tested at a record 577,000 units, crossing the boundary from food into weapon. By comparison, a taste of pure capsaicin, the hot chemical itself, would blast off the scale at 16 million Scoville units.

FAST FACT

Researchers are using hot pepper extract to treat—of all things—pain. At first, capsaicin stimulates pain receptors. But after repeated doses, nerve endings become desensitized or even die off. Capsaicin cream is used to quell the itching of psoriasis and the burning pain of shingles. And by eating taffy with capsaicin inside, cancer patients have reduced the pain of mouth sores caused by chemotherapy.

What is cholesterol?

What's white and waxy and toted around your bloodstream in neat little packages day and night? If you answered "cholesterol," you win a double cheeseburger. But after you read this, you may not want one.

We think of cholesterol as something in food, but it's also an important part of each one of us—as important as our hearts, livers, and lungs. Cholesterol is a member of a family of rather greasy substances called lipids. Besides waxy cholesterol, lipids include fats (such as butter and olive oil), beeswax, and vitamin A.

In our bodies, cholesterol is a building block of all cells, certain hormones, and bile

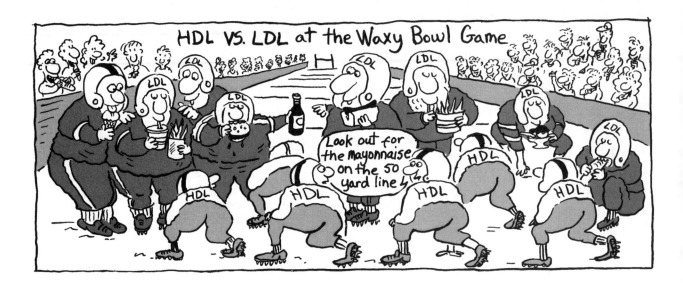

(a substance made in the liver that helps us digest the fat we eat).

Each one of us has about 5 ounces of cholesterol inside us—an amount that would fit into a small tomato paste can. We must have cholesterol to live, and so our bodies—mainly our livers—make about one-sixth of an ounce a day to replace the cholesterol used up making cells, hormones, and bile. Our bodies also get cholesterol from the animal foods we eat—eggs, milk, meats.

So why all the fuss about cholesterol? If it's so good for us, why do people say it causes heart attacks?

Cholesterol, like fat, won't dissolve in blood—it just blobs up. So it is towed around the body by molecules called lipoproteins. Low-density lipoproteins (LDLs) carry cholesterol from the liver to various organs and tissues. High-density lipoproteins (HDLs) carry cholesterol in the opposite direction—away from organs and back to the liver, to get rid of the excess.

Over history, much of the world has gone from eating the low-fat, high-fiber diets of our ancestors (fruits, vegetables, beans, grains, lean meat) to eating high-fat, mushy foods (double cheeseburgers, cream sauces, butter, cake with icing). We have gone from hard physical labor all day (farming, building, hunting) to sitting in schools and offices. The heaviest object we lift may be a bookbag.

The more saturated fat we eat, the more cholesterol the liver makes. (Saturated fat is the kind that's solid at room temperature, such as butter, the fat in meat, egg yolks, cheese, and whole milk.) Starting when we are young children, some of the excess cholesterol and fats may lodge in the walls of arteries.

Cholesterol, like fat, won't dissolve in blood — it just blobs up.

Later in life, the damaged, fat-streaked artery walls may form scar tissue and blood clots, and there will be less room for blood to flow through. Sometimes arteries will be so clogged that blood flow to the heart is blocked nearly entirely. The heart will be starved for oxygen, making even a brisk walk an ordeal. One tiny blood clot breaking off from the pileup in the artery will be enough to seal it shut. A heart attack will be the result.

Extra cholesterol should be carried away by HDLs. But because we don't exercise much, eat the wrong things, and weigh too much, our HDL levels may be low. So LDLs run amok, dumping their excess cargo in artery walls.

Here are five good ways to trick your body into loading more of its cholesterol onto HDL garbage trucks, so it will be disposed of rather than stuffed into arteries.

1. Substitute olive oil, avocados, and nuts for much of the saturated fat in your diet. These foods have "monounsaturated" fats that prompt the body to make more HDL without churning out more LDL.

2. Lose weight if you are overfat. Too much body fat, especially around your belly and chest, raises LDL and lowers HDL levels. Lose weight slowly and safely by eating a little less and exercising a little more. As you get lean, your HDL should rise nicely.

3. Get moving. Real exercise, the kind that makes you break a sweat, can raise HDL levels by 5 to 15 percent or more. Thirty to 60 minutes of brisk walking, swimming, running, biking, or other sports, preferably every day, should do the trick. (The average person may have an HDL level of 45; some runners' HDL levels are 110!)

4. Get more vitamin C and E. Vitamin C hides in many fruits and vegetables, especially oranges, cantaloupe, and broccoli; vitamin E is found in vegetable oils, nuts, yams, and other veggies.

5. Avoid smoking, including breathing in other people's smoke. Smoking dramatically lowers HDL levels—perhaps one reason why smokers have more heart disease than nonsmokers.

Why is cigarette smoking bad for the lungs?

Cigarette smoke contains 2,000 to 4,000 separate chemicals, some naturally present in tobacco leaves, others added to the tobacco to flavor it or make it burn more evenly. Many of the chemicals that emerge from a burning cigarette are classified as dangerous or cancer-causing substances. Among these poison gases are cyanide, formaldehyde, and carbon monoxide, the deadly, odorless gas found in car exhaust. Smoke sucked into the lungs also contains the pesticides sprayed on the tobacco plants.

The burned materials from smoking are called tars. When you draw in and then exhale tobacco smoke, only 30 percent of the burned particles are blown back out again. Most—70 percent—collect as black soot in your lungs.

Over years of inhaling burned particles and poisonous gases, the lungs change. Air sacs are the places in the lungs where the blood carries carbon dioxide to be exhaled, and new oxygen from the air goes into the blood. Smoking causes air sacs to bulge or even break open.

Smokers may notice an irritating cough, especially when they get up in the morning. As years go by, some smokers develop emphysema. Their air sacs become so distended that they can't get enough oxygen. As emphysema gets worse, they find themselves gasping for breath with the slightest exertion— even walking across the room. Emphysema sufferers can eventually die of the disease.

After someone smokes for years, the cells that line the main airways into their lungs begin to look peculiar. Tissue becomes tough, fibrous. Scientists call such cells "precancerous." Eventually, many smokers go on to develop full-blown cancer. Cells begin to divide like crazy, losing their function as lung cells and forming useless tumors. Tumors can spread throughout the lungs. Cancer cells can

When you draw in and then exhale tobacco smoke, only 30 percent of the burned particles are blown back out again. Most—70 percent—collect as black soot in your lungs.

break off, and, carried through the blood, spread into the bones and brain. Lung cancer is one of the most difficult cancers to treat; most people who get it die.

Smoke gets in your mouth and throat, too, of course, and can cause cancer there on its way down. If all that weren't bad enough, smoking can cause artery disease. Some chemicals in burning tobacco speed up the process of clogging arteries with cholesterol, fats, blood clots, and white blood cells. Heart attacks and strokes can be the result.

Smoking also impairs the body's immune system, perhaps because it must work overtime detoxifying poisonous chemicals from tobacco smoke. The immune system can't keep up with other diseases. So smokers have higher rates of other cancers, and they get more colds, flu, and bronchitis.

The children of smokers suffer, too. When mothers smoke during their pregnancies, their babies are often born with reduced lung capacity or other lung problems, making them more likely to suffer from asthma and lung disease later.

Inhaling the smoke from others' lit cigarettes can damage the lungs and hearts of nonsmokers as well. When we breathe in "secondhand smoke" we are inhaling the unfiltered smoke from the cigarette's tip, which has even more tar and pollutants than the smoke going into the smoker's mouth. Studies show that people exposed frequently to secondhand smoke have a higher risk of lung cancer and heart attacks than people in smokefree homes or workplaces.

Scientists in smoggy Los Angeles decided to find out just how much cigarette smoke is in city air. They took samples of L.A. smog and tested it for certain chemicals that waft out of smoldering cigarettes. To their surprise, they found that 1 out of every 100 smog particles comes from the end of someone's burning cigarette—a visual reminder, in the dark cloud over L.A., of cigarettes' power to choke us.

How does alcohol affect the body?

Alcohol is a drug that, for better or worse, has been used by human beings for thousands of years to relieve anxiety and physical pain, and to create a relaxed, uninhibited feeling.

Although beer commercials often show happy drinkers on sunny beaches, the reality of alcohol is sometimes darker. At the very least, alcohol can make you nauseated and give you a splitting headache. And for some, drinking can become a habit; they come to rely on alcohol to get them through each day. At its very worst, alcohol can cause death.

Thousands of years ago, the basic recipe for alcohol was invented: People mixed fruit, honey, and cereals or other plants with water. Then they let the gloppy mixture sit in the sun for days to ferment. Yeast cells living in the mixture dine on nutrients in the food. Then they give off waste products, such as carbon dioxide gas and ethanol (a kind of alcohol). Day by day, ethanol seeps out of the yeast cells and dissolves in the liquid of the mixture.

More and more ethanol builds up as the yeast cells feast. As time passes, the yeast find themselves swimming in their own waste. When the ethanol around them increases to 12 to 18 percent of the liquid, the little yeast cells get sick and die, sinking to the bottom of the bowl. By making alcohol, they have engineered their own destruction.

Alcohol has similarly powerful effects on the body, starting with the first swallow. Mucous membranes in the throat absorb alcohol on its way down. The lungs suck in its vapors. The stomach and small intestines soak up the rest. Through all these passageways, alcohol makes its way into the blood.

If the stomach is full of food, it may take up to 6 hours for the alcohol in a single drink to be completely absorbed. But if the drink splashes into an empty stomach, all the alcohol can seep into the blood in less than an hour. Since alcohol dissolves in water, it also dissolves in blood, which is mostly water. Soon, alcohol is flowing freely throughout the body. Organs that use a lot of blood—like the brain—quickly get a dose of alcohol, too.

Hear Nothing, 'cause your head's throbbing...

A little alcohol in the blood acts as a stimulant. But as more and more alcohol mixes into the blood and circulates through the brain, it disrupts the activity of nerve cells. The brain becomes sluggish, depressed.

Muscles become uncoordinated; it becomes hard to walk straight. Someone speaks, and you have trouble figuring out what he is saying. You find your own words slurring; your tongue and lips don't work right. (All this explains why a car driven by a drunk driver becomes a lethal weapon.)

When yeast cells make alcohol, they engineer their own destruction.

If you continue drinking, your responses get slower and slower. You may cut yourself and feel no pain. Finally, you may lose consciousness.

But alcohol poisoning can happen swiftly, too. People betting they can quickly down a pint of liquor can collapse and die as the nervous system, which controls breathing and heartbeat, goes down like power lines in a storm.

Speak Nothing, 'cause you'll sound stupid.

Pfff!

Why does our breath smell bad, especially in the morning?

The Smelliest Clouds on Earth...

A post-pizza exhalation...

An after-peanut-butter emanation...

Or an early morning "haven't-brushed-yet" aeration.

For thousands of years, people have worried about their breath. More than 3,500 years ago, the Greek physician Hippocrates advised rinsing out the mouth with a mixture of wine and herbs to sweeten the breath. And a young cosmetics manufacturer in ancient Rome became a rich man when he started producing breath mints.

Most of us—if not all of us—have bad breath now and then. And we humans aren't the only ones to breathe out smelly air. Dog breath can be pretty foul, too. And if we got close enough, we'd probably discover there was squirrel breath, giraffe breath, and hippopotamus breath, too.

Luckily, the body makes its own antibacterial mouth wash to keep things sweet smelling: saliva.

One cause of smelly breath is the pungent food we eat. For example, after we digest garlic, its odor will perfume air in the lungs (and even seep through the pores in our skin).

Some diseases and conditions can cause bad breath, too—a fruity odor from diabetes, a fishy odor from kidney problems, a cheesy smell from tonsillitis.

But 90 percent of bad breath comes from everyday conditions in the mouth, which can resemble the environment in a reeking garbage can on a summer afternoon. Tiny particles of food collect between or under teeth, braces, and dentures. And there they sit, rotting—sometimes for days on end. Not surprisingly, this creates a smelly situation.

Bacteria that live in the mouth and feast on the tiny leftovers actually create the bad smell. As they chow down, their waste products emit sulfur gases—the same gases that give rotten eggs their unlovely odor. These bacteria especially like to hang out on the back of the tongue, creating that carpet of white we sometimes see when we wake up in the morning.

(By the way, it's hard to know whether you have bad breath, unless someone tells you so. A dentist suggests this test, best performed in private: Lick your own wrist, licking from the back of the tongue to the tip. Let dry for 10 seconds, and sniff. If you don't like the smell, neither will anyone else.)

Luckily, the body makes its own antibacterial mouthwash to keep things sweet-smelling: saliva. The mouth bacteria that cause bad breath are anaerobic, which means they like to live where there's little or no oxygen. Saliva, among other ingredients, contains lots of oxygen. Morning breath, that delightfully foul breath that often follows a full night's sleep, develops when bacteria run wild.

The salivary glands slow their production to a trickle during the night, since you're not awake and eating. The mouth dries out, bacteria multiply, and your breath smells like last night's rotting dinner.

What can you do about bad breath? Brush and floss your teeth, to get all the between-teeth food particles out. Then gently brush your tongue, especially the rear part, with your toothbrush. To increase saliva and keep your mouth from drying out, chew gum (preferably sugar-free).

Snack on carrots, apples, and other fibery, teeth-scrubbing foods. Drink a lot of water. And have your teeth deep-cleaned at the dentist's office about twice a year.

Your mouth makes about 2 quarts of saliva a day!

Why do people burp?

It happens to all of us. We drink a fizzy soda, or eat a huge meal. And there comes the burp. It may be so small you can barely hear it. Or it could be a big, embarrassing belch. In some cultures, burping is like paying a compliment to the cook. But in many cultures, burping is considered rude. And that's probably why kids of all ages have belching contests, to see who can make the loudest, most disgusting noise.

Here's what happens when we eat or drink. Say you are eating a banana. You bite off a chunk and begin chewing. Your teeth tear and grind the fibery banana. Liquid saliva seeps out of glands in your mouth, and its enzymes break apart some of the banana's starches. Then you swallow. The muscular esophagus, a tube that stretches from the back of your mouth down to your stomach, begins to squeeze and release, forcing the food down.

When you swallow, a little valve at the bottom of your esophagus immediately relaxes, so that the food can get into the

stomach. Then the valve tenses again, keeping food and stomach acid from pushing back up into the esophagus.

Safely in the stomach, your mashed-up banana is doused with acids whose enzymes make it disintegrate still further. Your banana has been churned into banana soup, which drips down a tube into the small intestine. There, nutrients like vitamins, minerals, protein, and some sugars are shunted into the bloodstream. What's left of the banana—fiber, some sugars, and some complex starches—passes on into

When we open our mouths to eat or drink, air comes in along with food.

the large intestine, or colon. There, millions of bacteria break down the leftovers.

The process of eating involves not just saliva and stomach acids and bacteria, but also gases. Some gas, such as hydrogen, is produced by bacteria as they work on food. But other gases enter the body through the mouth—we actually swallow them.

When we open our mouths to eat or drink, air comes in along with food. Air is a mix of gases: nitrogen, oxygen, argon, etc. Each swallow adds about 2 to 3 milliliters, or about one-tenth fluid ounce, of air to the stomach.

We usually swallow more air when drinking than eating—up to twice as much—especially if we guzzle the drink from the small opening on a can. Sucking on a straw can also mean more swallowed gas. But we also put more air in our stomachs when we gulp down food, or when we are tense.

We can even swallow food that has gases already trapped in it. Soda contains carbon dioxide gas to make it fizzy. Whipped cream has air beaten into it.

Gases can make the stomach feel bloated and uncomfortable. Belching gets rid of some gases, by forcing them up the esophagus and out the mouth. Gases that remain behind get absorbed by the body. Oxygen is used, just as if we had breathed instead of swallowed it. Most nitrogen goes into the blood and then is exhaled by the lungs. Some swallowed gases pass on into the lower intestines.

Burping on purpose to relieve a bloated feeling can backfire. When you try to burp you swallow air, and the burp doesn't get rid of as much air as you swallowed. So each deliberate burp only adds to the air making your stomach swell and hurt.

What makes your stomach growl?

Listen to your own or someone's else's stomach, and it sounds like there's something alive in there, rumbling like distant thunder and creaking like a rusty door hinge.

Your stomach is most likely to make a growling sound when it is very empty, and you feel very hungry. When the stomach is empty (except for a little air and some stomach juices), it contracts and expands rhythmically. These contractions really get going when you smell food, or even think about it. That growling you hear is your stomach rippling and squeezing. You may feel hunger pangs, too—dull to sharp pains that urge you to eat, right now.

But the stomach also makes noises when it's full of food and working hard—and so do the intestines.

Have you ever eaten a huge meal and then sat back to relax, only to hear your stomach gurgling and your intestines rumbling? Digesting food is hard work. Imagine your stomach, stuffed with food after a holiday feast. Dumped down into your stomach sac might be a sweet potato, a lump of stuffing, a mound of peas, several dinner rolls, some turkey, and a piece of pumpkin pie. It's no wonder that your body gets a little noisy as it goes into overdrive like a food processor, liquefying the food by squirting it with acid juices and then extracting some nutrients.

Adding to the din may be air swallowed along with food and drink. Air, a mix of gases, creates turbulence as it mixes with liquids in the stomach.

Your Stomach Speaks

More fries
Where's the Ketchup?
Do another burger...
EAT! EAT! EAT!

Noises in the intestines likewise come mainly from gas—the gas produced by bacteria as they further digest food. Think of the noises coming from stomach and intestines after a meal like the noises of a radiator as it starts to heat up, clanking, hissing, and rumbling from trapped water and steam.

Aside from noises, there are odd feelings in the stomach, too. Have you ever had to speak in front of a group and felt a fluttering in your stomach, like butterflies beating their wings?

What causes stomach "butterflies"? According to Henry Janowitz, a physician and professor at the Mount Sinai School of Medicine in New York City, the source may not be in your stomach at all. Instead, your anxiety over what you are about to do causes your body to release a surge of adrenaline, the hormone that prepares us to "fight or flee" in a dangerous situation. Adrenaline makes your heart beat faster. And you may feel the rapid beating in your abdominal aorta, a large blood vessel that runs by your stomach. That, according to Janowitz, may give rise to that "fluttering" feeling.

But there may be more to such "gut feelings" than was previously thought. When people are upset, they may experience more than butterflies. Some people get diarrhea; others vomit. Scientists have begun to realize that the gut is like a second brain. The esophagus, stomach, and intestines are connected in an elaborate nervous system, using the same chemicals to communicate as the brain in our heads. So the digestive tract can react on its own to all the events in our lives, by speeding up, slowing down, breaking down— or even, in happy times, by working exceptionally smoothly.

Your Stomach Speaks

You ate too much!
I feel sick...
yuk!
I'm stuffed
Don't you have a math test today?

How come acids in the stomach don't destroy it?

In some cultures, human beings actually make a meal out of the stomachs of other animals. (The Scottish dish *haggis*, for instance, is a sheep's stomach stuffed with organ meats and oatmeal, boiled up on the stove.) Our stomachs digest these stomachs with ease. Yet our own stomachs emerge unscathed after the acid bath of each meal. How come?

Here's how it works. The stomach makes a lot of digestive juice a day—about 6 cups of the acidic brew. The juice is so acidic because one of its main ingredients is scary hydrochloric acid.

Just how strong is the stomach's hydrochloric acid? In the exact strength as that made in the stomach, hydrochloric acid can eat right through a piece of zinc metal and will kill living cells. (That's why spilling hydrochloric acid on skin causes terrible burns.) Hydrochloric acid not only breaks down food, it neatly kills incoming bacteria.

In the exact same strength as stomach acid, hydrochloric acid can eat through a piece of zinc metal.

But stomach juices contain more than just acid. The acid is dissolved in a mix of water; electrolytes such as sodium, potassium, and calcium; and enzymes called "pepsins" that break down proteins.

Like acid, pepsins are also threats to living cells.

This potent digestive juice goes to work on chewed-up food as soon as it arrives from the esophagus (food pipe). Food begins to break down into an almost-liquid mass rather like stew. There's even a name for the stew that food becomes in the stomach: chyme.

Where do the acid and pepsin come from? When you begin to chew and swallow food, it sets off a hasty chain reaction of events in your stomach. The swallowing stimulates the vagus nerve that runs down your chest, your stomach senses food entering, and the incoming food dilutes the acid balance of your stomach.

In response to these mealtime events, the stomach quickly releases some hormones into the bloodstream. One of these hormones is called "gastrin." Gastrin zips through the blood to special acid-producing cells in the stomach called the "parietals," arriving like an out-of-breath messenger with a message: "It's time!" The parietal cells then swing into action, using bits of hydrogen atoms and chloride, a chemical found in table salt, to manufacture hydrochloric acid.

Meanwhile, other stomach cells, called the chiefs, begin churning out a substance called pepsinogen. The hydrochloric acid helps water enter the pepsinogen. And like

magic, pepsinogen is transformed into the lean, mean, protein-chomping enzyme known as pepsin.

What protects the stomach from acid and pepsin? Mainly, our yucky old friend mucus. Mucus in the stomach lubricates food so it can move around easily. But it also forms a thick lining on the inner surface of the stomach, to protect it from being digested by its own corrosive juices. As acid and pepsin eat through the mucus, it is continuously replenished by the tireless stomach wall.

And here's a surprise: The stomach lining also makes its own antacid, secreting bicarbonate—one of the main ingredients in Alka-Seltzer—to neutralize threatening acid.

FAST FACT

The stomach's hydrochloric acid is one million times stronger than saliva.

Do we really need an appendix?

Some of the body's organs boldly make their presence known. You're hungry; your stomach growls. You run fast, and your heart pounds.

But other organs are stealthy; we could live a lifetime without knowing they were there. For instance, take the appendix. We notice the appendix only when something goes terribly wrong with it. What are some symptoms of appendicitis? Pain in the lower right abdomen, nausea and vomiting, and a fever.

If the ailing appendix is removed, it seems like no great loss. So for many years, medical researchers thought the appendix was a "vestigial" organ—some small fragment of us that once played a part now long forgotten.

Today, researchers have put the appendix in its rightful place in the cast of organs. The appendix, they say, seems to be part of the body's immune system. That means it helps to fight infections, by secreting antibodies into the intestines to fight off invading germs.

What does an appendix look like? On the right side of your lower abdomen, where the small intestine empties into the large intestine, the appendix protrudes from the large intestine like the tail on a dog. The appendix is usually about 3 inches long, and only one-third inch across. However, some people have long, skinny appendixes— more than 10 inches, snaking around in their lower right sides.

Where the appendix hooks up with the intestine, there's a little door called "Gerlach's valve." The appendix, like the nose, produces mucus. It gets rid of mucus by letting it flow through Gerlach's valve into the large intestine.

But if something at or near the opening blocks the way, there's big trouble. As mucus builds up in the passageway leading out of the appendix, so does pressure (think of a stuffy nose). The walls of the appendix and the blood vessels crisscrossing the walls are squeezed.

To make a long story short, bacteria that live in the appendix (but usually aren't a problem) begin multiplying like crazy. And the overwhelmed little appendix soon has a raging infection.

What blocks up the valve? Maybe something you've swallowed—a bone, a cherry pit, a piece of bubble gum. (Or even, sometimes, one of your own loose teeth.) More often, the culprit is feces from the intestine, which sometimes get into the appendix opening and dry up there.

The appendix seems to be part of the immune system, helping the body fight off infections.

That's how appendicitis starts. And sooner or later, one out of every 15 people gets it. Leave appendicitis alone, and it usually gets worse. The appendix can swell and burst, spilling feces into the body. That can cause a deadly infection called "peritonitis."

Fortunately, appendicitis is usually easily treated. The infected organ is removed in an operation, and the patient takes antibiotics to stop any infection that has spread. And despite its role in the immune system, we can get along just fine without an appendix if we must.

Where do our voices come from?

All the voices of the world—from the high soprano of some opera singers to the deep baritones of some television announcers to the babble of kids on a playground—start in the voice box, a hollow chamber suspended in the throat.

The voice box, or larynx, is really a kind of valve—an air valve. The larynx sits atop the windpipe, where it receives blasts of air from the lungs. The larynx is made mainly of cartilage, the semihard stuff that also shapes the nose and ears. Lining the inside of the box is mucous membrane—a surface studded with mucous glands. The mucous helps keep the larynx from drying out in the constant breeze of air blowing through.

Inside the larynx are the vocal cords, stretched like a V between the front and back of the box. Like the strings on a violin,

vibrating from the rubbing of the bow, the cords vibrate from the in-rushing air.

The lungs are the engines of voice. They act like the bellows in an old blacksmith's shop, pushing a stream of air up the windpipe to the larynx. (That's why people with lung disease often have such weak voices.)

Lungs are the engines of voice.

When you are sitting quietly, your vocal cords stay relaxed and open, letting air pass silently in and out of your body as you breathe. But when you begin to speak, muscles tug at the cords, shortening them to make higher sounds and lengthening them to make lower ones. (For a personal demonstration of your vocal cords in action, touch your fingers to what feels like a lump in the front of your neck. Now say "Aaaaah." That vibrating feeling comes from the vocal cords, quivering in the voice box inside your neck.)

The vibrating cords produce sound waves. On their way out to the world for all to hear, sound waves must pass through the pharynx, a cone-shaped tube connecting the esophagus with the mouth. The pharynx molds the sound, making it more full-bodied.

But if lungs, larynx, and pharynx were all there were to voice, we'd all go around making humming and grunting noises. To actually talk, we need articulators—structures that shape noise into speech. To see the articulators, open your mouth and look in the mirror. There they are—your hard jaw, teeth, and front roof of your mouth; and the softer lips, tongue, and rear roof.

Have you ever seen a person doing yoga? He gets into one pose after another, arms, legs, and body positioned differently each time. Well, each time we need to make a new sound, the mouth parts reposition themselves. By shifting our mouth structures through thousands of combinations and positions, we can make all the sounds we need for speech.

To glimpse the yoga of speech, try making first an "EEE" sound, and then an "EMM" sound, while looking in the mirror. You'll notice how differently jaw, lips, and teeth are positioned in each sound, and how the palates actually vibrate differently depending on which sound you are making.

Why do people snore?

Snoring can turn a mild-mannered sleeper into a trumpeting, window-rattling sound machine. In fact, many snorers bleat so loudly, they can be heard in the next room. How loud can a snore get? Researchers have measured the sound of snoring, and some snores reached 80 decibels. That's about as noisy as a jackhammer breaking up cement on a sidewalk.

When it comes to snoring, there is a difference between the sexes, with men snorers outnumbering women at least two to one. Snorers snore loudest when they are deeply asleep. But snoring seems to fade away when a dream begins.

How does a snore start? After you fall asleep, your muscles relax. If you are lying on your back, your tongue and jaw slide backward a little. The opening from the nose at the back of the throat may be partially covered. This makes it harder for air to travel through your nose and into your lungs.

So instead, you breathe mainly through your mouth. The incoming air makes the tissue of the soft palate (the roof of the mouth, near the back) vibrate. That makes a soft snoring sound. But the longer you breathe through your mouth, the more the tissues dry out. So the rattling sound gets louder and louder.

Anything that makes it harder to breathe normally can make even a nonsnorer pick up the habit, at least temporarily. Snore-starters can include colds, allergies, and swollen tonsils.

Occasionally, snoring may be a symptom of a more serious problem called "sleep apnea." Apnea is a breathing problem in which the sleeper stops breathing entirely, for a few seconds to a

Alternative Uses for Snoring.

SSSSnore

An accompaniment for lightning...

... Demolition ...

few minutes. Then, when the sleeper finally takes a breath, there is an explosive snoring sound. Apnea sufferers are often overweight men over 40 years old. This condition must be treated by a doctor.

How to reduce snoring? Doctors say snorers should keep their weight down. And they can try sleeping on two pillows, or raising the head of the bed with blocks. This may make breathing easier.

For the irritated others who must sleep in the same room with snorers, there's the old-fashioned quick fix: elbowing the snorer in the ribs, or pushing him over on his side. Here's one old home remedy: Sew a golf or tennis ball into the back of the snorer's pajama top. Then, when he flops onto his back, he'll have an uncomfortable incentive to turn onto his side again. (The trick is making him wear the booby-trapped pajamas!)

New antisnoring devices are always being brought to the patent office. One wristwatch-type contraption has a microphone that picks up snoring sounds, and then sets off a buzzing noise when snoring reaches a high level. This is supposed to remind the snorer to turn over. Another is a little adhesive strip that

Some snores can reach 80 decibels, as noisy as a jackhammer breaking up cement on a sidewalk.

holds the snorer's nose open, so he doesn't need to breathe as much through his mouth. Still another gives the snorer a small electric shock. Bedtime, anyone?

... Torture ...
(May be against Geneva Convention)

Why do we need sleep?

Sleep is a mysterious thing. After moving around all day long, we suddenly feel the desire to lie down and close our eyes. And then it's as if our minds go somewhere else, while our bodies remain on the bed. No one knows for sure why we sleep, but as you read this, billions of people around the planet are lying still, their eyes closed, their brains dreaming.

Babies sleep the most—sometimes 16 hours a day, including naps. By the time we become adults, 7 to 9 hours a night is about right for most of us. But as we get older, we sleep less and less. In our 80s, we may sleep only 6 hours a night.

Scientists have come up with a lot of theories about why we sleep. For example, there is the evolutionary theory. For animals (and humans) that naturally sleep at night, sleep can have survival value. Moving around in the dark is dangerous—it's easier to have accidents, and harder to avoid animals that want to eat you. Also, the night is colder than the day. Curl up in a warm, sheltered place, and the body will conserve energy until the sun rises once again.

Recently, however, researchers have found what may be one of the most important pieces of the puzzle of why we sleep. Sleep, they say, is the key time for the body to repair itself. Sleep is restorative. Strange, isn't it, how science eventually comes around to the things your grandmother always said?

An immune system without sleep is like a tree without sunlight or a car without gasoline.

How does this work? Sleep seems to be the essential ingredient for the immune system to function properly. We can eat well, take our vitamins, and get lots of exercise, but if we don't sleep, none of that will matter. An immune system without sleep is like a tree without sunlight or a car without gasoline. Eventually, it comes to a screeching halt.

Just how important sleep is was proved by scientists in experiments with mice.

Scientists forced healthy mice to stay awake day after day. Soon, the sleepless mice began dropping dead. By taking blood samples, the scientists discovered that the mice had died of a massive infection of the blood.

Why? Bacteria, both the helpful and the harmful, are always present in the bodies of living creatures. What happened with the sleep-deprived mice was that bacteria got out of control. The mice's immune systems apparently "crashed" due to day after day of wakefulness. Bacteria multiplied and over-whelmed their blood, and the mice died.

Getting too little sleep may damage people, too. Scientists in a sleep lab made sure 23 men got 4 hours' fewer sleep than normal on the third night they spent in the lab. The day after their semisleepless night, the natural killer-cell action of the men's immune systems had dropped about 30 percent.

Sleep seems to be the time when our immune and other defensive systems take care of business—putting a lid on multiplying cold germs, healing cuts, repairing tiny tears in muscles, and nipping cancer in the bud. Getting a good night's sleep may be one of the most important things we can do to stay healthy and live long.

Why do people sleepwalk?

Sleepwalking Runs in Families

I remember it vividly: I was about 9 or 10 years old, and I found myself in the middle of the night at the end of the dim hallway of my house on my way into the pitch-dark kitchen, reaching out for a red aluminum tumbler that sat on the counter.

But I wasn't awake, nor was I dreaming. Instead, I felt like a ghost, weightless and floaty, as I glimpsed objects through a tunnel-vision haze. Somehow I ended up back in bed, and the next thing I knew it was morning.

At least a quarter of all kids sleepwalk once in a while, even if they don't remember doing it. Fewer adults do, perhaps only 1 percent. And sleepwalking is genetic—it runs in families.

How does it work? All night long, the brain alternates between periods of dreamless sleep and dreaming. Dreaming sleep is called rapid-eye-movement, or REM, sleep because our eyes jerk back and forth

At least a quarter of all kids sleepwalk.

under our closed lids while we dream. During dream (REM) sleep, all muscles are paralyzed except for eyes and breathing.

A sleepwalker is stuck in a bewildering in-between state—half-asleep, half-awake, completely confused. Sleepwalking occurs because of a little glitch in the sleeping brain.

Ordinary sleepwalking takes place when people are asleep but not dreaming. Since they are not in REM sleep, their muscles are not paralyzed. Their nighttime ramblings may be uneventful—a stroll around the bed, or into the closet. But some people do hurt themselves or others, walking into dressers, falling downstairs, punching walls.

Such episodes of sleepwalking can include so-called "night terrors." A child or adult may sit bolt upright in bed, let out a horrifying scream, and then race around the house, karate-chopping imaginary enemies. The person is not dreaming, so they are not having a nightmare. Instead, they are in a half-awake state, with scary thoughts and feelings of danger rising to the surface with no conscious mind to stop them. After a few minutes, the person is back in bed, and usually doesn't remember what they did in the morning.

In another, rarer kind of "walking" during sleep, something goes wrong with the mechanism that paralyzes the body during dreaming. So people can and do move around while they dream. They may attempt to act their dreams out, with sometimes disastrous consequences.

While we inherit the tendency to sleep-walk, some things can make an episode more likely: Getting too little sleep for several days in a row. Drinking too much caffeine or alcohol. Being under great stress. And having a job that causes us to work odd, shifting schedules—6 P.M. to 2 A.M. one day, midnight to 8 A.M. the next, and so on.

What do you do with a sleepwalker or someone in the grips of a night terror? Without trying to wake them up, simply lead them gently back to bed.

What causes headaches?

Have you sat staring at your computer for hours, eaten a cold bowl of ice cream, had a cold, not eaten for 8 hours, slept too long, slept too little, eaten a hotdog, gone up in a plane, or had a fight with your brother? Any of the above, plus dozens of other ordinary events, can give you a headache.

Although headaches hurt, they are not usually a sign that something is seriously wrong. It's perfectly natural to get an occasional headache. Some headaches are major pain events, while others are just annoying dull aches. How a headache gets going is not fully understood, but scientists are learning more and more of the details. (There is even a scientific journal called *Headache.*)

What happens in a headache isn't a single event, but a cascade of events. The brain itself can't feel pain. But chemical changes in the brain can affect blood vessels and muscles in and around the head. Blood vessels swell or shrink, muscles knot, and head pain is the result.

These changes in the brain occur when amounts of chemicals called "neuro-transmitters" rise or fall. Neurotransmitters are the chemicals that carry messages across nerve cells, allowing the brain to think thoughts, direct actions, store memories, recall emotions. Neuro-transmitters can be tiny amounts of hormones (like noradrenaline) or even gases (like carbon monoxide).

Neurotransmitters rise and fall depending on what we eat, how we sleep, what medications we take, whether we are under stress or not, and so on. Fluctuations in neurotransmitters can make blood vessels swell or contract in spasms. This irritates surrounding nerve endings, and you feel pain. That's a headache.

Most headaches are considered to be minor. If you miss a meal, you may get a pounding pain in your head. (Blood vessels swell when your blood sugar level drops.) Eyestrain, from working at a computer or reading too long, can cause a headache around the eyes. Nitrites in hotdogs and bacon can make the head pound. So can very cold foods. Deciding not to drink coffee or tea anymore can trigger a headache that lasts for days. (Caffeine makes blood vessels constrict; without the usual dose, vessels swell instead.)

Major headaches include migraines, tension, and cluster headaches. Migraines, which usually throb on one side of the head and can include vomiting, may be caused by everything from red wine and alcohol to monthly hormone changes. Like hair color, the tendency to get migraines is inherited.

Tension headaches are often caused by stress or by holding the head and neck in a bent position too long. The back of the head and neck may be gripped in a viselike pain.

Cluster headaches can crop up with changes in the weather or from alcohol and other foods. They appear as a sharp pain in or near one eye, and mostly affect boys and men.

FAST FACT

Occasional headaches are a normal part of life. But severe headaches with a stiff neck and fever or double vision could signal a serious problem. Any unusual headache calls for a visit to a doctor.

Some headaches signal a serious problem... ...so see a doctor.

How do muscles work, and how do you build muscle?

Like a mummy in its white wrappings, your entire skeleton is wrapped in red muscle. Muscle is hidden under fat and skin; the less fat covering them, the more visible muscles are. (Think of the body of a very lean ballet dancer.) Your heart is also a muscle, and there is muscle tissue in your organs and blood vessels.

If you want to see what muscle really looks like, take a trip to the meat department of your grocery. A red steak, surrounded by a layer of fat, is simply a slice of muscle encased in the same white fat that covers your muscles.

How does a muscle work? When you want to bend your arm to hoist a grocery bag, a nerve impulse from the brain zips down the spinal cord and speeds into the bicep muscle in your upper arm. The nerve impulse triggers the release of chemicals called "neurotransmitters" in the muscle fibers. The fibers seize up, shortening the muscle and lifting the load. (If your muscle fibers don't relax and stay seized up, that's a muscle cramp.)

Muscles can also lengthen (to set the bag down) and exert steady force (to hold the bag without moving it).

How do muscles get stronger? When we lift more weight than usual, the nervous system "recruits" groups of muscle fibers that weren't doing much before. Called into action, they increase the available strength of the muscle. After the weight lifting ends, the muscle repairs microscopic tears it suffered, in the process adding new cells. Repeat the weight lifting, and the muscle will enlarge over time. (Surprisingly, it's the

lengthening/lowering part of weight-lifting, done slowly, that strengthens muscles most.)

With stronger muscles, it's easier to do everything—even to sit taking notes! Muscle training means fewer aches and pains, even for people with arthritis. Energy increases; balance improves. Bones, which are attached to muscle, get stronger and thicker.

If you want to see what muscle really looks like, take a trip to the meat department of your grocery and look at a red steak, surrounded by a layer of fat.

With more muscle and less fat, you'll look slimmer—muscle takes up less space than fat. And for each pound of muscle you add, your body burns 30 to 50 extra calories a day—so you can eat a normal amount of food without worrying about your weight.

In the past, scientists thought we naturally lost a lot of muscle as we age. Now they realize that much of the loss may simply be due to using muscles less. To test this theory, scientists asked frail nursing home residents, ages 86 to 96, to work out with weights three times a week. After just 8 weeks, the men and women had increased their average strength by an amazing 175 percent. They also were walking nearly 50 percent faster, and their balance improved by the same amount.

But you don't have to buy weights. Simple exercises using your own body weight will strengthen all major muscles. Push-ups, from your knees or with legs extended, work chest, triceps, and shoulders. Chin-ups on a bar work biceps and back. Curl-ups with bent knees tone stomach muscles. For the lower body, try squats and lunges.

FAST FACT

Surprise: The strongest muscle in your body isn't the bicep, which helps your arm lift a heavy weight, or the big quadricep muscles down the front of your thighs. It's the muscle in your jaw—the masseter—which moves your jaw and its attached teeth to grind and chew your food.

How does the heart work?

First, some heart facts. The heart is suspended in the middle of your chest. An adult-sized heart is about the size of a man's fist and weighs about 12 ounces. The bigger you are, the bigger your heart. (A blue whale, 100 feet long and 200,000 pounds heavy, has a heart that weighs in at 1,000 pounds.)

Each minute of each day your heart beats about 72 times—less if you're very fit, more if you're out of shape or very young. So in a year, your heart beats nearly 38 million times.

That may not seem so remarkable, but think about this: Your heart is a muscle just like the bicep muscle in your upper arm. Try lifting a small weight (5 pounds), curling it up and down, 72 times in 1 minute. Your bicep will quickly tire, becoming more and more painful. Finally, it will begin to tremble and give out, refusing to lift the weight at all.

Each time you lift the weight, your bicep contracts (squeezes together), and then lengthens again as you lower the weight to your hip. And that's exactly what your heart muscle is doing, 72 times a minute—contracting and releasing, contracting and releasing. But, unlike your bicep, your heart isn't pausing to rest and isn't getting too tired to go on. The heart is a very impressive muscle.

The heart's job is to push blood around the body. With each muscular squeeze, blood, with its load of oxygen and nutrients, is shoved along to the distant reaches of legs and arms, and to vital organs like the brain and liver. During an hour of just sitting around watching TV or reading, your heart will circulate about 300 quarts through its chambers and out its blood vessels.

Here's how it works: The heart is a hollow muscle, with four chambers (rooms). The passage of blood from one chamber to the next is controlled by four doors called "heart valves."

The top chamber on the right (the right atrium) collects the used-up, oxygen-poor blood streaming in from all parts of the body. Blood then drops into the chamber below (the right ventricle), which pumps the blood

During an hour of sitting, watching TV or reading, your heart circulates 300 quarts of blood through its chambers.

to the lungs. There, it picks up a fresh supply of oxygen from the air we breathe.

The lungs send the revitalized blood back to the heart, where it is collected by the top chamber on the left (left atrium). From there the blood goes down into the chamber below (left ventricle), where the blood is pumped out to all the body's waiting tissues and organs (including the wall of the heart muscle itself).

What keeps the heart contracting so regularly? A small area of specialized cells in the heart muscle acts as the pacemaker, generating electrical impulses to keep the heart beating in just the right rhythm.

What is high blood pressure?

Have you ever played with a garden hose on a summer day? With no water running through it, the hose is limp, bendable. Turn on the water, however, and the hose becomes rigid; with the faucet open all the way, the hose may feel as if it will burst. The difference is water pressure.

Your blood vessels are much like garden hoses, with blood pushing through instead of water. Large arteries branch out into a network of about 100,000 teeny-tiny arteries called "arterioles." It's hard for the heart to squeeze blood into these miniature vessels. When there's a large amount of blood, and when the arterioles are constricted, the pressure of blood against blood vessel walls everywhere in your body rises. (Imagine a blood vessel as a garden hose again—instead of being flexible and softened, the vessel is inflated and more rigid.)

A doctor uses an inflatable arm cuff to measure how hard your blood is pushing on the walls of your vessels. Let's say your blood pressure is found to be 110/70. The higher number (systolic pressure) is the pressure of your blood when your heart contracts (beats) and squeezes blood forcefully through the vessels. The lower number (diastolic pressure) is the pressure your blood exerts between beats, when heart and blood rest.

Your blood vessels are much like garden hoses, with blood pushing through instead of water.

The numbers measure the distance a column of mercury rises on the gauge (which looks like a thermometer). The mercury rises due to the pressure of your blood pounding against the inflated cuff, which is squeezing your arm and the vessels inside it. A systolic pressure of 110 means the mercury rose 110 mm, or about 5 inches. Blood pressure up to 120/80 is considered normal. High blood pressure starts at 140/90.

What's the worst that can happen if blood is constantly pressing too hard against vessel walls? Severe kidney damage. Heart attacks, since high blood pressure damages artery walls and makes them clog with cholesterol faster. Strokes, from blocked or hemorrhaging arteries. Aneurysms, in which blood vessels balloon and burst.

Here are some proven methods to reduce our risk of high blood pressure or to lower pressure if it's elevated:

• Lose weight if you are too heavy. Carrying extra weight makes your body produce more blood and your heart work harder, which can raise blood pressure.

• Get moving. Blood pressure falls after exercise like brisk walking, swimming, or biking, and can stay lower if you keep at it.

• Eat less fat and less salt. Both fat and salt raise blood pressure in some people. Eat more fruits, vegetables, and low-fat dairy foods.

Why do we run out of breath when we run?

Breathless...

PANT PANT

gasp!

gasp!

Is he running for a train?

Climbing the Washington monument?

Or reaching for the remote?

Sitting watching TV, you might breathe 12 times a minute, taking in 2 cups of air each time. But go out for a brisk walk, and you'll find yourself breathing about 35 times a minute—and inhaling 8 cups of air with each breath!

With all that air coming in to fill the lungs, it's hard to understand why we feel breathless as we move faster and faster. But keep in mind that oxygen must dissolve into the blood and then be carried all over the body— to the heart and other muscles and organs—for us to feel like we have enough air.

When you sit on your couch, each one of those 2-cup breaths delivers enough oxygen to the blood for all of your lazing-around muscles to feel comfy. But when you run in the park, your leg muscles, the largest in the body, need a big load of oxygen, pronto. Even the rapid 8-cup or bigger breaths you take often can't supply oxygen fast enough.

If your muscles aren't used to running, they won't be very good at extracting oxygen from the blood they get.

For quick energy, muscles make use of glycogen, a sugary fuel they store up. Without enough oxygen, muscles burn glycogen incompletely, leaving a waste product called "lactic acid" behind. Lactic acid builds up in muscle fibers, making your legs feel like lead.

If your heart isn't well conditioned from brisk exercise, it can't pump as much blood. And if your muscles aren't toned and used to running, they won't be very good at extracting oxygen from the blood they do get. Your body will yell for more and more oxygen—and you may be gasping for breath.

If you are gasping, you've probably reached your maximum heart rate. Maximum heart rate is the fastest the heart can beat and still pump blood. (Each "beat" is your heart muscle contracting to push out blood and then expanding to fill again.) Your resting heart rate might be 60 to 80 beats a minute. Your maximum heart rate is much higher.

Your average maximum heart rate is easy to calculate. Just subtract your age from 220. For a 10-year-old, maximum heart rate is about 210 beats a minute. For a 40-year-old, it's about 180. Maximum heart rate changes as we age because the older we get, the less flexible and elastic the heart and all the other muscles tend to become.

To strengthen your heart and other muscles at any age, brisk walking, jogging, cycling, dancing, skating, and swimming are all good exercises. Training enables your heart to pump more blood, increasing the oxygen sent to the rest of your muscles.

How? Working muscles push more blood back to the heart. So the heart is filled with more blood than usual when it contracts, and must push harder. This strengthens it, just like lifting a weight strengthens your biceps. Also, your body actually makes more tiny blood vessels to feed muscles like your calves, so blood can get into the muscles faster. And muscles burn fuel more cleanly, creating less lactic acid buildup.

Get your heart rate up to at least 60 percent of maximum, three or four times a week, for 20 minutes or more. You should soon be able to rush up hills—no panting required.

How does sweating work?

Humans are a sweaty bunch. Compared to other mammals, like dogs and cats, we would win the grand prize in any sweat gland contest. In fact, the average person has between 1.5 and 3 million separate sweat glands peppering his skin. Each foot alone sports about 250,000 of the tiny holes. (And you wondered why your feet smell.)

Sweat glands come in two varieties: apocrine and eccrine. The apocrine glands are the bigger glands, located mainly in the armpits but also in the chest, ears, and a few other spots. The apocrine glands are attached to hair follicles in the skin and secrete a milky-white sweat. Sweat from the apocrines is the kind we associate with body odor in people, and the familiar scent of other animals (like your unwashed family dog). These glands first start producing sweat with the hormone surges of the teen years.

The average person has between 1.5 and 3 million separate sweat glands peppering his skin.

The eccrine glands are smaller, but there are many more of them, covering your entire body. They are especially numerous on the hairless palms of your hand and soles of your feet. What does a sweat gland look like? A long twisty tube runs from the opening at the skin's surface down into the skin's deep dermis layer, where it coils into a bunch like a pile of string.

The sweat that travels up these tubes to the skin is clear and colorless, about 95 percent water and 5 percent other chemicals. One of these other chemicals is salt, which gives sweat its seawater taste. Others are albumin (a protein found in muscle, blood, and egg whites), various sulfates (chemicals related to sulfuric acid), and fatty acids (otherwise known as fats). There is even urea (a nitrogen compound found in urine) and skatole (a foul-smelling substance found in the intestines).

Since sweat contains all these substances, some of them quite nasty, you might think you'd found the answer as to why some sweat has such a strong odor. Actually, as sweat wells out of the body—from both apocrine and eccrine glands—it is virtually odorless.

The real culprit is the bacteria that live on our skin. Once these little beasties begin to feast on apocrine sweat by breaking it down, a smelly situation can ensue as their waste products build up. That's why daily bathing makes the world a sweeter-smelling place.

What's the point of sweat? Sweating eliminates some body wastes (but only a little). Also, slightly moist palms and feet give a better grip than bone-dry appendages. And the odor of sweat from the apocrine glands may actually attract the

FAST FACT

Human and animal breasts are actually modified, overgrown apocrine glands, secreting milk instead of milky sweat.

opposite sex. But sweating's main job is to keep the body from overheating.

Sweat glands swing into action on orders from the hypothalamus, the part of the brain that regulates body temperature. When the hypothalamus gets word, through the nerves, that the skin and blood are getting too warm, it in turn signals the sweat glands. First, the glands secrete salt, which attracts water from inside the body. When the water seeps out on the skin, some of the salt is reabsorbed into the sweat glands, to be used again.

As air evaporates sweat, the skin and the blood running through the tiny blood vessels in its dermis layer cool off. Evaporation of just 2 cups of sweat can lower body temperature by 10 degrees. (Of course, the dramatic cooling effect of sweating is offset by heat, so your temperature doesn't really drop below normal.) In the heat of the tropics, someone working outside may sweat a gallon an hour.

Where does the fat go when you lose weight?

With all the fat lost from dieting, it seems as if it should show up somewhere. Like in storage in seedy waterfront buildings. Or on your worst enemy.

The truth is, all that lost fat simply disappears. To see how it happens, we first need to know what fat is doing on our bodies to begin with.

Most body parts are obviously useful. The heart pumps blood from toes to head. The lungs breathe air in and out. The eyes let us see the purple flags of sunset, the ears let us hear the birds' chirping chorus at dawn. The bones hold us up, so we don't collapse into a formless heap. The brain thinks, reasons, remembers—and runs the rest of the body. And fat—well, fat just sits there . . .

Your FAT will be right with you...

You lose 10 lbs. It gets deposited in the Fat Bank, where it waits for you

bye bye

to overeat and lie around the house.

Your fat is then returned by automatic transfer, usually with interest.

But not really. Fat is actually just as important as every other body part. In fact, we can't live without it. Fat is the body's portable grocery, providing free food when supplies are scarce. Fat insulates us in cold weather, helping keep our internal organs at a steady temperature. It cushions our bones from breaking. It can secrete hormones, and having enough fat enables us to reproduce.

When fat disappears from your body, it doesn't retire to a fat farm. The truth is, most of it is burned up in your muscles.

Fat is the body's grocery.

Here's how it works: Muscles prefer to use sugar for fuel, because it burns easily. Sugar is available from three places: Some is stored right in the muscles, some in the liver, and a little circulates in the blood. Only about 750 calories' worth of sugar fuel is on tap for the muscles at any given time.

So muscles burn a mix of fuel: sugar and fat. The mix varies—the slower you move, the higher the percentage of fat burned. (The greatest percentage of fat is burned when you sleep.) However, the slower you move, the smaller the total amount of fat and sugar

burned. You may burn less than 60 calories an hour sleeping, but you will burn at least 600 in an hour of slow running.

The body's sugar supply is scant. But a mere 30 pounds of body fat provides nearly 105,000 calories of energy to a hungry body (enough to survive several months). Body fat came in handy for much of human history, when food was scarce. It is still critical for the millions of people who face famines on a regular basis.

What happens to burned fat? When sugar is completely burned, all that is left is water and carbon dioxide. The same is true of fat burned in muscles. However, some fat may be processed by the liver instead. There, fragments of partially burned fat—called *ketones*—are left over.

The carbon dioxide is carried by the blood to the lungs and breathed out into the air. (Plants use carbon dioxide, so your burned-up fat makes the world a little greener.) The water is used by the body or excreted through breath, sweat, and urine. Ketones travel from the liver through the blood and get burned in the muscles and the brain for energy. Or they're broken down in the kidneys. The end result: carbon dioxide and water—and disappearing fat.

What is the difference between identical and fraternal twins?

When you look up at the night sky, you can see shining evidence of the long human fascination with twins. Follow the bottom stars of the Big Dipper away from the handle, and you will find the constellation Gemini—the Twins.

The constellation's two brightest stars, Castor and Pollux, are the twins' "heads." Castor and Pollux are named after twins in Greek and Roman myths: two helmeted, spear-carrying horsemen.

Twins pop up all the time in mythology,

often performing extraordinary feats and having amazing adventures. Also, German stories gave us the idea of the "doppelgänger." A doppelgänger is your ghostly twin; according to the legend, seeing him or her on the street means something bad is going to happen.

Why are we so fascinated by twins? Probably because they are rare. Ordinarily, human mothers give birth to one baby at a time. (Unlike cats and dogs, which have litters of two, four, many babies.) When two or more human babies were born at once— sometimes looking exactly alike—people in the past often found it downright spooky.

Today, we know how twins get started, although exactly why identical twins form is still a mystery.

Fraternal twins are the least mysterious. Normally, a woman's body releases one egg cell each month. But some women occasionally release more than one. (They inherit this tendency from their parents.) If both eggs are fertilized by sperm, then two babies may grow. Because they are made from two entirely different eggs and two entirely different sperm cells, the babies are two unique individuals. They are just brothers and sisters who happen to be born at the same time, but who don't look any more alike than any two kids from the same family.

Identical twins are more complicated. A single egg is fertilized and begins to divide and grow. But somewhere early on— perhaps as a glitch, perhaps on purpose— the fertilized egg splits into two, essentially making one individual twice. (The egg can split more than once, making triplets, quadruplets, or quintuplets, all of them "twins.") Identical twins are nature's clones.

Fraternal twins are just ordinary brothers and sisters who happen to be born at the same time.

As they grow, identical twins do develop some physical differences, both internal and external. But identical twins are the same sex. They look alike, sound alike, and often think alike. Even parents can have a hard time telling them apart.

Scientists have studied identical twins who were separated at birth and adopted by different parents. As adults, the twins' similarities can be striking: They often turn out to like the same foods, colors, cars, and vacation spots, have similar careers, and marry similar people.

What makes our eyes the color they are?

"Don't It Make My Brown Eyes Blue?" "Brown-Eyed Girl." "Jealousy has green eyes." In songs, poems, and aphorisms, human beings have focused on one tiny, lovely facet of the body: the iris, that circle of color seemingly floating on the white sea of our eyes.

The iris is named after the Latin word for rainbow, and eyes do come in a rainbow of colors. Pale gray as an overcast sky, blue as robins' eggs, sea-green, brown like rich earth, copper-colored with wedges of gray, hazel with starbursts of gold, black as a moonless night.

The iris is peacock-showy, and it should be: It's the curtain that opens and closes on the light of the world. The iris is a curtain made of muscle, sandwiched between the cornea and the lens, with a hole (the pupil) in its middle. The iris's two muscles, one expanding, the other contracting, control the size of the hole. Sometimes the hole is widened to let more light in, as when we enter a shadowy room at night. Other times the hole is shut down to pinpoint tiny, as when we glance at a glaring-bright sky on a summer's day.

Eyes with very little pigment appear blue.

The color of the iris depends on how much pigment, or coloring chemical, is deposited there. The pigment, melanin, which also colors our skin, is yellow to dark-brown in color. With very little pigment, eyes appear blue; with thicker layers, the eyes appear hazel or brown or black.

Newborn light-skinned babies usually have blue eyes, which may stay blue or darken as pigment builds up over the weeks to come. Dark-skinned babies are usually, but not always, born with dark eyes.

How much pigment builds up in the iris is controlled by our genes, which we inherit from our parents. Genes order specific amounts of pigment to be manufactured and deposited in the iris. Scientists say that there is a gene "switch" they call "brown/blue," with brown being dominant over blue.

Two brown-eyed parents who also carry genes for blue eyes can pass on different combinations of eye-color genes to their children. Brown from both parents will produce a brown-eyed child. Brown from one parent and blue from the other will also produce a brown-eyed child, since brown dominates. Only if a child beats the odds and inherits blue from both will she have blue eyes.

But what about green eyes? Scientists say there is a separate gene switch they call "green/blue." Just like brown, green is dominant over bossed-around blue.

Although this simple model can help to explain eye color, scientists say the true process is more mysterious and complicated, and eye color is also affected by other, unknown genes. For example, some people whose eyes appear blue actually carry the gene for dominant brown eye color. But a group of "modifier" genes apparently interfered, turning off the process of laying down pigment in their eyes. So their eyes never became truly brown. That may be one explanation for why two parents with apparently blue eyes can be surprised with a brown-eyed child.

Why do we giggle when we hear jokes?

What's the one universal human language? It's not Esperanto. Clue: Its most popular expressions are tee-hee, ha-ha, and ho-ho.

Laughter—among New York City cabdrivers, New Delhi doctors, and São Paulo sailors—is truly universal. Even the very sad will sometimes manage a chuckle, when faced by a fat cat capsizing off a coffee table, or an old Marx Brothers film.

Lately, scientists have been studying laughter—how it makes us feel, what changes it produces in the body, and how it might have evolved. Although they don't have all the answers, what they've found is that laughter is one of the few things that is as genuinely good for us as it feels.

Human beings start laughing very young—at age 2 or 3 months of age. Mother loudly kissing baby's tummy, which previously provoked a wide grin, may at 3 months unleash a torrent of excited giggles.

As children, one scientist says, we laugh more than 400 times a day; as adults, he claims, only 15 times.

But we may laugh many more times a day than this if we include the laughs that occur naturally when we speak. People laugh before they tell a funny story, or to highlight what they've just said, funny or not. And listeners laugh throughout conversations as a friendly way of encouraging the speaker. So one of the reasons why we laugh may be as means of facilitating conversation, and communication, between us.

Bad People to Tell Good Jokes to...

oh boy that's a good one.

Laughter is contagious, too, just like yawning. Someone breaking up over something in a quiet room can start a chain reaction, with whole rows of people giggling uncontrollably. Researchers say laughter brings people closer, making for a closer, more successful human society.

(And a footnote: Although we laugh all day long, we are least likely to laugh in the hour just after we get up. It seems we humans are all a bit grumpy in the mornings.)

We can speculate about why we laugh, but what we find funny varies from society to society and time to time. Researchers note that some societies at some times favor long, rambling, humorous tales, while others prefer snappy one-liners. However, pratfalls and other mishaps—a slip on a banana peel, a bowl of spaghetti dumped on the head— were probably always considered funny, and probably always will be.

What happens to the listener as a joke starts? The left side of the brain swings into action, beginning to intellectually analyze the joke. Then the right side joins in to find any overall patterns in the joke. (Damage to the left side of the brain sometimes results in a total inability to find anything funny.)

Brain activity spreads to an area associated with processing information from our senses. "Delta"-type brain waves build. Finally (as an EEG tracing the activity shows), a "surprise" wave crests as the brain gets the joke, and giggling starts.

But don't tell jokes to the driver of the car you're riding in. When the brain produces a lot of delta waves, we get distracted, and don't pay attention to what's going on around us. Laughter should carry a warning: Don't giggle while operating heavy machinery.

Laughing also improves our blood circulation, reduces pain, and lowers levels of stress hormones in the body. Of course, we don't laugh because we think it's good for us, like eating our vegetables. We laugh because, despite all its tragedy, the world is still a pretty funny place.

Laughing Is Good Medicine

In 1983, author Norman Cousins wrote about how he came to lead a vigorous life after a heart attack. As he had in an earlier serious illness, Cousins relied in part on laughter as his favorite medicine for healing. Cousins prescribed a program of low-fat foods, exercise, and belly laughs for himself. He walked, spent hours on the tennis court, and watched funny movies or listened to comedians on tape. Gradually, his heart grew stronger along with his spirits. Cousins made a truce with his heart by having more fun.

Research over the last 20 years has tended to confirm the link between mind, body, and disease. In 1993, scientists found some exciting physical evidence for such a link. It turns out that nerve endings jut up against certain immune cells in the skin.

Nerve cells seem to "talk" to the immune system cells, called the "Langerhans cells," by using chemicals. How might this work? A chemical released by nerves, called CGRP, can dampen the activity of the nearby immune cells. Changing emotions might cause the brain to order the nerve cells to release less or more CGRP.

This could explain why certain skin diseases flare up under stress. Or why a wart on a kid's leg may suddenly disappear when his mom tells him it has to be removed. In such cases the nervous system, which is mediated by our emotions, may actually communicate with the immune system in a direct, hands-on way.

Of course, there is more to the immune system than the Langerhans cells, and more to the nervous system than the nerves in the skin. But such studies provide tantalizing clues that body and emotions are inextricably linked.

For example, one study compared the arteries of mice who were fed high-fat diets. One group was fed high-fat meals and otherwise ignored. The other group was petted and stroked gently as they ate. Researchers found that the mice who were left alone had significantly clogged arteries after months on the diet. But the mice who had been held and petted had nearly clear arteries—even though they ate the same high-fat foods.

This seems to show that the body has some control over the amount of damage done to itself in some circumstances. Illness apparently isn't cut-and-dried, a simple matter of bad diet or infection. Our sense of well-being— feeling generally happy, at peace, and loved and cared for—may have an effect on our illnesses.

And it seems that laughter is indeed one of the best medicines. Laughter increases the amount of oxygen in the blood, just as running does; relaxes us; reduces pain, possibly by causing the body to release natural painkillers; and prevents stress.

One study by William Fry, a gelotologist, or laughter researcher, found that people in the throes of laughter show more activity of white blood cells. White blood cells are a key part of the immune system, particularly important for fighting bacteria.

Whether or not laughter makes us live longer, it is certain that it makes us live happier. That living with joy and laughter turns out to be useful in healing disease is like the frosting on the cake.

Why do we sometimes feel that what we're experiencing has happened before?

It's called "déjà vu," which is French for "already seen." It's that overwhelming feeling that washes over you for a moment, telling you "been there, done that"—when you actually haven't. The feeling can be so intense when it is happening that it may be impossible to believe it isn't real.

Flashes of déjà vu seem to tell us that we are leading bits and pieces of the same life over and over again. This is probably what has led many over the ages to see déjà vu as evidence for reincarnation, the idea that our souls live many lives.

Others see déjà vu as a kind of evidence for precognition—knowing what's going to happen before it happens—and the fluidity of time. This view sees the future as coexisting with the present and the past. It says that we sometimes have a strong feeling of familiarity with an experience because on some unconscious level, we knew it was coming.

Scientists take a more down-to-earth view. They have come up with dozens of different explanations of déjà vu, but no one is sure which (if any) is correct. Although scientists don't profess to know what causes déjà vu, many think it involves the brain's memory system. Déjà vu, they say, could be a kind of faulty memory. Reinforcing this view is the fact that déjà vu often occurs when we are very tired or under a lot of stress.

Some scientists suggest that déjà vu occurs when one part of the brain registers an experience a split second before another part does. So you feel like the experience has happened before.

An intriguing new idea about memories is that they may be stored as kinds of holograms in the brain. A hologram is a photographic image made using lasers that looks three-dimensional. The interesting part about a hologram is that the entire holographic image can be reconstructed from any small part of it.

How could memories be like holograms? Scientists say that information from any one memory is stored in various sites in the brain. A section of the brain known to contain a part of the memory can be removed, but the patient will still be able to recall the whole

Déjà vu is that feeling telling you, "been there, done that"— when you actually haven't.

memory. Why? Like a hologram, even a fragment of a memory can be used by the brain to recall the whole memory.

In this theory, déjà vu may be provoked by having an experience that shares some features with one or more real past experiences. The brain may take bits and pieces of several different memories that may be nearly identical to each other (two memories that involve a dog in a red sweater, say) and combine them into a new, totally false memory—a déjà vu.

Whatever its cause, the déjà vu experience can involve some strange coincidences. A dermatologist named Steven Kohn wrote about an encounter he once had with a young man in New York City. The man was standing in front of a clothing store with a confused look on his face.

He told Dr. Kohn that this was the first time he'd visited New York. But he was overwhelmed by the feeling that he had stood in this spot before, looking at the exact suits in the window, while telling this

FAST FACT

Your brain has between 10 billion and 1 trillion neurons (nerve cells). Every single neuron has about 1,000 synapses, which connect it to other neurons. It's no wonder the brain is able to make and store a seemingly endless number of memories from the past.

stranger, Dr. Kohn, about his feeling of déjà vu. So the man's experience was a sort of déjà vu within a déjà vu.

But what the young man couldn't have known was that the man in his "double déjà vu" wasn't just any bystander. In a strange twist, Dr. Kohn had done his medical school thesis on—you guessed it—déjà vu.

FACTORY FIELD TRIP

Take a good look at this book you're holding in your hands: the printed words, the colorful covers, the pages glued together. We human beings love to make things. Our closest primate relatives, the chimpanzees, use tools such as twigs to pull ants out of anthills, leaves to collect rainwater from tree trunks, and sticks as weapons. Our bigger, even more specialized brains gave us the ability to make tools of every description—from spoons to carry cereal to our lips to robot space probes to carry our experiments to nearby planets. So take a factory field trip, and find out how we've made everything from chocolate bars to microwave ovens to mysterious mummies.

How is chewing gum made?

Kids love it. Teachers frown on it. So do dentists. Hard lumps of it can be found lurking under the seats in movie theaters—or on the bottom of your shoe. In some places, chewing it is a crime.

Gum is sold all over the world, in every shape and size. It comes by the stick, by the chunk, by the ball, by the tiny pellet. Gum comes in dozens of flavors, from peppermint and spearmint to cinnamon, clove, and fruity. There is even gum that tastes like violets.

Bubble gum is gum with something extra. You chew, you blow, you pop—sometimes all over your own face.

But all gum is peculiar. It goes in the mouth, it gets chewed—but it's not really food. You're not supposed to swallow it, although you might, by accident. You simply chew and chew. Until the flavor is gone, and the gum is a tasteless rubbery lump in your mouth. Yuck. You spit it out, and it may end up on someone's shoe. (Which is why, in some places, gum is banned.)

Gum isn't a recent invention. Both the ancient Greeks and the Mayan Indians enjoyed a good wad of gum. But it wasn't until about the 1860s that familiar modern gum was manufactured.

What's the key ingredient in a stick of gum? A clue can be found in the brand name of one gum: Chiclets. Chewing gum has traditionally been made from chicle, which is a gummy sap from the bark of a special evergreen tree. The tree, known scientifically as *Achras zapota*, grows naturally in Central America. Other natural gums may also be used, along with cheaper synthetic materials—polymers made from petroleum products.

Machines blend the chicle or other material with latex (rubbery) products, waxes, and other ingredients to make the gum base, the part of the gum that stays solid no matter how long you chew it. Each manufacturer has its own blend, controlling the sticky chewiness of its product. (Bubble gum is ordinary gum with extra latex added, for stretchiness when blowing.)

The gum base is ground up, melted, sterilized, and purified until it is a thick, clean syrup. Other machines add ingredients like sugar, corn syrup, or artificial sweetener; color; plus flavorings to give each gum its distinctive taste.

The gum is mixed in huge vats until it has the consistency of bread dough. Then it is flattened by rollers into thin sheets, which are left to cool and harden before they are cut into small pieces. Gum pieces may then be sprinkled with powdered sugar, wrapped in paper by another machine, and stuffed into little packages.

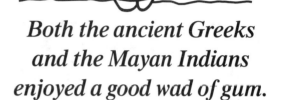

Both the ancient Greeks and the Mayan Indians enjoyed a good wad of gum.

Why chew gum? Because it's fun. It's a burst of sweet flavor. It's something to do with your mouth between meals. Some say chewing gum increases concentration, relieves boredom, and relaxes. (Time for a trip to the candy store!)

How is chocolate made?

The world loves chocolate. Chocolate companies measure the amount of cocoa beans they grind up, and have found that human beings consume about 3 billion pounds of the stuff each year. Most chocolate is eaten in cool climates; in the tropics, it's too steamy to keep chocolate solid and fresh.

But ironically, the tropics is where chocolate comes from. Chocolate is made from the ground-up beans (also called seeds) of the cacao tree. Cacao trees grow in places like Brazil, Ghana, and Nigeria. A cacao tree stands about 25 feet high when full-grown. Hanging on the trunk and branches are pods, each packed with 20 to 40 almond-shaped seeds.

(If you've ever had plain baking chocolate, with no sugar added, you know that the taste is very bitter. In fact, the word *cacao* comes from two Mayan Indian words meaning "bitter juice." Likewise, the word *chocolate* comes from the Mayan words for "sour water."

People chop off the pods with long knives, slice them open, and scoop out the beans. Beans are piled up, covered with

Human beings consume about 3 billion pounds of chocolate a year.

burlap or leaves, and allowed to ferment for a week or more. Then they are uncovered and left to dry in the sun or under heat lamps, and are finally shipped to chocolate factories. (For example, the Hershey factory, in Hershey, Pennsylvania, where the whole town smells of roasting chocolate and the streetlamps are shaped like chocolate kisses.)

At the plant the beans are roasted and shelled. The shelled beans are about 54 percent fat, in the form of cocoa butter. When beans are ground into pieces, the cocoa butter seeps out. The liquid combination of cocoa butter and floating bits of cocoa bean is called chocolate liquor.

Baking chocolate is simply solid, cooled blocks of chocolate liquor. Cocoa powder is made by removing some of the cocoa butter and pressing and grinding what's left. Milk chocolate, the kind found in most candy bars, is made of chocolate liquor, extra cocoa butter, dried milk, and sugar, with vanilla added for flavor. Dark chocolate, often known as sweet or semisweet, has everything but the milk.

What is white chocolate? Technically, it isn't really chocolate. White chocolate has cocoa butter and sugar, but no ground-up bits of cocoa beans. So it has all the fat, but little of the chocolate flavor.

White chocolate is also missing something else: caffeine. One ounce of dark chocolate can have as much as 35 mg. (A 5-ounce cup of coffee has more than 100 mg.) Eating a giant-size bar of dark chocolate can produce the same jittery feeling as a cup of coffee. Eating a big bar of white chocolate, however, will probably only make you sleepy.

FAST FACT

English-speaking people call cacao beans "cocoa beans" because many years ago, an English chocolate importer misspelled "cacao" as "cocoa."

How is decaffeinated coffee made?

Call it coffee, java, or joe—Earth must have its morning coffee. About one of every three people on the planet drinks the dark brew.

Coffee seeds—otherwise known as beans—naturally contain caffeine. Caffeine is a chemical stimulant, one of a group called "alkaloids." When you say a cup of coffee wakes you up, it's mainly due to the caffeine. Caffeine causes the body's nervous system to release adrenaline, making your heart pump faster and making you more alert.

Many people like the taste of coffee or the custom of drinking it, but don't want the stimulating effects of caffeine. Caffeine, especially in large doses, can make people anxious, fearful, or jittery. A cup of regular

De-jitter, De-quiver Dem Beans !!!
(taking the jump out of java)

soothing music

relaxing games

That feels better.

Beans are given 6 months relaxation therapy...

Followed by a looooooong cruise...

...and a move to the country.

coffee has 60 to 180 mg of caffeine, but a cup of decaf has only 1 to 5 mg.

Coffee makers use several different methods to pry the caffeine out of the bean. They extract the caffeine when the bean is still green, before roasting turns it brown.

Caffeine causes the nervous system to release adrenaline, making you more alert.

One decaffeination process uses a chemical called "methylene chloride." First, steam is used to soften the beans, causing caffeine to rise to their surfaces. Then, the beans are rinsed for about 10 hours in methylene chloride, which bonds to the caffeine and draws it out. Finally, the beans are washed and dried.

In a variation on this method, the beans are soaked for hours in very hot coffee water. This draws out caffeine and coffee oils (including those that give coffee much of its flavor). The coffee water is separated from the beans and treated with methylene chloride (or a chemical called "ethyl acetate"), which absorbs the caffeine.

Then the coffee water is heated, and the caffeine–methylene chloride evaporates into the air. The water is then returned to the beans, which get most of their oils and flavor back.

Still another method uses activated charcoal or carbon filters, like those used in home water filter systems, to clean the water-coffee mixture of caffeine before returning it to the beans.

Sometimes, manufacturers use coffee oils to decaffeinate coffee. First, the beans are soaked in hot coffee water, bringing the caffeine to the beans' surfaces. Then the beans are put in a heated container of coffee oils taken from old coffee grounds. After several hours, substances in the oils called "triglycerides" bond with the caffeine and pull it out of the beans. Then the beans are taken out of the oil and dried.

Finally, some beans are decaffeinated using carbon dioxide gas. First, steam brings caffeine to the surface of the beans. Then the beans are dunked in the gas. The gas is kept under extremely high pressure, which makes it act like a liquid. The carbon dioxide seeps into the beans and hooks up with the caffeine. Then, the carbon dioxide/caffeine is drawn off. When the beans cool, any leftover carbon dioxide floats off into the air—just as it does when we exhale.

Why does rubber bounce?

Bandleaders on old TV shows and movie shorts used to ask viewers to "Follow the bouncing ball" as it skipped across song lyrics for a sing-along. Well, if it weren't for rubber, balls wouldn't bounce. Basketball players wouldn't be able to dribble, and hair bands wouldn't hold ponytails. And sadly, you wouldn't be able to shoot rubber bands at unsuspecting friends and family. Not to mention the fact that cars and school buses would have to come up with entirely new kinds of wheels.

We think of rubber as coming from a plant, but most of today's rubber is tailor-made by people. However, it all started with trees, and an oozing, milky-white substance called

"latex." People discovered that if they collected liquid latex and dried it over a fire until it thickened and solidified, they would have an elastic material: rubber.

When we say a material is very elastic, we mean that a piece of it can be stretched to several times its own length—and not only not break, but snap back to its original size. Another word for highly elastic? Bouncy. Rubber, both natural and man-made, is very, very bouncy.

The tall, slender tree most natural latex comes from—*Hevea brasiliensis*—is a native of South America (you'd probably guess that from the "Brasil" in its name). Some 2,500 years ago the Mayan Indians of Mexico were making rubber balls. One way they

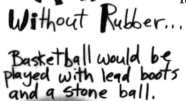

A World Without Rubber...

Basketball would be played with lead boots and a stone ball.

ugh!

A World Without Rubber...

Ponytails would be held up by a stick and string arrangement.

used the balls was on courts with hoops, much like modern basketball courts.

For many centuries, only people who lived in South and Central America and the Caribbean knew that rubber existed. Then the European explorer Christopher Columbus noticed the curious, bouncy balls people were playing with in Haiti and brought a few home with him in 1493. With that, rubber was launched on its career as an international superstar.

What makes rubber so bouncy is the unique way its molecules are arranged. Natural rubber is made of long, flexible chains of carbon atoms, connected here and there to hydrogen atoms and coiled up into a spaghetti-like mass. In other long-chain materials like plastic, chains are rigid. But in rubber, the chains can twist, flex, tangle. When a piece of rubber stretches, the molecular chains uncoil; when the rubber is released, the chains retract by curling back into place.

It wasn't until World War 2 that people started making rubber synthetically on a wide scale. The United States needed millions of rubber tires and other rubber products for the war. It couldn't get natural rubber from Asia, where most of it was produced. So the United States began to make vast quantities of rubber in factories.

Today, most rubber is man-made from petroleum products. Some rubber facts: Sulfur is usually added to rubber to vulcanize (stabilize) it. A filler like sooty carbon is often mixed in to make the rubber even stronger and stiffer (that's why tires are black). Besides tires, rubber is used to make sneakers, surgical gloves, and—look around the room—a million other things, from raincoats to chair cushions to rubber duckies.

A World Without Rubber...

Bicycles would run on tank treads.

How is glass made? How is it shaped into drinking glasses and pop bottles?

If you want to know where glass comes from, go to the beach. Almost all glass is made from sand—silica sand, which is really ground-up quartz.

Sand has a little iron in it. The iron gives glass made from plain sand a greenish cast. To make absolutely clear, colorless glass, glassmakers add some selenium. This mineral gives the glass a slight reddish tint, which cancels out the green, making the glass appear clear.

(To make glass of other colors, glassmakers add other elements to the sand—cobalt for deep blue, manganese for purple, chromium or more iron for green.)

Once you have the sand, you must melt it. As you might guess from walking through very hot sand on a sunny day, sand must be heated to a very high temperature before it melts. An ice cube melts above 32° F. Sand doesn't melt until it reaches 3,100° F., or nearly five times as hot as the highest temperature most kitchen ovens can reach. Heating something to more than 3,000° takes a lot of energy and is very expensive. So to make most kinds of glass for everyday use, glassmakers add a chemical to the sand to help it melt at lower temperatures— anywhere from about 1,500° F. to about 2,500° F. Usually, the chemical is soda ash.

However, the recipe of sand plus soda ash creates a peculiar kind of glass—one that dissolves in water. (Not a particularly good choice for a drinking glass.)

So a third ingredient must be added, to make the glass hold together better. Glassmakers mix in some ground limestone with the sand and soda ash. (You may have seen this lovely white stone in old hotels or monuments.)

The glass usually made into windows, mirrors, drinking glasses, bottles, and light bulbs is called "soda-lime glass." Soda-lime glass is durable and easy to shape when hot. Besides the sand, soda ash, and lime, the formula calls for some magnesia, alumina, and boric acid, along with chemicals to keep bubbles out of the glass mixture.

Once the ingredients are combined, the mixture is dumped into a giant furnace.

Ice melts just above 32° F; sand melts at 3,100°.

Tremendous fires in the furnace heat the mixture until it melts from a solid mass to a flowing liquid. (The biggest of these furnaces may hold almost 3 million pounds

He's such a show-off!

of liquid glass.) The liquid glass is kept at the highest temperature until all bubbles and streaks disappear, so that objects made from it will be perfectly clear.

Once the glass is nice and smooth, the fire is turned down a little, so that the glass thickens to a gooey mass—like hot taffy. Then the glass is poured out of the front of the furnace into a forming machine, where it is pushed and prodded into molds, pressing it into shapes.

However, to make some hollow objects, such as bottles, the glass must be blown like a balloon. Glassblowing is sometimes done at fairs and carnivals. You may have seen someone blowing into a gob of hot glass at the end of a tube, creating little glass animals. Glassblowing is also done by machine. The idea is to blow into the glass until a bubble of air forms in the middle, making the finished hard object hollow.

After glass is shaped, the danger is that the new glass object will crack as it cools to room temperature. Glassmakers control the cooling by giving the hardening glass a heat treatment to remove stress. Putting on the finishing touches, workers may grind off little pieces of glass on the handle of a glass mug, or use special chemicals to polish a glass pie plate until it is perfectly smooth.

FAST FACT

Scientists are still debating whether glass is a solid or a very viscous (syrupy) liquid. Since very old windows are often thicker at the bottom than the top, some claim the glass flowed over time. However, old windows weren't made perfectly flat, and people set them in the frames with the heavier ends down. Also, the oldest Roman glassware shows no signs of "flow." So looking at old glass won't settle the question of whether glass is really a liquid.

What is perfume made of? And where do they come up with the fragrance names?

Question: What does perfume have to do with smoke? Answer: "To perfume" comes from the word *perfumare*, which in turn comes from the Latin word *fumare*—meaning "to smoke." Primitive perfumes were created by burning woods and bark. Scented smoke (incense) that floats up and away into the air was seen as a way of reaching the gods.

Throughout history, people have used perfume in religious ceremonies, to mask odors, and to attract others. Napoleon would only go into battle if he was equipped with dozens of his favorite scents. The Egyptian queen Cleopatra had the sails of her boat perfumed, so that the winds over the Nile River carried her scent near and far. (Among the favorite perfumes of ancient Egypt: white lily.) And the Romans may have invented aftershave lotion.

Today's perfumes are made from natural oils of plants, synthetic chemicals, or both. A typical complex perfume, whose formula is strictly guarded, may contain jasmine, violet,

rose, orange blossoms, sandalwood, patchouli, cinnamon, oak moss, and other scents, as well as alcohol.

> ### *Perfumers say that creating a new fragrance is like composing a piece of music.*

Here's how it works. Plants and flowers contain essential oils, which are intensely fragrant. Oils may be removed by using steam (a method invented in ancient Arabia) or chemical solvents, by pressing, or by allowing oils to soak from flowers or leaves into a layer of fat. Today's perfumers, using sophisticated chemical analysis and computers, can even incorporate scent molecules from a piece of flannel to add the smell of a men's suit to his cologne, or the ozone in sea air for a nautical scent.

Traditionally, perfumes might also contain animal scents: ambergris from the sperm whale, musk from the musk deer. Today, sparing the animals, these musky scents are almost all made in labs.

Perfumers say that creating a new fragrance is like composing a piece of music. Most perfumes release their fragrance in scent layers, called "notes."

Top notes are the scents you notice first, which quickly fade. Then come the middle notes, and finally the long-lasting bottom notes—the traces of scent left on the skin after hours.

Perfume makers invent names whose images appeal to how customers would like to see themselves. For example, take these men's fragrance names: Iron (strength), Stetson (a cowboy hat), Chaps (more cowboy wear), Grey Flannel (an expensive suit), Tsar (a king), Boss, Gentleman.

In contrast, women's fragrance names often evoke floaty images of loveliness: Poème, Allure, Beautiful, Longing, Dreams, Youth Dew, Diva, So Pretty, Blonde.

Some fragrances are named after their maker, often a well-known clothing designer: Chanel No. 5, Lauren, Dioressence, Escada, Lagerfeld, Armani. Other names refer to scents in the fragrance: Vanilla Fields, Cool Water, White Musk, Old Spice, Bay Rum.

Actress Elizabeth Taylor's perfume, White Diamonds, reflects her fondness for wearing the large gems. White Linen reminds us of summertime. And Lasting, perhaps the most practical perfume name of all, simply means that the scent will still be evident 10 hours after it's applied.

How are diamonds formed?

You may know that diamonds are usually found by miners working underground. But did you ever in your wildest dreams imagine that the glittering diamond in your mother's wedding ring may once have been a dinosaur?

Recently, scientists have been debating long-held theories about how diamonds are created. First, here's the traditional story:

Diamonds form 80 to 300 miles below Earth's surface, where the heat is blazing (about 1,650° F.) and the pressure is colossal (about 40,000 times the weight of Earth's atmosphere).

The combination of blasting heat and crushing pressure causes carbon atoms to crystallize into pockets of solid diamond. Diamonds usually form in rocks called

"kimberlite," which are made of minerals like iron and magnesium. Kimberlite often comes in the form of long, green pipes, formed and thrust up toward the surface millions of years ago in volcanic eruptions. A kimberlite pipe isn't exactly a king's scepter, studded with jewels; a pipe may contain one diamond crystal for every 40 million parts of kimberlite.

If you stumbled across a natural diamond washed up on a beach, you might not recognize it as a valuable stone. Before it is cut and polished, a diamond is usually a dirty, lumpy crystal, ranging in color from white to canary yellow to brown or black. But diamond miners know what to look for; they dig up kimberlite pipes, break them into pieces, and sort out the diamonds. (Later, those good enough to make gems are cut and polished.)

Look at the lead in your pencil for a clue as to what diamonds are made of. The lead is graphite, a material made of carbon—just like diamonds. But unlike graphite, which breaks annoyingly each time you write too hard, diamond is the hardest natural substance known in the universe.

What makes diamond so hard is how it is built. Think of the Egyptian pyramids, those sturdy triangles set in the desert. Unlike a rectangular building, a pyramid can't sway and topple over. Likewise, diamonds are made of pyramids of atoms. Each carbon atom is bound tightly to four others, making the five points on a pyramid. A diamond is made of many of these pyramids, interlocked like Tinkertoys. Since pyramids are the strongest structures known, and since each pyramid in a diamond is a part of the next, a diamond is unbelievably hard and virtually indestructible.

Look at the lead in your pencil for a clue as to what diamonds are made of. The lead is graphite, a material made of carbon—just like diamonds.

But mysteries about diamonds remain. For example, in Norway, microscopic diamonds were found in rocks that weren't volcanic and didn't come from Earth's depths. Instead, the tiny diamonds were embedded in rocks that originally lay on Earth's surface, as sediment.

How did these diamonds form? One theory is that as ancient continents collided, the sedimentary rocks were carried deep into Earth, where they formed diamonds. Later, they rose back up to the surface. Another theory is that the minidiamonds formed in the crust when continents smashed together, since thin films of diamonds have been grown in labs at similarly low pressures.

Here's another new idea: The forms of carbon found in some diamonds are the same forms found in living tissue. So some diamonds may be made of long-gone plants and animals, including dinosaurs.

But diamonds aren't only found on Earth. When a meteorite drops from space, diamonds are often embedded in its stony depths. Scientists think they form when meteorites collide or slam into planets, creating the heat and pressure that are the recipe for diamonds. So old meteor craters (rather than the bottom of the sea) may be the best place to look for buried treasure.

Although we associate diamonds with expensive jewelry, most (the run-of-the-mill diamonds) are used in factories like auto plants for cutting and drilling.

How do gems form, and how do they get their color?

oday's jewelry-store browsers are part of a long line of human beings intrigued by gems. In fact, as soon as people began writing things down, gems were among the first objects mentioned.

Take the lovely purple amethyst. The stone's name comes from the Greek word *amethystos*. Surprisingly, *amethystos* doesn't mean "purple," as one might expect. Instead, it means "without drunkenness."

Why the connection with alcohol? Greek legends feature a nymph named Amethyst. The god of wine, Bacchus, was smitten with Amethyst. To protect her from Bacchus, the goddess Diana turned Amethyst into a glittering gem. Sad but still lovestruck, Bacchus poured his wine over Amethyst's stony form, tinting the gem a beautiful violet.

That's how, legend says, amethyst got its color. And that's why, according to legend, the stone was believed to have the power to keep its wearer sober (out of the wine god's clutches). Believing in the gem's power, ancient Egyptian soldiers wore amethysts to remain calm and collected— another meaning of "sober"—when they went into battle.

Where does real amethyst come from? You may have seen quartz, the sparkling crystal mineral often found embedded in ordinary rocks. Amethyst is a kind of quartz. What makes this quartz purple, however, is not Bacchus's wine, but the elements manganese and iron. Mixed into quartz, they color its glittering crystals in hues from palest violet to deepest purple.

Like amethyst, most gems are minerals—

crystalline solids found in Earth. There are a few exceptions, however. Pearls grow around sand or other irritants in oyster shells; golden amber is ancient tree resin

If the right minerals are present, diamonds, sapphires, and garnets may crystallize in hot liquid (molten) rock under great pressure.

hardened into a fossil by the passing of the centuries. But when people say "gems," they usually mean red rubies, green emeralds, white diamonds, and the rest of the rainbow of glittery minerals we wear in rings, necklaces, and bracelets.

Gems form under the ground when Earth and heat conspire in special ways. If the right minerals are present, diamonds, sapphires, and garnets may crystallize in hot liquid (molten) rock under great pressure. Certain gems, such as rubies, may form when molten rock seeps into solid rock, changing and recrystallizing minerals found there.

The dazzling hues of gemstones depend mainly on their different compositions. For example, take the gray-white mineral corundum, made of aluminum and oxygen molecules. Substitute chromium for some of the aluminum, and the mineral turns blood red—making a ruby. When small amounts of iron and titanium turn up in corundum, the result is a deep blue tint—a sapphire. A gem's color depends on how different elements absorb and reflect different wavelengths (colors) of light.

Light's antics in gemstones create many unusual effects, such as the rainbow iridescence of opals or the softer iridescence of pearls, called "orient." Gems can even change color depending on what sort of light strikes them. So a pale amethyst might appear pink in bright sunlight and purple under a fluorescent lamp.

What releases a gem's glittery brilliance is the cut. By carving the stone's sides into facets, light is bent (refracted) and reflected inside the stone and back to the viewer. So we see sparkling colors and fiery flashes; the gem seems lit from within.

How is silk made?

Silk's past is shrouded in mystery. But the Chinese say silk was first discovered and woven into cloth 5,000 years ago—by a teenage girl.

The 14-year-old, named Hsi-Ling-chi, was said to have been married to an emperor named Huang-ti. No one knows whether Huang-ti was a real man who was the emperor of China, or a figure in legends. As the story goes, the girl not only discovered silk but also created the device to spin it into yarn—the silk reel.

No matter who discovered it, Chinese royalty soon began wearing closetfuls of silk clothes, keeping the secret of where silk came from to themselves. Eventually, people in places like Rome and Greece heard stories about the royal fabric being worn in China and later saw it firsthand. Most believed the fiber came from special Chinese trees.

Save the Worms

60,000 silkworms gave their lives to make this dress!

I didn't know...I'm so ashamed! sniff!

It's difficult to imagine today, when TV and newspapers reveal many "secrets" in a matter of days. But here's the astonishing truth: the Chinese kept the secret of silk from the rest of the world not for 10 years, but for 3,500.

Who let the cat out of the bag? Two monks from Persia (today called Iran), living in China, got wind of how silk was made. In the year 552, the men hid some tiny silkworm eggs and mulberry tree seeds in their hollow bamboo canes, and made their exit—quietly, because removing silkworm eggs from China was a crime.

The rest is history. Silk-making spread around the world, sometimes violently. In 1147, for example, King Roger II of Sicily invaded Greece and sent his soldiers to kidnap a bunch of silk weavers and bring them home.

To make silk, you need silkworms. Any caterpillar that spins a silky-fibered cocoon is dubbed a silkworm. But the caterpillar most often used is *Bombyx mori*, common in northern China, because this worm makes the thinnest, whitest silk. (Many wild silkworms make a thick brown silk, called

For 3,500 years, how silk was made was a secret only people in China knew.

tussah.) The *Bombyx mori* worm eats the leaves of the mulberry tree, which is why the monks stole those seeds.

Silkworms are raised on trays in warm rooms, and fed mulberry leaves around the clock. After 5 weeks, the worms are about 3 inches long and ready to spin cocoons on beds of straw. (A silkworm builds a cocoon to have a safe little cave where it can develop for several weeks as a "chrysalis"—its final shape before becoming a moth.) As a worm spins out

threads in a figure eight around itself, the filaments are glued into place by sericin, a gelatin-like protein made in the worm's body.

Unfortunately, since their struggle to emerge from the cocoons will break the silk threads, the silkworms are not allowed to grow into moths. The cocoons are heated in ovens, killing the worms inside, then soaked in hot water to soften the sericin.

The silk filaments (threads) are only 1/1000 inch thick. But unraveled from the cocoon, one may stretch 5,000 feet. Filaments from 5 to 10 cocoons are twisted together on a reel, making a thicker yarn, held together by the melted sericin. These yarns are then twisted together to make an even thicker yarn.

The result is silk: the strongest of all natural fibers, light-weight but warm, with a soft sheen and a slippery feel.

How does detergent get clothes clean?

Whatever their name, scent, and advertising budget, detergents work pretty much the same way. Laundry detergents use the attraction between certain molecules to draw dirt out of clothing and whisk it down the drain.

To understand how detergent works, we first must reveal water's strangest secret: it's not very good at getting things wet.

Have you ever poured water onto wax paper, and watched it roll off in little beads? Something similar, though not as dramatic, happens with many fabrics. Water mostly sits on the surface, instead of soaking in. And that's a real problem, if you're trying to draw out dirt and grease.

Water acts this way because of its "surface tension." The electrical attraction of water molecules on the surface for water molecules underneath is so strong that the water can seem to have a kind of "skin." This lets water ball into drops. And it also allows certain insects to run across the surface of a pond as if it were springy solid ground.

Detergent molecules look like tiny tadpoles. The "heads" love water; the "tails" hate it.

The first task of a detergent is to reduce the surface tension of water, so that it will soak into clothes easily instead of beading up. The main chemical in liquid or powder detergent, called a "surfactant," actually weakens the electrical attraction between the water molecules. Balls of water collapse and spread out, soaking into the fabric of the dirty clothes. So detergent actually makes water wetter.

Besides surfactants, there are ingredients called "builders," usually phosphates, which soften the wash water, chemicals to control suds, whiteners and brighteners, and chemicals that stop dirt from glomming back onto clothes as they wash. Not to mention perfumes, to create those "spring shower" and "ocean breeze" scents.

So how does a detergent actually get the dirt out of clothes? Take a pair of pants. Under a microscope, your cotton pants would look like an explosion in a spaghetti factory: tangled fibers, like strands of linguine. And trapped in the fibers would be particles of greasy dirt, the size of meatballs.

Water itself will dissolve away salts and sugars; you know that from stirring sugar or salt into hot water. So we say water is a good solvent for salts and sugars.

But water is not a good solvent for fats and oils. Remember the old saying "Oil and water don't mix"? Fat molecules don't bind well to water molecules, which is why homemade salad dressing made from oil and vinegar separates seconds after it's shaken.

Most food stains are pretty greasy— think hamburger grease, melted cheese, mayonnaise, chocolate bars—so water alone won't get them out. Detergent to the rescue! The surfactants in detergent, usually made from petroleum chemicals, tend to dissolve fats, because part of each surfactant molecule is very similar to a molecule of fat or oil.

Surfactants are made of long molecules. A good image for a surfactant molecule is a tiny tadpole, with a round "head" and narrow "tail." The head of each molecule is attracted to water molecules. (Many surfactant heads have a negative electrical charge, while the water molecules have a slight positive charge on one end.) So the heads are "hydrophilic"—water lovers.

The tails, on the other hand, are hydrophobic—water haters. The tails are similar to grease in their chemical structure—and, once again, oil and water don't mix.

So when dirty clothes are dropped in water containing detergent, the "tails" of the surfactant molecules dissolve in the fabric's greasy dirt. The grease loosens and breaks apart as it is coated by the detergent molecule heads. In effect, the surfactant molecules surround particles of greasy dirt and carry them away from the clothes and into the water. (The agitated shaking of the washing machine helps loosen the dirt.) Like helium balloons, the water-loving heads float out into the water carrying their tiny loads of dirt. Dirt flows away with the detergent as the washer drains its water. More detergent exits in the rinse water. What's left? Clean clothes, their fibers "vacuumed" by the electrical attraction of molecules.

FAST FACT

Protein stains—like blood, milk, and eggs—are immune to ordinary soap. That's why special enzymes that break down protein molecules are added to detergents.

How does a refrigerator work?

Refrigerators are an enigma: Plug them into an electric outlet, turn them on, and mysteriously, heat begins to vanish from the inside. Most things we plug in soon heat up—from toasters to televisions. Refrigerators cool down.

To work their cooling magic, refrigerators use liquids that normally turn to gas at very low temperatures. (Think about water, which becomes a gas—steam—when its temperature is raised to 212 degrees F. Water wouldn't make a good candidate.) Most home refrigerators use chlorofluorocarbons (CFCs) as their cooling chemicals.

Built into a refrigerator is a maze of sealed, connected tubes, through which CFC circulates over and over again. The CFC changes from liquid to gas and back again—but never escapes.

Heat from the food inside warms the air

Refrigerator Abuse...

Remove butter and eggs... *good evening* ... invite Dracula in for a nap!

Insert shelves vertically... ...for a great penguin house!

Leave door open, turn to wall, and... ...voilà! a totally inefficient space heater!

inside the refrigerator, and this heat radiates through the inner refrigerator walls and into wide tubes containg CFC. As the liquid CFC absorbs heat from the food, its temperature rises and it vaporizes into a gas. (Meanwhile, the temperature of the food falls.)

Like a washcloth being wrung out, heat radiates through the refrigerator coils.

At the bottom of the refrigerator, the gas is sucked by an electric motor into a pump called a "compressor." There the gas is squeezed, increasing its heat. The heated gas is then forced into thin tubes on the back of the refrigerator, which you can see if you look. (But don't touch; these coils get very hot from the gas.)

Like a washcloth being wrung out, the heat radiates through the coils, dissipating into the air of the kitchen. So the next time you notice that the air behind a refrigerator feels unusually warm, you'll know that the heat you feel was siphoned out of the food stored inside.

As it loses its heat, the gas, still under high pressure from the walls of the thin tubes,

changes back to a liquid. The liquid CFC is pushed through a tiny tube back into the wider tubes in the walls of the refrigerator. Where, once again, heat from the food turns the liquid to gas. Then it's back to the compressor for another good squeeze. And so it goes, over and over, hour after hour, day after day.

(Because CFCs, when released into the atmosphere, harm Earth's ozone layer, scientists are searching for new gases to use as refrigerants.)

Many different people had a hand in inventing modern refrigerators. In 1834, a man named Jacob Perkins obtained a patent in Great Britain to make things colder by using a liquid in a closed cycle. Another man, L.W. Wright, got a similar patent for a device using compressed air. In 1844, an American doctor named John Gorrie designed a compressed-air refrigerator that was soon used in a Florida hospital. In 1851, James Harrison of Australia developed an ether-cooled fridge and installed it in a brewery. The first home refrigerator was developed by German engineer Karl von Linde around 1875, using ammonia as the coolant. More than 100 years later, refrigerators come in all shapes and sizes, from tiny dorm-room cubes to big side-by-sides with automatic ice makers to industrial refrigerators the size of houses.

How does a microwave oven cook food?

They Strap you in, turn it on and you give yourself a sauna!

HOT POTATOES!

Regular ovens seem simple to understand. You can see the blue flames in a gas oven or the glowing red coils of an electric range. The whole oven gets hot to the touch, inside and out, as the heat penetrates both the food and the oven walls.

But microwave ovens are mysterious. There is no fiery glow, and the oven stays cool, even as the food heats to boiling. It's as if the microwaves were smart—as if they only aim for food.

Actually, the microwaves aren't that different from the infrared rays that cook food in a regular oven. Both are forms of electromagnetic radiation. (Visible light is a kind of electromagnetic radiation, too.)

All electromagnetic radiation is made of streams of particles called "photons." The difference is in their energy. X rays, for example, are made up of photons of fairly high energy and short wavelengths. Visible light is a stream of photons of medium energy and medium wavelengths, just right for our eyes to see. Infrared rays are just past the red of visible light, too low-energy for our eyes to see.

Microwaves are lower-energy still, part of the stream of radiation we call "radio waves." The wavelength of microwaves is much too long for our eyes, so microwaves are invisible to us.

In an ordinary oven, the burning of natural gas or the heating of a metal coil makes electrons in the gas or metal atoms give off photons of infrared radiation. We can't see it, but we can feel it—our skin, as well as the food, will heat up if we get too near.

Microwaves are not as energetic as infrared rays. Yet they can cook most foods much faster. Scientists think this happens because water in the food absorbs microwave energy very quickly.

Inside a microwave oven is a device called a magnetron. The magnetron is a bit like a TV picture tube. It uses the household electrical current to spit out electrons. Pulled by magnets in the magnetron, the electrons travel in a circle. As they do, they

Microwave ovens are mysterious. There is no fiery glow, and the oven stays cool, even as the food heats to boiling. It's as if the microwaves were smart—as if they only aim for food.

emit photons of microwave radiation—microwaves.

The microwaves are steered into the oven chamber by a metal "waveguide." At the end of the waveguide is a rotating "stirrer," which spreads the microwaves evenly throughout the oven.

The oven is made of metal. Metal reflects microwaves like a mirror reflects visible light. So the microwaves stay inside, and the oven itself stays cool.

Glass, on the other hand, lets microwaves pass straight through. That's why there's a metal grill behind the glass door. The microwaves are too big to squeeze through the holes. But visible light, which has a smaller wavelength, can easily pass through. The result? We can see what's cooking.

Microwaves penetrate only about an inch into food. They work mainly by rapidly heating water trapped inside food. Scientists say that the electric field of a microwave causes water molecules to spin. The molecules begin jiggling more and more rapidly.

Temperature is just a measure of the movement of molecules. So as the molecules move more, the temperature of the water rises. The water soon gets boiling hot, and the heat spreads in a chain reaction of jiggling molecules throughout the food, cooking it. DING!

How does a radio work?

Radio seems mysterious. We can't hear the voices or music coming from a radio station by just standing outdoors and listening for it. It's not sound waves that are traveling from the station's big antennas to us. Instead, it's electromagnetic radiation—light—carrying the imprint of sound. But instead of ordinary, visible light, the antenna emits invisible light—radio waves.

The visible light we see streaming from lightbulbs or the Sun is medium-energy light. But there is also high-energy light, such as ultraviolet and X-ray light, and lower-energy light, such as infrared light and radio waves. All are forms of electromagnetic radiation—photons, zipping along at 186,000 miles (300,000 km) a second.

The tiny waves of visible light measure about 0.6 micrometers from crest to crest, or about 1/200,000 inch. Radio waves, by comparison, are giants measuring from a few centimeters or inches to 300 feet (91 m) or more across.

Our eyes are equipped to welcome in and process medium-energy light—that's why we call it "visible light." But radio waves are just the wrong size and frequency for our eyes to admit. So we can't see the radio "light" around us.

(In fact, at this very moment, radio waves are invisibly penetrating the walls of your building and zinging through your room—and through you. Too bad you can't see all the excitement.)

Here's how we use radio waves to send music and conversations across the sky. The station transmitter has a long antenna to send off radio waves to listeners many miles away. Each listener's radio is equipped with its own, smaller antenna—a rod, or a piece of wire.

Radio waves pulse out in all directions from the station and can be picked up by the antenna of any radio in their path. Radio stations broadcast their programs in either AM or FM. AM stands for amplitude modulation; FM means frequency modulation. AM waves are longer than FM waves. An AM wave may measure more than 300 feet from the peak of one wave to the peak of the next.

When you are driving over a large bridge, you may hear an AM station on your car radio fading in and out. That's because those big AM waves are hitting the bridge. The bridge is acting like a giant metal antenna, and the waves don't all make it to the little antenna stuck on the hood of your car.

By contrast, FM waves may measure only one or several feet long from one wave peak to the next. They can pass through gaps in a bridge, so FM stations may come in more clearly.

FAST FACT

While radio stations use radio waves as carriers for sound, broadcast television uses radio waves to carry both sound and pictures. Airplanes and submarines use radio waves like car headlights, beaming them out to illuminate hidden objects. (We call this radar.) The medical procedure called MRI uses radio waves to map the inside of the body.

Whether FM or AM, radio works the same way. Microphones pick up the disk jockey's voice and convert the sound waves into an electrical signal. This electrical signal vibrates in the same pattern as the original sound waves, so it is called an "audio (sound) signal." An amplifier at the station strengthens the audio signal.

At this very moment, radio waves are invisibly penetrating the walls of your room and zinging through you.

Meanwhile, an electrical circuit at the station—an oscillator—is continuously producing its own electrical signal, called a "carrier wave." The audio wave, vibrating in the pattern of the voice or music, "modulates" the carrier wave, changing its pattern, too. The total electrical signal—audio plus carrier—is further amplified and then sent on to the station's antenna.

The electrical signal excites the metal atoms in the antenna. Their electrons begin vibrating to the pattern of the electrical signal. The electrons begin to give off invisible light—radio waves—that spreads out from the antenna into the sky. Since the electrons in the antenna are vibrating in the special pattern created by the voice, the outgoing radio waves are imprinted with that pattern, too.

When the radio waves strike the antenna on your radio, they are converted back into an electrical signal—the audio plus carrier. Your radio receiver automatically separates the audio signal from the carrier wave. What was assembled at the station is disassembled in your radio. It then feeds the audio signal to a speaker.

The speaker acts like a microphone, but in reverse: It turns the electrical audio signal back into sound waves. And, like magic, you hear the disk jockey's voice as he introduces the next song.

Natural Radio Stations in the Sky

Think of all the visible light we take for granted every day. Visible light shoots out of the Sun, and from all the other stars. It reflects in silver off the rocky surface of the Moon. It beams out of streetlights and neon signs. It radiates from lightning, and from glowing toadstools. It comes from molten lava, the red-hot burners on your electric stove, and the blue-hot flames on your gas stove. It flashes from meteors as they burn up in the upper atmosphere; it glows from ghostly fish in the ocean depths. Visible light comes from here, there, and everywhere—not just from our man-made lamps.

Radio waves come from everywhere, too. The universe is aglow in radio light, but we are all blind to its presence.

Some of the natural objects that give off radio waves: our Sun, other stars, the planet Jupiter, and the gas and dust between the stars, to name a few. How can we see some of these objects glowing in invisible radio light? We can build giant "radio eyes" to do the looking for us. Those giant eyes are called "radio telescopes."

Go to Arecibo, Puerto Rico, and you'll find the largest single radio telescope in the world. The telescope's main part is an aluminum dish 1,000 feet across. Radio telescopes image the universe in radio light, and computers translate their findings into pictures we can look at. So some parts of space that appear dark and empty reveal themselves to be lit up like Las Vegas in radio waves.

How does a compact disc play music?

Remember vinyl records, which scratched, warped, and broke? A compact disc is an echo of a record, in a shinier, tinier, sturdier package. Records used a needle dragging through ruts to reproduce their hidden sounds. Compact discs use a weightless beam of focused light—a laser—to "read" tiny bumps on the disc.

How does it work? Pick up a CD and turn it upside down, to the plain side. Under the clear plastic surface you'll see a layer of shiny aluminum—like aluminum foil, but much, much thinner. The aluminum is so thin that if you hold the CD up to the light, you can dimly see through it.

The aluminum has tiny raised ridges that curve around the disc in a spiral pattern. If you could see them up close, the ridges would look like the broken lines down the center of a highway.

The landscape of a compact disc is impossibly tiny. Scientist Louis Bloomfield, in his book *How Things Work: The Physics of Everyday Life*, reveals just how tiny. Each ridge, Bloomfield says, is 110 nanometers high, 500 nanometers wide, and 833 to 3,560 nanometers long. (A nanometer is a billionth of a meter.) Near the center of the disc, for example, the circular rows of ridges are so tiny and close together that 40 rows could fit side by side on the edge of a piece of paper.

When a CD plays, a laser beam "senses" the pattern of ridges and valleys as they whirl by, rather like a blind person feels the raised dots and dashes of Braille with her fingertips. The laser works its way from the center of the spinning disc to the edge, just the opposite from the needle on a record.

When the laser light hits a ridge, its reflection weakens. So as the disc turns, the amount of light reflected back changes constantly. By noting these changes, the CD player measures the ridges and valleys. It decodes the measurements into numbers and, ultimately, sound.

Using numbers to represent sound is a key difference between CDs and records. Such a method is called "digital recording." The numbers actually represent the changing air pressure in the recording studio, as sound waves from the musical instruments and voices pass into the microphones.

In the studio, microphones convert sound waves, or changing air pressure, into a fluctuating electric current. An analog-to-digital converter then measures the microphone's current 44,100 times each second and converts the result into a series of numbers. Each number has a total of 16 ones and zeroes, arranged in different orders. The numbers, in turn, are represented by the different-sized ridges on a disc, which the laser "reads."

When a CD plays, a laser beam "senses" the pattern of ridges and valleys as they whirl by.

When you listen to a CD, the player uses a digital-to-analog converter to take the ever-changing numbers and create an ever-changing electric current. The current flows to the stereo amplifier and speakers. The speakers convert the current back into sound waves—and you hear music, just as it sounded when it was made.

How does a mercury thermometer work?

Picture a slim glass thermometer, the kind sometimes used to take your temperature. At one end is a little bulb full of silvery mercury. On the side is a temperature scale. As the mercury warms (say, from the heat in your feverish mouth), it slowly rises up the column. The amount it rises corresponds to a particular temperature in your mouth.

Galileo Galilei, the Italian mathematician and astronomer, usually gets credit for inventing the thermometer around 1592. But guess who invented the mercury thermometer in 1714? A physicist, born in Poland, named Daniel Gabriel Fahrenheit. (Of course, what Fahrenheit is most remembered for is the temperature scale he devised, which bears his name. On the Fahrenheit scale, water freezes at 32° and boils away at 212°. A Swedish scientist named Anders Celsius was also busy during the 1700s, inventing a rival temperature scale that today is used in most of the world.)

If you've ever dropped and broken a glass thermometer, you know that the mercury escapes in shiny silver drops, which roll around the floor like something living. So it's very fitting that mercury's common name is "quicksilver."

This flowing quality is very important for thermometer makers. In fact, mercury is the only metal element that is a liquid at ordinary room temperatures, just like

What I wouldn't give for a good 103° fever...

...Feel that mercury pumping through me...

water. (Most metals, such as iron, copper, and aluminum, are frozen solid at room temperature. If they weren't, we couldn't make iron frying pans, copper wire, or aluminum cans.) Mercury must be cooled to about minus 39° C. (minus 38° F.) before it freezes into a soft solid rather like lead.

Water clings annoyingly to glass, as anyone knows who's tried to shake the last drops out of the bottom of a drinking glass. Glass and water are attracted to each other. Mercury, on the other hand, isn't fond of glass, so it doesn't wet glass or cling to it. In a glass thermometer, mercury rises and falls smoothly rather than sticking to thermometer walls.

All substances expand when they are heated. That's because their molecules get a burst of energy, and jiggle outward in all directions. But liquid mercury is a particularly good choice for thermometers because it expands so rapidly and evenly when it is heated.

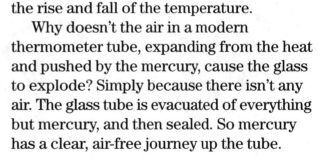

The temperature inching up and up and up...

Don't ya love flu season!

Using mercury, Fahrenheit experimented until he had devised an accurate thermometer scale: one that corresponded to how mercury expanded and shrank according to the rise and fall of the temperature.

Why doesn't the air in a modern thermometer tube, expanding from the heat and pushed by the mercury, cause the glass to explode? Simply because there isn't any air. The glass tube is evacuated of everything but mercury, and then sealed. So mercury has a clear, air-free journey up the tube.

How does hot air lift a balloon?

We've all seen them, or seen pictures: huge, colorful balloons, floating up and away into the blue sky until they become a flock of distant colorful shapes. They seem clean and pure—what could be purer than heated fresh air, right?

But in the past, hot-air balloons were a lot weirder. In June of 1783, a couple of French brothers, Joseph and Jacques Montgolfier, did some of the first experiments with hot-air balloons. They noticed that smoke rises. So they gathered a bunch of damp straw and wool, and set it on fire. Then they used the sooty, acrid, choking smoke to launch a balloon, 35 feet across, made out of paper and cloth.

Several months later, in September, the balloon brothers got even more inventive.

They went to Versailles to demonstrate their invention to the king and queen of France. For some reason, the brothers decided to throw some old shoes and rotting meat onto the pile of burning straw and wool. Great idea. As the king and queen walked over to look, the terrible smell coming from the balloon sent them running royally in the other direction.

A gallon of hot air contains fewer molecules than a gallon of densely packed cool air.

But the balloon's passengers had no such choice in the matter. The Montgolfiers tethered the stinky balloon to a duck, a rooster, and a sheep, and sent the three aloft. Fortunately, they landed with feathers and wool intact.

In November, the brothers' balloon was taken up by human beings, two men who balanced at opposite ends of a wicker basket while they frantically stuffed straw into a burning oven suspended above their heads. Strangely, the brothers themselves chose not to ride.

Today's balloons are a lot safer—and a lot less smelly. Propane burners in the basket heat the gases in the balloon above. Modern balloons usually use hot air, or, for long, record-breaking flights, a combination of helium and hot air. Helium is the second-lightest element in the universe. (Look what happens to a helium-filled party balloon when you let go of the string.)

Why not use hydrogen, the very lightest element, in a balloon? It's been done, but hydrogen is extremely flammable and explosive. (Think of the *Hindenburg*, the German dirigible filled with hydrogen that burst into flames and burned to a cinder in New Jersey in 1937. Or the U.S. space shuttle *Challenger*, whose hydrogen fuel exploded.)

A balloon floats because it and the gases filling it together weigh less than the air surrounding it. How can a plastic or silk balloon, full of air, weigh less than the air around it? Simple: Gas expands when it is heated. So a gallon of hot air contains fewer molecules than a gallon of densely packed cool air. Thus, a balloon full of hot air weighs less than the cooler air it is taking the place of—and rises.

The ancient Greek scientist Archimedes figured out the scientific law for this: Any body immersed in liquid or floating in air tends to be pushed upward, by a force that is as strong as the weight of the fluid or air whose space it is occupying. If this force is greater than the weight of the body, then the body will rise.

See this principle at work for yourself by trying to push an inflated balloon into a bucket of water. Since the balloon, including the air inside, weighs less than a balloon-sized amount of water, the balloon floats.

FAST FACT

Balloons carry scientific instruments high into the air (up to 130,000 feet, or nearly 4 times as high as a passenger jet flies). Then the balloon bursts in the low pressure; and the instruments begin falling, taking readings as they go.

How do jet airplanes fly?

Have you ever put your hand out the window of a moving car and let the air, streaming by, lift it up? If so, you already know something about how a wing makes a plane fly. As your hand rises and dips in the onrushing wind, you feel the force of the air, streaming over the top and bottom of your hand.

But a hand's floppy "flight" shows that it doesn't make a very good wing. Hands are oddly shaped and bumpy, and air can't flow smoothly over them. So no amount of flapping will turn us into birds.

However, a thin, curved plate, designed much like a bird's wing, can lift even a heavy plane (with us inside) high into the air. Passenger-jet wings are all similarly shaped: The front of the wing, facing into the wind, is rounded. Behind the hill, the wing tapers to an edge. We call such structures "streamlined."

As air strikes the gently rounded part, it breaks smoothly over, flowing down the wing's hill and sliding off. Meanwhile, air is also flowing steadily across the bottom of the wing.

Under the wing, the streaming air pushes upward, lifting the wing. But surprisingly, most of the lift comes from the air flowing across the more steeply curved top.

How come? Because it travels faster on the roller-coaster-hill top of the wing, the speeded-up air creates less pressure on the top of the wing than on the bottom. (This principle was discovered in the 1700s by a Swiss mathematician named Daniel Bernoulli, long before there were airplanes in the sky.) The

Wings that Won't Work

They came with a big drink and a toy!

Curly fries...

higher pressure underneath pushes the wing up to the area of lower pressure above. That's the "lift" that lets a plane fly.

How much lift a plane really gets depends on the shape of the wings, the angle at which the wings meet the flow of air, and the plane's speed. The weight of the plane is also important, since gravity is always tugging the plane downward. Airplane designers try to make planes as lightweight as possible. And pilots must make sure that the combined weight of passengers, fuel, and freight isn't too much.

Wings that Won't Work

Drag 'em down the runway. Only your appetite takes off.

Limp Noodles...

Obviously, the streamlined shape of its wings is critical to a plane's being able to fly. But sometimes, the weather can cause a disastrous change in wing shape. How? On the ground during winter, or high up in the clouds, where it is often cold and wet, snow and ice can build up on wings. Even a thin layer of ice or sprinkling of snow changes the shape of the wings, making them rough.

Instead of passing smoothly over the wings, like water down a slide, the air will break up into random, whirling currents, useless for lifting. On a runway, a plane with ice-coated wings may be unable to take off, or may lose lift on takeoff. If it's already in the air, a plane may drop.

Surprisingly, most of an airplane's lift comes from air flowing across the tops of its wings, not the undersides.

That's why wings are de-iced at the airport in winter. And once in flight, hot air directed from the plane's engines or from special heaters flows through the wings, keeping them frost free and streamlined.

A jet takes off by using its powerful engines to build up to high speeds on a runway. Air flows into the engines, which have open fronts. Some of this air is compressed (squashed together), and then mixed with high-powered jet fuel. The fuel burns, reaching temperatures of 1,400° to 1,900° F., making very hot gases. Eventually, the hot gases shoot out of the rear of the engine, thrusting the plane forward.

As the plane picks up speed, with air rushing furiously over and under the wings, it lifts off. The plane is able to fly because the lifting and pulling force of the air on its wings is greater than or equal to its weight. Since weight is just the force of gravity pulling the plane to earth, flight happens when the two forces balance.

Wings that Won't Work

Cruises at 350 mph, on the ground!

Big Bumps...

It seems incredible that air, which seems weightless and barely there, can lift a 700,000-pound jumbo jet. But air is nothing to sneeze at. As you sit reading this, nearly 15 pounds of air are pressing on each square inch of you. Think of air as an invisible ocean. Just as water can hold up a swimming child, so air cushions a soaring bird, or a plane.

How is paper made?

Paper always surrounds us, but it seems most obvious at the start of a new school year. Trips to the store to buy notebook paper; endless forms to fill out; tests to take; notes to pass in class, folded neatly to foil prying eyes.

Most paper is made from wood. But modern paper is also made from cloth rags, straw, and bamboo. With recycling, new paper is made from old—even from old money.

Ever since writing was invented, people have looked for surfaces to write on. They scratched symbols on stone, and on bones. Words were traced in clay. Later, writing was etched onto hammered-out sheets of copper and brass.

Some 2,300 years ago, people in Egypt wrote on pressed strips of the papyrus, a plant that grows in swamps. (*Papyrus* is where we got the word *paper*.) Others put their words on animal skins, stretched thin and dried to make a material called "parchment."

In China, where paintbrushes and ink were used more than 2,200 years ago, people wrote on cloth. Then, around 1,900 years ago, the first real paper was made there, by using cloth fibers to make thin sheets. Until the mid-1800s, most paper around the world was made from cloth. How? Rags were beaten until they fell apart. Then the cloth fibers were put in a vat of water. A screen was dipped in, collecting the fibers in a thin layer and letting the water drain away. The fibers dried into a mat, which was cut into sheets of paper.

But people also tried making paper from wood, and it worked very well. After all, as some observed, wasp nests are simply papery structures made from wood fibers. If wasps could make paper from trees, maybe we could, too.

Today, there are several processes to turn trees into paper, but all follow a similar plan. First, a tree must be sawed down and cut into logs. The logs are moved into a huge, turning drum, which shaves off their bark. Then the bare logs move on to a chipper, which—no surprise—whittles them into small chips.

Then mechanical grinders or strong chemicals—or both—break the wood chips down into their individual fibers. The wet fibers are called "pulp," a yellowish or brown mush. (Pulp may remain that color if it is to be used to make something like brown paper bags. Or it may be bleached to make newspaper or writing paper. If you look closely at a paper bag, or at this page—a magnifying glass helps—you can see the individual wood fibers.)

Until the mid-1800s, most paper around the world was made not from trees, but from cloth rags.

The pulp fibers are washed to get rid of chemicals, then beaten and rubbed. Finally, they may be treated with a material such as rosin, which makes them water-resistant. That way, ink won't soak through when pulp becomes writing paper or newspaper. If the paper is to be colored, dye is added.

Then the fiber, mixed into lots of water, flows across a moving wire screen. The fibers collect into a wet web on the screen, while the water drains through. Now the pulp is officially—TA-DA!—paper. Presses flatten it, and then it is pulled over huge drums and dried. Once dry, the paper—often 20 feet wide—is rolled out and cut to size.

How does glue work?

Have you ever tried to wash dried egg off a dish, only to find it cemented to the plate? Have you ever picked up a piece of paper, only to find it glued to another piece by dried honey? Or held a pine cone, and found your fingers covered with a sticky substance that attracts lint—and is almost impossible to wash off?

Congratulations—you've met Nature's Adhesives, a line of glues created with no help whatsoever from meddling humans.

Adhesives are substances that can bind one thing to another. Like a stamp to an envelope. Or a Band-Aid to your knee. People have used adhesives for thousands of years; ancient Egyptian carvings show people gluing wood. In World War 2, the dried-egg adhesive, albumin, was used to make a strong glue that literally held together airplanes.

We use the word *glue* to refer to adhesives of all types. But strictly speaking, real glue is made by—are you ready?—cooking leftover animal parts like bones, skin, and blood into gelatin. Glue makes a strong bond, but dissolves easily in hot water.

Mucilage, the golden liquid that comes in cute containers with rubber tops, is a mixture of water and plant gums—not as strong as glue, but good for sticking stars to paper in class projects.

And, of course, there's good old paste, a mixture of flour or cornstarch and water. (Now you know why a sauce with too much cornstarch tastes so gluey.)

Different adhesives work in different ways. An adhesive can seep into the cracks and crevices of two surfaces, sticking them together like burrs stick to socks ("mechanical bonding"). An adhesive's

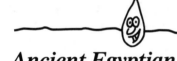

Ancient Egyptian carvings from thousands of years ago show people gluing wood.

molecules can be attracted to the molecules of the two surfaces ("intermolecular bonding"). Or an adhesive can fuse chemically with the molecules on the surfaces ("chemical bonding").

Today's artificial glues are much stronger and work much faster than natural glues.

Superglues, made from petroleum chemicals, harden in seconds, making a bond so strong that it's hard to undo when a mistake is made. When superglue touches a trace of water, its molecules instantly link up into long chains. This is called "polymerization," making superglue a "polymer."

Every surface has some water from the air, so super-glues can get supersticky almost anywhere. They especially like moist skin. That's why people show up at emergency rooms with fingers superglued together—or attached to that broken plate they were trying to repair. (Meanwhile, in the same hospital a surgeon may be using a superglue spray to close a wound without sewing.)

Today's adhesives can be engineered with just the right amount of sticking power for the job. Post-It notes use polymers to create a piece of paper that sticks lightly in place—and can be moved to another spot later. So your mother can leave a note— "PLEASE CLEAN YOUR ROOM!"—first on the refrigerator, later move it to the door of your room, and finally press it to your pillow if all else fails.

How does a magnifying glass work?

A magnifying glass seems almost magical. Peer through a simple chunk of glass and the pores on your arm loom like tiny craters. Now search for that splinter that you can feel, but can't see. There it is, jutting out of your skin like a stick of wood.

Magnifiers help us squeeze more information into tinier spaces. For example, the *Compact Oxford English Dictionary* crams 20 books' worth of words into one fat volume. Open the book, and the type is so teensy it appears written for dollhouse dictionary-browsers. So each book comes equipped with its own handy magnifying glass.

Magnifying glasses come in all sizes, from tiny plastic toys to heavy Sherlock Holmes–style glass magnifiers with long handles. Some magnifying glasses are simply chunky rounded domes, flat on the underside.

This last type of magnifying glass resembles a paperweight. Looking through a domed paperweight, you may have noticed that words on the papers underneath are magnified. You may also observe that objects inside the paperweight, such as dried flowers, are likewise enlarged.

What do paperweights and store-bought magnifying glasses have in common? Look closely, and you'll notice they're both curved. This curve, and the varying thickness of the glass, are the keys to magnification.

A magnifying glass is a kind of lens—a converging lens. When things converge, they come together, like two side-by-side lanes on a highway converging into one. A converging lens forces light rays, traveling side by side, to squeeze together.

When light enters an object from the air, it bends a little as it encounters the molecules of the new material. When light travels through a converging (convex) lens's bulging middle, it bends hardly at all. But the light that enters through the thin top and bottom of the lens, which curve steeply

away from the center, bends a lot, toward the center.

The result? Light rays shooting through the top of the lens bend down. Those zipping through the center go straight ahead. And light rays traveling through the bottom bend up. The result is a cone of light. This cone converges a little distance away from the lens. (The place where light converges after traveling through a lens is called the "focus.")

Many common objects made of curved glass act like weak magnifiers. A goldfish in a round fishbowl will look bigger than the same goldfish in a rectangular aquarium.

This makes an object under the magnifier look bigger, since you, the viewer, are at the wide end of the cone. The steeper the curve of the lens, the bigger the image you'll see. The strongest magnifiers make an object look 25 times larger than it really is.

Many common objects made of curved glass act like weak magnifiers. Check it out with a glass of water and a straw. See how the straw appears swollen when you look through the curving side of the glass? And a goldfish in a round fishbowl will look bigger than the same goldfish in a rectangular aquarium.

With so many natural magnifiers surrounding us, it's no wonder that people discovered and have been using magnifying glasses for many thousands of years. (Five-thousand-year-old magnifiers made of rock crystal have been dug up in Egypt.) Besides using magnifiers to glimpse the very small, people have also long used chunks of curved glass to get fires going. Since a magnifying glass makes rays of sunlight converge to a point, it creates a hot spot on a piece of dry wood or brush that can easily start smoldering.

How does camera film record pictures?

You've undoubtedly drawn a picture with a pencil or a pen. Well, a camera draws a picture with light. That's what the word *photograph* means: "a light drawing." Light etches an image on a piece of film in the back of the camera, like pen on paper.

No matter what their size or shape, nearly all cameras use the same basic parts:

a lens, to focus incoming light; behind the lens, a shutter that opens and closes; and behind the shutter, the film.

Film is usually a plastic strip coated with a thin layer of silver salts, chemicals sensitive to light. The film is kept in the dark inside the camera. When you take a picture, the button you push trips the shutter open. A burst of light passes

Say cheese! Pick the Musts and Must-nots to get the picture!

A. Remove the lens cap.

B. Drop camera in bathtub!

C. Shine bright lights 'n your eyes.

D. Press shutter button.

E. open film cannister, add honey... then have Ralphie lick the film.

through the lens and strikes the film. Photographic film is so sensitive that it usually needs only a fraction of a second to record an image—from 1/1000 second in blindingly bright light to about 1/30 second in a room indoors.

The brief blaze of light triggers chemical changes in the silver particles on the film. Say you are taking a picture of your dog. Your dog, the grass he's sitting on, and the trees behind him, all reflect different intensities of light. So different silver particles get differing amounts of light, "painting" a picture of your dog on film.

When the shutter snaps shut, the film moves. A new, unexposed section stands ready in the dark behind the lens. Time to take the next picture. After all the film has been exposed and rolled onto a spool, a whole line of images waits to be developed. The camera then rewinds the film into its canister.

But be careful: If you open the back of the camera before rewinding is finished, a burst of unfocused light will flood onto the film, "overexposing" it and ruining your pictures.

When you take your film to be developed, it is unrolled in a darkroom and dunked in a series of chemicals. The chemicals react with the silver particles that were exposed to light. Particles that got the most light will remain in dense layers; particles that got less light will wash away more easily.

Gradually, a pattern appears, forming a picture. The objects that were bright in real life look dark on the film (where the particles are built up); the darker objects look almost clear (where the particles washed off).

"To photograph" means "to draw with light."

The next step is to take this "negative" and make prints. The film is put in an enlarger, a machine with a bright light and a lens. Light shines down through the film; the lens focuses the light on a sheet of photographic paper (coated with its own layer of light-sensitive chemicals). Lots of light flows through the negative's lighter areas, so they will be darker in the print. Less light flows through the negative's darker areas, making them light in the print. When the paper is developed in chemical baths, there he is: your dog, sitting in the sun.

How do electric lightbulbs emit light?

Campfires Go Incandescent and Fluorescent...

The original... | Hey, what's that white thing?

The warm... | It's toasting up nicely...

The cold... | Sixty hours to toast a marshmallow?

For thousands of years, people used fire to illuminate the darkness: first campfires and torches, then candles, oil lamps, and gas lights. As night fell, something was always burning.

Electric lightbulbs changed all that. In 1879, Thomas Edison, an American inventor, built a lamp that used thin filaments of carbon sealed inside a glass bulb. (Edison had removed the air from inside the bulb, using a vacuum pump.)

The bulb was hooked up to an electric current, which Edison turned on—and gradually turned up—until the carbon filaments heated up and began glowing. Supplied with a steady current, the filaments glowed for 40 hours, until they disintegrated.

The kind of lightbulb Edison designed is called "incandescent." When an object gets so hot that it begins glowing, that's incandescence. The idea behind incandescent lightbulbs is simple: Use electric current to heat a wire until it glows. Encase the glowing wire in a glass bulb; scatter the bulbs in lamps around a room. Voilà: Portable artificial light, placed right where you need it.

Up to 95 percent of the energy supplied to an incandescent bulb ends up wasted as heat; only 5 percent is emitted as light.

Modern incandescent bulbs have metal filaments made out of tungsten, which lasts longer than carbon and can be heated to a higher temperature. (A typical 60-watt lightbulb today glows for about 1,000 hours.) But tungsten can't get as hot as the surface of the Sun (about 10,000° F); it melts at 6,170° F. So glowing tungsten gives off light that is redder than natural sunlight, more orange-white than white.

(To understand this, think of an iron poker placed in a flame. As it heats, it first glows dull red, then orange, then yellow, and finally white—giving us the adjective "white-hot" for something that is very hot.)

Today's incandescent bulbs, including superbright halogens, are filled with inert gas (gas that isn't chemically active), usually a mix of nitrogen and argon. The gas keeps the very hot filament from disintegrating too quickly, by pushing some of the escaping tungsten atoms back onto the filament.

But there's more to artificial lighting than hot wires. People began using blue-white fluorescent lamps in the 1930s. Why? Up to 95 percent of the energy supplied to an incandescent bulb ends up as heat radiated from the lightbulb; only 5 percent is emitted as light. So most of the lamp's energy is wasted.

But most of a fluorescent's energy goes into producing light rather than heat; the bulbs are actually cool to the touch. So a 40-watt fluorescent emits far more light than a 40-watt incandescent. Lower electrical bills make fluorescents a favorite for big buildings like hospitals, schools, and offices.

Fluorescent tubes stay cool because they use excited gases rather than hot wires to emit light. Fluorescents are part of a group of lamps called "discharge tubes," which use glass tubes filled with gas like argon, neon, and/or krypton. Mixed with the gases are a few drops of liquid mercury, which evaporate into mercury vapor. As electric current passes through the tube, the mercury atoms get "excited." Settling back into normal energy states, the atoms emit photons of light.

But like a dog whistle that can't be heard by human ears, most of the light the mercury produces (ultraviolet) can't be seen by human eyes; its wavelength is too short. Plus, glass blocks much of the ultraviolet light that strikes it. So the inside of the fluorescent tube is coated with phosphor powder. When the photons of light hit the powder, it luminesces, giving off lower-energy photons of visible light. (To luminesce means to produce light at low temperatures, unlike a hot, incandescent light source.)

This process of using invisible radiation to produce visible light is called "fluorescence." And now you know where fluorescent lights got their name.

How does a telephone work?

Pesky telemarketers calling just as you sit down to dinner? Blame Alex Bell. Alexander Graham Bell patented a good working telephone in 1876, beating many other inventors to the finish line. The basic premise has never changed: the idea that sounds can be converted into electrical signals, shot over wires, and changed back into sound in a telephone across town (or across the ocean). "Telephone" is a good name for such a device; it comes from two Greek words meaning "far sound."

How does a phone work? The telephone is plugged into a special wall outlet that needs electricity to run. The electric current is carried by wires that run from the phone

company office, over telephone poles or under the ground, all the way to your house.

When you pick up the phone from its switch hook to call your grandmother, electric current suddenly streams into the phone. Sensing this, a special switching machine back at the telephone office sends you a dial tone, letting you know that the office is ready to process your call.

Let's say your grandmother's number is 555-2468. You dial the first number, 5. If you are using an old rotary phone, when you turn the dial with your finger and then release it, you will hear five clicks interrupting the flow of current. Down at the office, the switching machine counts the clicks. If you are using a Touch-Tone phone, the dialer sends a unique tone to the central office for each number that has been dialed, so that the switching equipment can tell a 5 from a 2.

FAST FACT

Alexander Graham Bell patented the telephone in 1876. By August of 1877, there were already 700 telephones in use in the United States.

When it gets the whole number, the switching machine checks your grandmother's phone to see if she is already talking to someone. If so, your phone is

The basic premise of the telephone is that sounds can be converted into electrical signals, shot over wires, and changed back into sound in a telephone miles away.

sent an annoying busy signal. If not, the switching machine makes her phone ring. When your grandmother picks up her phone, current flows into it. This signals the switching machine to stop the ringing. And the two of you are connected.

In the bottom of each phone's handset is a cup crammed full of tiny pieces of carbon. When your grandmother picks up her phone, electric current flows into the carbon. Held against the carbon is a thin metal disk. When she speaks, the sound waves make the disk vibrate. The vibrating disk compresses the pieces of carbon, thereby changing the current through the carbon. Your grandmother's voice has a distinctive pattern, which makes a unique pattern in the electric current. Presto: Sound waves changed into electrical waves.

The electrical current, carrying the pattern, zips through the wires to the phone company office. There, the current is routed down other wires to your house— all in seconds—and carried into a coiling electromagnet in your phone's handset. The changing current causes the electromagnet to emanate a fluctuating magnetic field. And the changing magnetic field continuously tugs and releases a metal disk, which is held to a small permanent magnet inside the earpiece.

The moving metal disk makes sound waves in the pattern of your grandmother's voice, which travel into your nearby ear. And you hear your grandmother's "Hello."

How were mummies made?

The layers of wrappings on a mummy give it its air of mystery. What's under there, anyway? Looking at a mummy, you wonder if it could be looking back at you. And there's always the nagging fear that a mummy might suddenly sit up and walk stiffly across the room.

Mummies were a way for human beings to outwit nature, whose bacteria tend, over time, to turn dead bodies to dust. By mummifying a body, people could keep it almost intact—for thousands of years.

In the past, a number of cultures mummified some of their dead members, especially wealthy people and royalty. But it was in ancient Egypt that mummification reached its height as an art and science. It's Egyptian mummies that are wound in those layers of browning bandages.

The Egyptians mummified bodies from about 3000 B.C. until about 5 A.D. (Some 70 million mummies were created!) The

Egyptians thought that the spirit of a dead person needed its body to return to. Over the years, embalmers (who were also priests) devised a process to expertly preserve bodies after death. (Warning: Reading about this process isn't for the squeamish!)

Leaving soft, moist organs in the body would cause it to decay. So the lungs, stomach, liver and intestines were removed through a slit cut on the left side of the abdomen. The brain was pulled out bit by bit through the nose with a long, slender hook, and thrown away. The Egyptians believed that the center of thinking was in the heart, so they usually left the heart in the body.

The lungs, stomach, liver, and intestines were dried in a salt compound called natron. Then the dried body parts were put in a four-compartment box, or in four jars.

The nearly empty body was rinsed in wine, a natural bacteria-killer, then rubbed with spices and covered with natron. Salt packets were put inside the body, too. For 40 days the body would lie drying on the embalming table, until it was a blackened, shriveled shell.

The next stage was cosmetic, making the body beautiful again to attract its wayward soul. The skin was rubbed with oils, and the body stuffed with sawdust, linen, or resin to plump its contours. False eyes were attached, and makeup, such as rouge, was applied. Finally, warm resin was poured over the mummy. The body was then carefully wrapped in hundreds of yards of linen strips, cemented with resin. The wrapping served to further protect the mummy from decay.

Amulets, or charms, were tucked into the bandages to guard the mummy's soul. Then the mummy was slipped into a cloth shroud. The body was ready for its tomb, and, the Egyptians believed, a happy afterlife.

FAST FACT

Little bottles of medicine containing powdered mummy used to be sold as a cure-all. Downing a heaping teaspoon of 2,000-year-old dead body was supposed to make you energetic and fit.

INDEX

Special Thanks

Since in the world there are no complete or permanent answers, science is most truly about knowing what questions to ask. Thanks to the curious people of all ages who provided the wonderful questions in this book:

Argelis Alvares
S. Anand
Justin Applewhite
Denise Auer
Ryan Bachmann
Danny Battista
Scott Bernardo
V. Bhuvaneshwaran
Daniel Blake
Sean Bogdahn
Janine Bonacuso
Danielle Canizio
Brooke Causanschi
Winnie Chang
Eva Chrysanthopoulos
Anthony Cinquemant
Shannon Clark
Nilton Claudio Da Costa
Gerald Crippen
Jeremy Cruz
Juan Gabriel Cruz
Michael Cummins
David Dale
Kathryn Davies
Alfredo Diaz
Dennis Diond
Alex Dominguez
Eric Joel Dowling
Lauren Epstein
Stephen Albert Ertel, Jr.
Ana Escoboas
Meaghan Fitzgerald
Jason Flores
Peggy Fung
Mrs. Golden's class

Kumarie Gopal
Rayon Gordon
Gregory Grambo's class
Hussain Guru
Kristin Hall
Ana Hernandez
Michael Higgiston
Wendy Ho
Tiffany Holland
Christina Hsu
Russell Hyman
Jerry Jaffee's class
"Jason"
Shawn Jones
John Joseph
Edward Kang
Jonathan Kappel
Katherine Karamalis
H. V. Kavitha
Imran Kazmi
Joe Keegan
Lamia Khan
Lauren Kingston
Ayala Klein
S. U. Rethna Kumar
Brian Kushner
Celeste Labayen
Elizabeth Lackrai
Barry Ladizinski
Jessica Larcy
Andrew Lee
Raya Leefmans
Mrs. F. Levine's class
Jodi Levy
Laurence Llamosi

Mrs. Lufrano's class
M. Mahesh
Jessica Mahr
Juliana Martino
Stinsey Mathai
Abraham Matthew
Jackie Maura
Sean McGee
Kathy Meenan
Andrew Meny
Keith Miller
Susan Mintz's class
Mrs. Moir's class
Leslie Morris
Lauren Murnane
Chris Neal
Caroline Oakley
Nicholas Owen
Samantha Pazer
Pamela Perea
James Perr
Manuel Pica
Lisa Pierra
Christopher Pomo
Sashikala Prabhu
Stephanie Puczko
Danny Quirk
Vangala S. Ramachandran
Deepthi Rao
Justin Ratanaburi
A. Sunil Kumar Reddy
Bhavana Reddy
Tina Reinle's class
Jorge Reinoza
Cindia Rivera

Earth Science Rockie
Leticia Rodriguez
Ryan Rogers
Alexandra Rosen
Zachary Rubins
Gayle Ruderman
Elizabeth Scholl
Mrs. Schultheis's class
Abdool Shadi
Howard Shapiro
Ian Silverman
Samantha Singh
Aimee Smith
J. Smith
M. Someswar
Samuel Spiro
Carrie Stawski
David Sterling
Alyssa Streat
G. Sumana
Michael Tehomilic
Yevgeniya Traps
Andrew Trotta
Tatiana Tubis
I. Uma
R. Sree Vidya
N. Vijay
M. Vikram
Jenae Williams
Keenan Winn
Ian Wittman
Melissa Wong